FOR THE MOTHERLAND! FOR STALIN!

BORIS BOGACHEV

FOR THE MOTHERLAND! FOR STALIN!

A RED ARMY OFFICER'S MEMOIR OF THE EASTERN FRONT

Translated by
Maria Bogacheva

HURST & COMPANY, LONDON

First published in English in the United Kingdom in 2017 by
C. Hurst & Co. (Publishers) Ltd.,
41 Great Russell Street, London, WC1B 3PL
© Boris Bogachev, 2017
Translation © Maria Bogacheva
All rights reserved.
Printed in India

Distributed in the United States, Canada and Latin America by
Oxford University Press, 198 Madison Avenue, New York, NY 10016,
United States of America.

The right of Boris Bogachev to be identified as the author of
this publication is asserted by his estate in accordance with the
Copyright, Designs and Patents Act, 1988.

A Cataloguing-in-Publication data record for this book
is available from the British Library.

ISBN: 9781849047975

This book is printed using paper from registered sustainable
and managed sources.

www.hurstpublishers.com

This book is dedicated to my grandson, Konstantin

CONTENTS

CONTENTS

ACKNOWLEDGEMENTS

I would like to thank the following people for their valuable help and advice: my wife, Nina; Sarah Dixon; my daughter, Maria; Nigel Hawkins; my son, Anatoliy.

EDITOR'S NOTE

I have used internationally recognised spellings for place names such as Moscow, Prague, Kiev and the River Vistula. In Ukraine itself, I have used the Russian place names supplied by the author, as these were in use during the 1940s when Ukraine was part of the USSR. Their Ukrainian equivalents are supplied in brackets. I have followed the same principle for other places in the former Soviet Union, as well as places in modern Poland which had German names during the war.

TRANSLATOR'S INTRODUCTION

The greatest value of a memoir lies in recreating the atmosphere of a particular time, in this case the Great Patriotic War of 1941–45. Future generations may know about the history of the war and its causes, but they cannot feel what it was like to live through such a turbulent period. In his memoirs, my father Boris manages to convey the atmosphere of the war, in which he was a participant, while analysing the events that he witnessed.

My father started writing his memoirs when he retired in 1985. His memory of some episodes was amazingly detailed, as his wartime experiences were permanently imprinted in his young mind and would dominate the rest of his life. He had always taken notes, even at the front, writing them down on anything that came to hand. After the end of the war he collected war poetry, especially poems which reflected his own experiences and emotions during the war.

In the 1970s, my father joined a group of veterans from his assault sapper brigade and went to their reunions which were held every five years in the town of Zagorsk (now Sergiev Posad), near Moscow. In Odessa my father contacted other surviving comrades-in-arms who were still fit enough to attend regular reunions, and became chairman of a local group of veterans from the 4th tank army. After *perestroika*, there was greater access to state archives and my father was able to study wartime documents in the military archives at Podolsk and elsewhere.

So, over the next fifteen years my father wrote his book, using his notes and memories supplemented by conversations with fellow veterans, war poems and information from the archives and other memoirs. He felt compelled to write his memoirs as he wanted them to become a mouthpiece for those millions who had never returned from the war, or had died later, leaving no record of their experiences.

This book contains a powerful anti-war message: it asks us to remember people and events, but in no way does it glorify the war itself. It was written by a survivor who had an incredible lust for life. Its recurring message is this: such a devastating war should never happen again.

My father finished his memoirs in 2000. Since then many years have passed... The tragic deterioration in relations between Ukraine and Russia shocked him deeply: he could never understand why animosity should be encouraged between two brotherly nations so closely intertwined in their culture and history.

AUTHOR'S PREFACE

This book is dedicated to my grandson, Konstantin Bogachev. Time flies mercilessly. Years run by. Generations change. At the sunset of your life, you contemplate and analyse the past years and what you have done, and you feel an acute need to share your view of events with today's generation, to narrate what has been stored deep within you and is now ready to be written about.

The tempo of life today is so frenetic, the amount of information we receive is so vast and varied, and the differences in opinions and assessments of historical events are so great that it is difficult to determine what is the truth and what is a lie. That is why I have decided to write this book and give my version of the great historical events as an eyewitness and participant.

'Everyone can write a book about their own life,' Maxim Gorky said. I wrote this book about a period in my life which was the richest in events—the period of the Great Patriotic War.[1] A truthful book about this war can be interesting not only for our contemporaries, but for those who will research the lives of our generation in the future.

I happened to learn about the war's horrors and its day-to-day life when I was seventeen. You might say that I went straight from childhood into the war. I regard all those years after the war as a great gift which was received only by a few. I was a trench officer or, as they used to say, a *Van'ka vzvodniy* (platoon Jack).[2] Long ago I decided to carry out my sacred duty on behalf of my comrades-in-arms (and there were millions of them) who were killed when they were eighteen to twenty years old and rotted in the marshes near Rzhev, Novgorod and other battlefields.

With my own eyes I saw people die while defending their houses, villages, towns or relatives. Through their deaths those people stepped into immortality. Their heroic deeds will live on forever. In accordance with the vows we made at the time of our victory, we have a sacred duty to use our memories to tell future generations the whole truth about the war and its heroes, about the inferno which my contemporaries had to go through. It is even more important nowadays when Ukraine is finding its direction and making plans for the future. No matter how horrible the events of the war were, the past cannot be changed. It is necessary for the living to remember the past and to lay flowers on a hero's grave. War is too dirty and horrible to be admired. And God forgive me if I can't remember anything joyful, because there could be no joys in that inferno. I cannot write glorious words about the most terrible war in the history of humankind. And I don't set myself the task of analysing the professionalism of military actions—I leave this to competent military historians.

When the Great Patriotic War was over I developed an interest in the poetry of the front. Poets are special people. They can see what others don't and just pass over. They embody their vision of life in poetic form. With their poems they confirm my feelings, thoughts and emotions during wartime in the best way.

For a long time I collected poems by war poets without any intention of using them in printed material and very often I didn't bother to note down the author's name. That is why my book includes poems by known and unknown poets, and some anonymous poems. The fact that these poems live on and affect our imagination and emotions gives me reason to ask forgiveness from their unknown authors in advance. I also ask forgiveness for some inconsequential passages and the awkwardness of my narration, as well as some contentious political statements and views. As the poet Robert Rozhdestvensky wrote:

> I made some mistakes. Sorry—
> This was the first time I have lived on this planet.

FOREWORD

by *Geoffrey Roberts*

At the heart of Boris Bogachev's powerful memoir of the Great Patriotic War is a determination to communicate the truth about his experience as a combatant on the Soviet-German front. The story he tells is heroic and horrific in equal measure. His descriptions of battle and life on the front line are as graphic as they are compelling. Bogachev takes pride in the Soviet victory but criticises its extraordinarily high cost, much of it paid as the result of mistakes made by the Red Army's leadership. He understands but refuses to excuse the atrocities committed by his comrades and he is scathing about those who used their personal connections to avoid the front and sit out the war in the rear. Although a committed communist—he joined the party during the war and remained a member for forty-five years—he is an acute observer of the brutalities, absurdities and corruptions of the system for which he served.

Eight million Soviet soldiers, sailors and aircrew were killed during the Great Patriotic War—more than ten times the combined casualty numbers of American and British armed forces. The attrition rate among junior officers like Bogachev was particularly high. Being lucky to survive, he was among the 17 million troops, including a majority of officers, who returned to the front—often three or four times—after recovering from being wounded.

Bogachev was not yet seventeen years of age when Germany invaded the Soviet Union in June 1941 and was, at that time, living in Odessa where his father was a military commissar. The outbreak of war was not unexpected but the calamitous defeats suffered by the Red Army in the early months of the conflict were shocking. Before the German attack Soviet authorities had been confident the Red Army would successfully repulse any German invasion and this confidence was exuded in party propaganda. In the event, Minsk, the Belorussian capital, was captured by the Wehrmacht within two weeks of the invasion. Kiev fell in September and Leningrad was surrounded.

Bogachev's home city of Odessa, too, was besieged then occupied by the Germans in October 1941 and he was evacuated to a village outside Moscow. In November 1941, as the Germans closed in on the Soviet capital, he volunteered for service in the artillery but because of his age was not admitted as an officer cadet until 31 December. By this time the German attack on Moscow had been repelled and the Red Army was in the midst of a massive winter counter-offensive intended to chase the Germans out of Russia. At the core of this counter-offensive was an attack in the Rzhev-Viazma area—between two and three hundred miles from Moscow—aiming to inflict a crippling blow on German Army Group Centre. This winter operation failed but was resumed in July 1942 and was Bogachev's first battle as a junior lieutenant in charge of a mortar platoon—a seventeen-year old boy with thirty to forty soldiers under his command. He went into battle without ever being kissed or hugged by a girl. Bogachev had not even been trained to use mortars in artillery school but, of necessity, he soon learned.

FOREWORD

Before the battle Stalin's famous Order 227 was read out to the troops. Familiarly known as *Ni shagu nazad!* (Not a step back!) Stalin ordered a policy of no-retreat. As Bogachev notes the order was issued because in summer 1942 the Red Army was being forced to retreat again, particularly in the south where the Germans were advancing towards Stalingrad. Under pressure many units were breaking and running away in disarray. Stalin's order was intended to prevent any unauthorised or disorderly retreats.

To enforce Stalin's order, blocking detachments of the security forces were deployed to detain, arrest and, if necessary, shoot unauthorised retreating soldiers. As a junior officer Bogachev had the power to execute on the spot anyone refusing to obey orders. It was not a power he had personally to exercise but 157,000 Soviet soldiers were indeed executed during the war. In addition, some 994,000 members of the armed forces were convicted of offences by military tribunals. Many of them were sent to serve in penal battalions—units allocated to the most dangerous assignments—which afforded the sentenced transgressors a chance to redeem themselves in action. The possibility of redemption as well as the threat of death was characteristic of the Soviet system under Stalin.

The second Rzhev-Viazma operation (Bogachev refers to it as the first because he omits the winter offensive) failed as badly as its predecessor at the cost of hundreds of thousands of casualties including Bogachev, who was shot in the foot. He crawled from the battlefield and was eventually evacuated, but only as far as a frontline hospital. After recuperating, he was sent to a reserve division for a month before returning to combat as senior lieutenant of a mortar platoon. In February 1943 he was again wounded, shot in the shoulder and neck by a sniper. This time he took his fate into his own hands and after evacuation and initial treatment ran away to his father who was serving as a military commissar in Kazakhstan.

FOREWORD

Bogachev's memoir strongly criticises the privileged sons of the Soviet elite who manoeuvred to evade combat during the war. But he confesses here that, when fully recovered and discharged from the local hospital, he asked his father to pull some strings to get him a position in the rear. Alas, his father who was a staunch communist, refused to do so. But a reprieve of sorts came in the form of a posting to Tashkent, where the now eighteen-year-old Boris was placed in command of an artillery platoon that included forty officers. Mindful there were many officers who had never seen any action, Bogachev resisted being returned to the front on the grounds that he had already served well and been wounded twice.

But his resistance was to no avail. In May 1944 he was returned to the front as commander of a sapper platoon. Essentially sappers were infantry with engineering and technical skills who were deployed to spearhead offensives. They built bridges, cleared minefields, and destroyed enemy fortifications. During an attack they would ride on the outside of tanks and self-propelled guns in order to protect them from anti-tank weapons. In retreat, sappers were responsible for destroying any strategic structures that could be of use to an advancing enemy.

Bogachev's engineering battalion was part of Marshal Ivan S. Konev's 1st Ukrainian front. In summer 1944 the front took part in Operation Bagration—an attack to drive the Germans out of Belarus where they had been entrenched for three years. The 1st Ukrainian front's task was to penetrate into southern Poland to stop the Germans redeploying forces to support Army Group Centre in Belarus. It was during this offensive that Bogachev killed his first German face-to-face.

Bogachev recalls that during this offensive the Red Army came into conflict with the Polish Home Army—the resistance organisation of Poland's government in exile, which was anti-communist and intent on opposing Soviet occupation of the country. Curiously, Bogachev does not mention the controversy generated around the Warsaw Uprising of August 1944. The Home Army's insurrection in the Polish capital was savagely put down by the Germans, killing 200,000 of the city's inhabitants in the process. Stalin and the Red Army were accused of deliberately pausing their advance on Warsaw to allow the Germans to crush the Home Army. But, as Bogachev notes, Stalin was eager for the Red Army to cross the River Vistula in the 1st Ukrainian front's area of operations, this being essential to a successful assault on Warsaw by the 1st Belorussian front. But efforts to cross the Vistula in force failed and the Red Army did not succeed in capturing Warsaw until January 1945.

Bogachev took part in the 1945 Vistula-Oder operation in which the Red Army swept through Poland and into Germany. In this section of his memoirs Bogachev is frank about the war crimes committed by Soviet forces, including the killing of German prisoners. He also gives details about the pillaging of German property by all ranks—from the lowliest privates to the top generals. One subject on which he is reticent, however, is the Red Army's mass rape of German women, hundreds of thousands of whom were violated during the march to Berlin. The only allusion to what went on is a curious story that Bogachev tells of meeting two German women, an older woman and younger one who thought he was going to rape her. He didn't, only to return the next day to be told that his 'peaceful visit yesterday had affected her so much that her heart had failed and she had died'.

While rape was an atrocity committed by only a minority of Red Army soldiers, it was wide-spread and it is difficult to believe that Bogachev had no knowledge of what was going on. This reticence is shared by most other Soviet veterans, including Marshal Georgy Zhukov, whose memoirs Bogachev quotes frequently. Zhukov was commander of the 1st Belorussian front, which in May 1945 captured Berlin—the epicentre of the epidemic of Red Army rapes.

FOREWORD

It is important to understand the background to the rapes committed by the Red Army. Seventeen million Soviet civilians were killed during the war, most of them by the Germans. The Germans committed mass murder as well as mass rape during their occupation of Soviet territories. As the Red Army swept through Poland it had the gruesome honour of liberating a string of Nazi extermination camps at Auschwitz, Belzec, Chelmno, Sobibor and Treblinka. On the eve of the invasion of Germany Soviet soldiers were bombarded with inflammatory anti-German hate propaganda. The Red Army was not the only Allied army to commit atrocities against German civilians. American, British, Canadian and French soldiers were also guilty, although the scale of their rape and pillage was much less than that of the Soviets. But it was the Red Army that bore the main burden of the war against Hitler and the Soviet Union was the country whose lands were devastated by Nazi invasion.

In March 1945 Bogachev was wounded again by a shell fragment lodging in his right buttock, a potentially serious wound which meant that his war was over. So when the war did end on 9 May 1945 Bogachev was ensconced in a mobile hospital not far from Prague. Having recovered from his wound Bogachev feared being sent to the Far East to take part in the war against Japan but that conflict came to an end in August 1945.

Like many young warriors Bogachev feared death but did not believe he would be killed in the war. As an atheist he did not pray but confesses that when he was caught in the middle of an artillery strike he did call on God's help to survive. Miraculously, the bombardment lifted!

Bogachev notes that, contrary to myth, the Red Army was not fuelled by vodka not least because it was too dangerous to go into battle drunk. But alcohol was widely used as a sedative after battle.

In the postwar era Bogachev trained then worked as a military lawyer, retiring with the rank of Colonel after forty-three years' service. In retirement he became active in veterans' circles and began writing his memoirs. In Soviet times only generals had access to military archives for the purpose of writing their memoirs. Bogachev was fortunate that his retirement coincided with the political reforms introduced by Mikhail Gorbachev who was advocating a more honest approach to Soviet history. The archives became more available to researchers, a process that continued after the collapse of the USSR in 1991. Even so, restrictions remained on what researchers were allowed to see and record in their notes. Russian authorities were—and still are—keen to ensure that only positive stories get told about the Great Patriotic War and Bogachev shares a number of amusing anecdotes about his efforts to thwart them.

Bogachev undertook a lot of research for his memoirs so they contain much valuable information gleaned from military archives. He also highlights some lesser known aspects of the war, for example the role played by animals on the front-line. One of the minor heroes of Bogachev's narrative is a two-humped Bactrian camel who pulled his battalion's kitchen wagon and remained calm under fire. In an appendix—Hurray for Dogs!—he describes how German Shepherds and other dogs delivered messages, dragged wounded soldiers from the battle-field and helped clear minefields. Among those who took part in the great Victory Parade in Red Square in June 1945 was a detachment of dogs and their handlers. Grotesquely, during the war some dogs were strapped with explosives and trained to attack enemy tanks. In one of the most poignant passages of the book Bogachev relates how at the end of the war fifty of his brigade's dogs were abandoned because they were of no more use. As Bogachev writes, 'it was a cruel time with cruel ways'.

Soviet war memoirs published during the communist era tend to gloss over the harsh realities of the war and, hence, are bland and formulaic. In contrast and in line with other post-Soviet

Russian war memoirs, Bogachev's book is grittily realistic and brutally honest about his own feelings and attitudes. There is no heroic romance in fighting a war. He writes that 'the cruelty experienced during the war is impossible to describe—it has to be experienced' and he does a good job in sharing his personal experiences with the reader.

Bogachev's memoir is unusual in that it contains several strong strands of criticism of the Soviet war effort. He is adamant that the Rzhev battles resulted in little more than a pyrrhic victory, the enormous casualty toll being the result of incompetent top-level leadership. During the early years of the war, he says, 'Soviet generals could only achieve victory by shedding rivers of blood.'

He rails against the unfairness of decision-making about how medals and decorations were awarded both during and after the war, including his view that some were denied to him. He remains appalled by the endemic corruption, spying and petty bureaucracy of the Soviet system. And he is bitter that victory in the war did not deliver to the Soviet people the prosperity they deserved.

Although he took part in suppressing their revolt, Bogachev says he understands why, after the war, some Ukrainian nationalists conducted a prolonged insurgency to free themselves from Soviet rule. He is even sympathetic to the Vlasovites—the followers of General Vlasov who defected from the Red Army to form the German-backed Russian Liberation Army. Vlasov was captured by the Red Army in May 1945 and, according to Bogachev, the renegade general and his comrades in arms faced execution with dignity, insisting they were patriots who wanted to liberate their country from Stalin's dictatorship. He is highly critical, too, of Soviet and Russian jingoists who proclaim the peaceful character of their state when record shows that it has a history of expansionism.

All memoirs are limited as accurate historical sources. People tend to forget and to select and edit the memories and documents that chime with their beliefs. An individual's story is influenced by the memories and stories of others who shared the same experience or by powerful historical narratives about what apparently occurred. The past is viewed through the lens of what happened subsequently and the narrative is often shaped as much by present-day concerns and attitudes as by the realities of the past. Yet most memoirists consciously strive to overcome these handicaps and to tell the truth as best they can. Sometimes they succeed. The honesty and directness of Boris Bogachev's memoir give his words a ring of authenticity.

Of the many thousands of Russian and Soviet memoirs of the Great Patriotic War very few have been translated into English and, of those, most are the memoirs of generals. There are hardly any translated memoirs to provide a bottom-up view of the war and detail the experiences of ordinary soldiers. Bogachev's daughter, Maria Bogacheva, has done a fine job of translation ably assisted by editor Sarah Dixon (the book was published in Russian in Odessa in 2007). Bogachev had a particular interest in front-line poetry and the book contains many evocative verses, including one dedicated to the author. Bogachev's memoir is easy to read, well-illustrated with good photographs and bolstered by some highly informative explanatory footnotes.

BIOGRAPHICAL DETAILS

Boris, July 1940

Boris Bogachev was born on 31 December 1924 in the town of
Penza, Russia, into a military family. His father, Ilya Bogachev
(born in Moscow, 1899), was a rifle company commander who
participated in the Civil War (1917–22)[1] and the Great Patriotic
War. He served in the army for twenty-six years, retiring as a
colonel. Boris's mother, Maria (born 1904), had worked at the

Arsenal Factory in Kiev (the most revolutionary factory in the city) before their marriage.[2] Boris's father was frequently transferred from one garrison to another, which is how Boris ended up going to five different schools in five different cities. Before the war his father was the military commissar of Voroshilov (now Primorsky) district, Odessa.[3] By June 1941 Boris had finished eighth form at school.[4]

Because Odessa was under the threat of German occupation Boris, together with his mother and younger brother, Anatoliy (1930–53), was evacuated to his father's home village of Gumyonka, Ryazan region, south-east of Moscow.[5] In November 1941 Boris volunteered as a cadet at the artillery anti-tank school in Podolsk, outside Moscow. He left artillery school as a junior lieutenant in May 1942 and was posted to the Kalinin front. Serving as a commander of a 50-mm mortar platoon of the rifle company, he was lightly wounded by a bullet in his right foot during the Rzhev offensive on 30 July.

Boris recovered at a frontline hospital, then went on to take part in battles as a platoon commander of his regiment's 120-mm mortar battery. On 26 February 1943, he was severely wounded in the right shoulder and neck near Kholm, Novgorod region.

After recovering at a hospital in the rear at Kazakhstan he was considered fit for active service in a limited capacity and served as a commander of a 120-mm gun platoon of the 25th artillery training regiment for officers in Tashkent.

In May 1944 Boris was sent to the 1st Ukrainian front as a commander of an assault platoon and took part in battles for the liberation of western Ukraine, Poland, Germany and Czechoslovakia. On 16 March 1945, as a platoon commander of tank assault troops, he was wounded in the right hip by a shell fragment but remained in the army. After the war he served as a platoon commander in the 76-mm gun battery of the rifle division in Berdichev (Berdychiv) and took part in ensuring that the

Boris with a friend, Muhammet Tatanov, Petropavlovsk, 1943.

elections to the Supreme Soviet of the USSR in February 1946 went to plan in Rovno (Rivne) region, west Ukraine.

In August 1946 Boris became a cadet at the Military Law Academy in Moscow from which he graduated in 1951. He served both as a member and as the chairman of the military tribunal at the Baltic fleet's naval base in Świnoujście (Poland) and at the Black Sea Kerch-Feodosia fleet's naval base.

During 1955–58, he worked as a senior officer in the inspection department of the Military Collegium of the Supreme Court of the USSR in Moscow on the rehabilitation of those unjustly condemned during Stalin's Terror of 1936–38.[6] From 1958–84 he was a member of military tribunals in Chita, then in Odessa, where he retired with the rank of colonel of law, having been in military service for forty-three years.

In Odessa Boris was head of the council of veterans from his regiment of the 4th tank army. He married in 1949. His wife Nina was born in Moscow in 1927, and taught at schools and universities. His daughter Maria (born 1955) has a PhD in lin-

BIOGRAPHICAL DETAILS

Major Boris Bogachev, senior officer of the Military Collegium of the Supreme Court, 1956

guistics and was a senior lecturer at Odessa University. His son Anatoliy (born 1959) is a defence lawyer in Odessa. He has two granddaughters—Elena (born 1980) and Natasha (born 1985); a grandson, Konstantin (born 2003); and a great granddaughter, Daria (born 2011).

This book contains a truthful and documented description of the Great Patriotic War. This is why it does not resemble the types of memoir which have been published only after being checked and approved by bureaucrats and censors.

BIOGRAPHICAL DETAILS

Boris Bogachev 31 December 1924–14 September 2015[7]

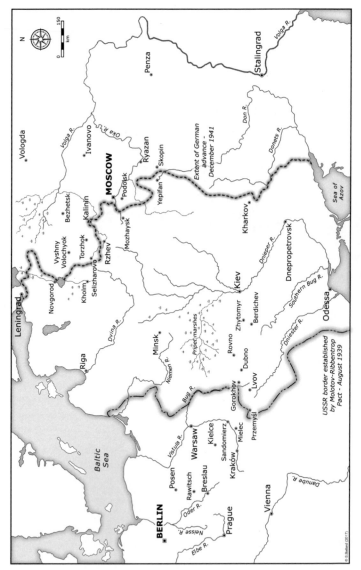

Eastern Europe and West European Russia 1939–45

Places on map: N, 0 km 150, Vologda, Leningrad, Riga, Baltic Sea, Novgorod, Vyshny Volochyok, Kholm, Selizharovo, Torzhok, Rzhev, Bezhetsk, Kalinin, Mozhaysk, MOSCOW, Podolsk, Ivanovo, Oka R., Volga R., Ryazan, Yepifan, Skopin, Penza, Extent of German advance – December 1941, Don R., Donets R., Stalingrad, Volga R., Sea of Azov, Kharkov, Kiev, Dnepropetrovsk, Dnieper R., Berdichev, Zhytomyr, Southern Bug R., Odessa, Dniester R., Rovno, Dubno, Lvov, Gorokhov, Przemyśl, Mielec, Sandomierz, Kielce, Kraków, Warsaw, Vistula R., Posen, Rawitsch, Breslau, BERLIN, Oder R., Neisse R., Elbe R., Prague, Vienna, Danube R., Minsk, Pripet marshes, Niemen R., Bug R., Dvina R., USSR border established by Molotov-Ribbentrop Pact – August 1939

© S.Ballard (2017)

1

EVACUATION TO GUMYONKA

WAR!

22 June 1941. War breaks out. People are gathering around the loudspeakers on the streets. The adults look worried, while we boys are cheerful—we are going to fight the German enemy on their territory, just as our leaders had assured us. Our courageous troops will defeat the fascists in two to three months 'with a powerful blow and little bloodshed,' as the song goes.[1] In Germany the working class will stage a revolution and their country will become a socialist republic.

How naive these judgements were! And how utterly wrong they proved to be! As early as the second day of the war, there were long queues outside the shops. People in Odessa had experienced war and bitter privation before, and it seemed a wise precaution to build up supplies.[2]

FOR THE MOTHERLAND! FOR STALIN!

Boris, September 1940

Everyone began to look out for spies. Anyone who seemed suspicious either in looks or behaviour—perhaps he had been looking in one direction a little too long—was ordered to show his papers and if the slightest inaccuracy was spotted, he was taken to the local militia headquarters, accompanied by a crowd consisting mostly of boys.[3]

I was unaware of this at the time. I was sixteen years old, staying with my eleven-year-old brother Anatoliy at a Pioneer camp in the suburbs.[4] One afternoon we saw a plane flying high in the sky. Suddenly, from behind the stone wall of the camp, anti-aircraft guns started firing. We had no idea that an anti-aircraft battery was there. Small black clouds of shrapnel burst around the plane, before it turned and headed west.

We were surprised: why were we shooting at our own plane?

Soon everything became clear: we were told that the war with Germany had broken out and the plane had been a German scout. Although we hadn't been in any danger it dawned on us that this war was not some exciting adventure but something really terrible. Later that day there were two or three air raid alerts, with sirens wailing and people running to the shelters. That night and over the following nights bombing raids took place in the centre of Odessa. During daytime only German scout planes flew over, but these escaped being shot down.

Soon our father brought us back home to our flat in the centre of Odessa. Father was the military commissar for Voroshilov district (he had the task of organising conscription after the outbreak of war) and he was a member of the district committee of the Communist Party. He was at work all the time—he even had to work through the night at the enlistment office. I would often visit him there, where I would deliver conscription papers and packages for him, help the soldier on duty and tidy the office.

Many houses were ruined by bombs and fires.[5] Once after an air raid, Anatoliy and I came home and saw that the neighbour-

Town hall, Odessa, 1941

ing house had been completely destroyed. Our flat was ten metres away. Our door and windows had been blown out in the blast. A huge bomb or a naval mine must have exploded. We found our mother in the flat; she was terribly frightened. This incident, as well as her constant stress and worries about father and us, affected her very badly. She completely lost her appetite and stopped eating. We had to beg her to drink a glass of milk at the very least. As a result she lost a lot of weight.

Evacuation from Odessa

The enemy was approaching the city. The evacuation began: father told us to be ready for departure at any time. We packed a few bags and two suitcases with food and necessities. Everything else that my parents had acquired during the seventeen years of their married life had to be left behind in the flat.

Later I was very sorry that I hadn't taken our family photographs with us. When my parents returned to our flat after the war, all their possessions had gone; their neighbours said that our photographs had been scattered all around the courtyard.

Father said he would remain in Odessa while mother, Anatoliy and I went to his home village of Gumyonka in Russia, about 1,000 kilometres north of Odessa, accompanied by a soldier called Kopich. Father's two sisters lived there, and we would stay with them and their families. The plan was to go most of the way in the goods van of a freight train, with the families of officers from the artillery school, and then carry on to Gumyonka by ourselves.

On 9 July we said goodbye to our neighbours, then got into father's *gazic* (jeep) and drove to the freight station. We hoped to come back home three or four months later, if not sooner.

We wanted to take our dog with us. She was a Doberman Pinscher. We had her for two years and she was very dear to us. But the rest of the passengers, fifteen women with children, protested, and we had to leave her behind. I remember her rushing about between the two windows of the *gazic*—she seemed to realize that we were leaving her for good.

We were all in tears as we said goodbye to father, who reminded us for the last time to behave ourselves and look after mother, then we said goodbye to our dog and our lovely city of Odessa, before we moved off slowly into the unknown.

It took us eleven days to reach Gumyonka. In normal conditions it would have taken two days. Even so, this was good—it could have been much worse. At first we went through Ukraine to Kharkov (Kharkiv), via Kirovograd (Kirovohrad), Dnepropetrovsk (Dnipropetrovsk) and Lozovaya (Lozova). But when we reached Lozovaya, there was a delay and then our train had to go on a long detour because the way to Kharkov was blocked. Our train was not bombed on the way, though once a German plane opened fire on us with a machine gun.

Soon we had to get off the train, which was heading to the east, as we had to go north. We went the rest of the way on a series of trains, travelling in open carriages by day and night. When it rained, all four of us would get under a blanket and lie there shivering from the cold. At night Kopich and I took turns to keep watch. We were eating the food we'd taken from home and whatever we managed to buy on the way, which was mainly milk. Sometimes we had to change trains several times in one day. The trains were moving slowly, giving way to the troop trains.

At last we reached Gumyonka. Having brought us there, Kopich went back to Odessa. But by that time the city was surrounded by Romanian troops.[6] We never found out what happened to him. After the war father sent an enquiry to his home address. They answered that he was missing.

Should we believe in fate or not? On our way to Gumyonka, we passed a small town called Yepifan. Little did I know that, there, in that town, at the very same time, was my future wife Nina, then a schoolgirl of fourteen. Her school had been evacuated to Yepifan as the Germans were advancing on Moscow. This turned out to be a mistake—Yepifan happened to be even closer to the frontline than Moscow itself. As the Germans approached Yepifan, the teachers took all the food, abandoned the children and made their own escape. Fortunately Nina's older sister Irina, who was twenty-two years old, turned up from Moscow to rescue her, walking the final fifty kilometres along the railway tracks. Irina arrived just in time: the following day the Germans captured Yepifan and if Nina had still been there, she would have perished.

Six months later fate tried again to bring us together. In May 1942 I visited a house in Moscow, which was right opposite Nina's home. But again we failed to meet. It proved to be a case of third time lucky when, again in Moscow, five years later, we finally met and we have remained together ever since.

An *izba*

EVACUATION TO GUMYONKA

Village life in Gumyonka

In Gumyonka we stayed in a wooden peasant's hut, or *izba* with Uncle Zudin's family. His wife was my father's sister. They had seven children. Their two sons were away in the army, but their five daughters still lived at home. Once we arrived, there were ten people in the *izba*. We spent the first few days getting used to life in the village. We rose at daybreak and went to bed when it was dark, sleeping either on the large Russian oven which heated the hut, or on *polaty*, the wooden sleeping platforms in the space between the oven and the roof. Zudin slept on a wooden bench with his winter jacket rolled up as a pillow under his head. We had lunch together around a scrubbed wooden table. We all ate *kulesh*, a kind of porridge cooked from millet, potatoes and milk, out of a big cauldron. We started eating when Zudin gave us the command. He would strike the cauldron twice with his spoon, then we were allowed to eat. As the cauldron was in the middle of the table, we had to bring each spoonful of *kulesh* to our mouths with a piece of bread held underneath so that nothing spilled onto the table. If anyone tried to eat before the command or dropped *kulesh* on the table, he was punished—Zudin hit him on the forehead with a spoon. But this seldom happened, because everybody tried to behave at the table.

Mother stayed with us for a week or two, but then she had to be put in a psychiatric hospital because of her mental state. The hospital was in the town of Ryazan, about 100 kilometres away.

Zudin worked at a collective farm and found me work there too.[7] I tried to scythe and thresh rye, but I was clumsy and the village lads and girls I was working with teased me. I would also rake up hay, drive the horse and cart, and run other errands. On 1 September, Anatoliy and I started school in the neighbouring town of Skopin, two kilometres away. When I returned from school I would do my homework and help my aunt about the house.

In 1930–31 my father had been the military commissar of Skopin and the surrounding district, and they remembered him well in Gumyonka, so I was nicknamed 'commissar's son'.

The war was gradually approaching... In the west the artillery cannonade grew louder and louder. There was a constant droning and rumbling and there were reddish flashes in the sky in the evenings. Endless processions of refugees were moving slowly along the road from Skopin to the east. They were a sorry sight. Women, children and old people trudged along with bundles, suitcases and rucksacks, tired, dirty and smutted with wood smoke. Skinny cows, horses and goats were driven past. Household goods and possessions were piled in carts and wheelbarrows. A large group of kindergarten children passed by: exhausted teachers were carrying heavy bags with food; older children were carrying younger ones wrapped in shawls, kerchiefs or large pieces of fabric. They trudged in silence, they were not crying, they must have been walking for days... Tractors and combine harvesters rumbled alongside them, also heading east...

I go to Ryazan to visit my mother

I started worrying about my mother: what had happened to her? How was she? I made up my mind to go to Ryazan to see her. My aunt tried to talk me out of it: 'It's too dangerous for you to go so far by yourself at such a troubled time!' But I was adamant, so my aunt put some food into my rucksack and I set off.

There was a railway station at Ryazhsk, forty kilometres away from the village. But it was impossible to get to Ryazan by train. Passenger trains had already stopped running and I would not be allowed to board a military train. It was a time of extreme vigilance and secrecy.

Boris's mother, Maria, in 1948

The distance between Ryazan and Gumyonka is about 120 kilometres if you go by road. For the first time in my life, aged sixteen, I set off on my own. At villages, I would tell people my sad story and they would let me spend the night in their houses. Once I saw a marvellous sight about ten kilometres away. The ancient town of Pronsk stood on a high flat-topped hill in front of me, its golden church domes shining in the sun. The hill was almost completely encircled by a small river.

At last I came to Ryazan and found the psychiatric hospital. I saw my mother. It was heart-rending to see her, exhausted, skinny and ashen faced, with sad eyes. She recognized me and was very glad to see me. She asked me about Anatoliy and whether we had heard anything from father in Odessa, which was currently under siege. Our meeting lasted an hour. She couldn't be discharged from hospital yet, and it was time for me to leave. She grabbed hold of me and wouldn't let me go. Nurses

9

tore her hands off me but she grasped the half belt of my coat and it was impossible to release her grip. Then the nurses unbuttoned the half belt and I slipped free. So I left, distraught, my mother still holding my half belt.

The hospital was in the suburbs. As I left, the centre of Ryazan was being attacked by two dozen German bombers. At that time the Germans were thirty kilometres away. A state of siege was announced: anyone inciting disorder was liable to summary execution. About 200 types of armaments were manufactured in Ryazan, including mortars, mines, anti-tank rifles and shells. When the bombing was over, I went to the town centre to look at the aftermath. It was a horrible sight.

For the first time I encountered the cruel and destructive power of war. Some houses were completely ruined. Where once a house had stood there was now a huge pile of smoking rubble. The wall of another house was demolished and you could see the rooms on all four floors. Some objects from normal everyday life remained: an overturned table, a lamp shade swinging in the wind, wallpaper ripped from the walls, exposed flights of stairs. It's terrible to think about the fate of the inhabitants. Most of the contents of the rooms had been sent flying out into the street: I saw a samovar, dishes, tablecloths and brushes scattered on the ground; sheets and towels hanging from the trees; photographs, letters, documents rustling in the wind...

My journey back to Gumyonka

I decided to take the train to Ryazhsk, then walk along the road for the last forty kilometres to Gumyonka. One by one, train loads of evacuees were leaving for the east. The trains were also carrying plant machinery and other equipment on open flatbed cars to the army's rear, so it would not be difficult to get on, especially in the dark.

I hung around the centre of Ryazan for the rest of the day: it is one of Russia's ancient towns, founded in 1095, fifty years earlier than Moscow. In the evening I boarded a freight train to Ryazhsk. I travelled in the brake van. My only fellow passenger was a grubby man with shifty eyes who was anxiously looking around all the time. He turned out to be a patient from the psychiatric hospital who had been discharged because there was not enough food left for all the patients. For all three hours of our journey I was tense and worried. I expected him to attack me and throw me off the train when it was travelling at full speed, but all went well.

On arriving at Ryazhsk early in the morning, I saw an incredible scene. A military train pulled into the station from the east. There were Red Army soldiers in the freight carriages, and weapons and military equipment on the open cars. As soon as the train stopped, sentries with rifles were posted outside the carriages and cars. Some soldiers jumped out of the carriages and ran into the station to fetch boiling water for tea, while others walked along the platform to stretch their legs. I couldn't believe my eyes! All of them were wearing *lapti* on their feet![8] Hundreds of military men wearing *lapti*! The *lapti* had probably been hidden away in a military store after the Civil War and a military commander had ordered conscripts to turn in the shoes they were wearing and change them for *lapti* so that everyone was wearing the same footwear.

Jumping ahead of myself, I will tell you about another strange incident which I witnessed. In February 1945 our battalion was marching along an asphalt road in Germany. We called a halt for lunch. Suddenly I saw a regiment with mortars slowly making its way along the road. Each mortar was carried on a sled hauled by a pair of oxen. Soldiers walked alongside the oxen, shouting from time to time 'Tsob-tsobe!'[9] They were being overtaken by American military vehicles—modern Studebakers, Dodges, Fords

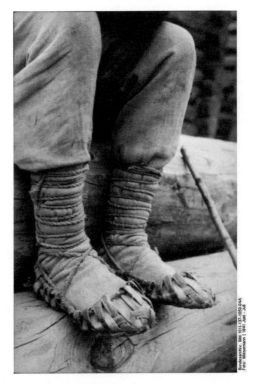

Lapti

and Willys MBs, not to mention French Chevrolets. Two centuries clashed—the seventeenth and the twentieth.

From Ryazhsk I headed west to Gumyonka by road. After twenty kilometres I was detained by soldiers. They were suspicious of me and interrogated me for a long time at their battalion HQ. Thankfully they believed my story and let me go. They could have simply shot me dead. The spy scare was widespread then. Stalin's rule, 'No man, no problem', was being applied everywhere.

During my interrogation I learned that the Germans had made a breakthrough and occupied Skopin, and that they could come here any minute. The soldiers had been digging trenches in frozen ground nearby to create a fortified line which they hoped would hold back an enemy attack.

I went out on the road again. By now it was night and I was alone; there was no one around and there was a hard frost. What should I do? Where should I go? There was nobody to ask for advice, so I decided to carry on to Gumyonka, to my brother and relatives. But what if I bumped into the Germans? I would not be of any interest to them, I told myself. I was just a sixteen-year-old boy with a few coins in my pocket.

I spent the night at the next village. There happened to be two marines from the naval rifle brigade staying in the hut with me.[10] When their platoon was crossing the river earlier, they had fallen through the ice so they had stayed behind to get dry. Their presence reassured me: it meant that our troops were still ahead.

When I reached Gumyonka, my relatives told me that the previous day German motorcyclists had turned up on the outskirts of the village, then there had been shooting for half an hour before they went away. Now a battle was under way for Skopin. The naval rifle brigade was mounting an attack on the town. The next day I went to the edge of Gumyonka and saw a real battle for the first time in my life. I had only seen battles before in films. Our marines were advancing across a snow-covered field towards Skopin, where the Germans had fortified their positions. They looked so awkward and out of place against the white snow. Their black uniforms provided excellent targets for the highly skilled German snipers, who were showering them with well-aimed bullets.

Some figures lay motionless on the snow, dotted over the field like chicken pox spots on a face; others were moving forward in short bounds. Then they all stayed down for a long time. I went home without waiting to see the end of the battle. I learned later that they succeeded in liberating Skopin.

The next day Uncle Zudin told me that the sailors had driven the Germans out of Skopin and were pushing them back to the west. There was no one to impose order in the town. People were rushing around, plundering shops and warehouses. 'Take the sledges, go to town and take everything you can!' my uncle ordered. So I went to Skopin. There I saw a terrible sight by the church wall. Ten tractor drivers in greasy sweaters and thick trousers had been shot dead by the Germans and left lying on the ground. Their corpses were frozen.

This scene affected me badly and has remained in my memory for the rest of my life. The drivers' dead faces were distorted by horror. I looked into them for a long time trying to imagine what ordeals the drivers had gone through and what their last thoughts must have been.

As it turned out, German motorcyclists had overtaken a tractor column which was moving east. Having neither the time nor desire to deal with the drivers, they simply shot them dead. There were spent cartridges around the bodies. I picked some of them up but lost them later. But this cold-blooded act of cruelty stuck in my memory.[11]

By the time I reached Skopin, numerous looters from the town and nearby villages had taken everything they could. All the shops and warehouses were empty. In the offices all the doors were either open or broken off their hinges, and the furniture was overturned. Annoyed with myself for having been unable to find anything worth taking, I set off home.

When I passed my school, I saw books scattered in the school yard: books by Thomas Mayne Reid, James Fenimore Cooper, Robert Louis Stevenson, Mark Twain, Alexandre Dumas, Victor Hugo, Arkady Gaidar and others.[12] This was more like it! I brought home a whole sack of wonderful books. But Uncle Zudin was not impressed. On learning that the only thing left in the town was some salt which was so hard that it had to be broken with a bar or an axe, he gave me an axe and sent me to fetch some straight away. To his great satisfaction I brought home half a sack.

2

JOINING THE ARMY

INTO THE UNKNOWN

My youth ended long ago
But still I ask why
I was among the three per cent
Of my age to survive.

A few days later at a collective farm meeting I made a critical
remark, then heard somebody from the back row say: 'Shut up,
you commissar's brat. Just wait, when the Germans come, they'll
sort you out.' I began to feel anxious: the frontline was rumbling
away somewhere near Skopin. Uncle Zudin advised me to leave
the village. I must say, I was not unwilling: I was bored with
village life and had never really adapted to it, having been brought
up in the town.

FOR THE MOTHERLAND! FOR STALIN!

I decided to volunteer for the army. And wholeheartedly too—it had always been my dream to become a regular officer like my father. I was not old enough to be called up yet, but, I assured myself, there is always an exception to the rule!

My aunt put some food into my rucksack and, saying goodbye to my relatives, I went to the enlistment office in Skopin. Nobody was there. The Soviet authorities had not arrived yet. Like all the other offices in Skopin, the doors were wide open, drawers had been pulled out of desks and windows had been smashed. The wind blew through the rooms, rustling the papers scattered on the floor. Eventually two lads turned up. They told me that they had been conscripted with many others the day before the Germans captured Skopin and sent to a military unit to the west of the town. On the way there, they came under fire from German motorcyclists and made their escape. After a discussion, we decided to go to the enlistment office in Sarai, fifty kilometres east of Skopin. On our way we called in on the home of one of the lads, where we had a light snack and drank some spirits. For the first time in my life, I drank half a glass of neat alcohol, so I can barely remember what happened next.

On leaving the town we took a snow-covered road across the fields. It was–20°C. I was so drunk that I couldn't walk and my companions dragged me under my arms as best they could, as they were also very drunk. If they had left me on the road, I would have died. After the war I tried to find them but failed.

The lads joined up at the enlistment office in Sarai, but I couldn't because I wasn't old enough yet, being sixteen years and ten months. The officials gave me two coupons—one for lunch at the state-run canteen and the other for a loaf of bread—and sent me away. I decided to see the regional military commissar at Ryazan, but he also refused to enlist me. Then I went further, to Moscow. On one leg of the journey I nearly froze travelling on the step of a brake van of a freight carriage. There was a severe frost and it was–30°C, but it felt even colder when the train was on the move and I was only lightly wrapped in an overcoat. Further on, I managed to board a passenger train where I happened to share a compartment with a senior lieutenant, an officer who taught at the artillery school in Podolsk, near Moscow. He turned out to come from the same part of the country as my father's family—he had lived in a village near Skopin before he was conscripted. I told him about my dream and he promised to help me volunteer as a cadet in the artillery school.

My dream comes true

As a child and a teenager I had always lived among military people, both officers and soldiers. My father, a professional mili-

Boris's father, Major Ilya Bogachev, commander of the 3rd rifle regiment of the 421st Odessa rifle division, July 1941

tary man since 1918, had served in seven garrisons before the war. Since childhood I was used to the tough military way of life, and grew up sharing troubles and quiet joys with soldiers.

I still can picture myself sitting with the soldiers at a long wooden table under a sunshade in summer, eating buckwheat *kasha* (porridge) copiously dressed in sunflower oil. Or my father lifting me, a five-year-old boy, onto the saddle of his horse and leading me around the parade ground. No wonder I looked forward to becoming a military man, a defender of my native soil, like the sons of so many other military professionals. Indeed, before the war, such men were treated with great respect and they were comparatively well off.

Why did I want to join the artillery? Because when I was in the eighth form at school, we lived next to the barracks of an artillery regiment and every day I would see the artillery officers in their smart military uniforms with black-banded peaked caps on their heads and lustrous calf boots with spurs on their feet.

How I loved to watch the Red Army soldiers marching along the street singing in chorus, the red banner flying over their ranks, the formidable artillery weapons, the beautiful horses, accompanied by the officers' loud commands, the martial music of the regimental band, the blare of bugles—all these things impressed my young romantic soul.

There was also an artillery school in Odessa, and groups of smart cadets with artillery insignia on their collar patches would walk along the streets. They were only two or three years older than me.

Actually, there were three specialised military schools in Odessa: the naval school, the air force academy and the artillery school, each with a curriculum based on those followed by the eighth, ninth and tenth forms at secondary school. When I finished eighth form and applied to the artillery school, I was not accepted because my grades for mathematics and physics were only 'satisfactory', and those are the most important subjects for the study of artillery. My father knew that I was trying to join the artillery. He suggested that he could help me enter naval school, or the air force academy, which were both in the district where he was military commissar. Their headmasters were his colleagues and he knew them well. But I only wanted to go to the artillery school. And indeed, my favourite writer Chekhov preferred artillerymen above all other military men.

And now my youthful dream was coming true! My fellow passenger had said that there was currently no accommodation in Podolsk and had told me to stay in Moscow for three days; meanwhile he would sort out my nomination. But because I was not quite old enough, things turned out to be more difficult.

Moscow in a state of siege

I'd never been to Moscow before. In the daytime I walked around the city; at night I slept at Kazan railway station, north-east of the centre. Moscow, the capital of the Soviet Union, was martially austere, forbidding and almost empty. The frontline city was in a state of siege. It was difficult to imagine that twenty-five kilometres away, within striking range, there was a cruel and treacherous enemy. At night Moscow was submerged in darkness. There was no light anywhere. But the radio was never turned off. At any time an air raid warning could sound. As soon as the sirens began to wail people would hurry to the numerous bomb shelters, or to the metro. Only armed patrols remained in the streets. There were plenty of them. Papers were checked all the time. A curfew was in effect. People could only go out between 6 am and 10 pm unless they had a special pass. There were anti-aircraft guns and searchlights on the roofs of big houses. At the attic windows women and teenagers were on duty; they had tongs with long handles for throwing incendiary bombs

An anti-aircraft machine-gun in Moscow, 1941

off the roofs. My future wife Nina, a fourteen-year-old school-girl, was among them (judging from what she told me). During air raids they had to notify their local air raid defence HQ where bombs had fallen, check whether blackout discipline was being observed and look out for saboteurs who might be using lights to signal to German planes.

Later Nina told me that she was an eyewitness to a terrible panic in Moscow on 15 October 1941. A woman on the radio was appealing to the people of Moscow to be firm and brave, and she said, speaking figuratively, 'The enemy is at the gates of Moscow.' At that time, the frontline was actually 100 kilometres away (a two-hour journey for a German tank column). But it was rumoured that the Germans were actually at the Red Gates in the centre of Moscow. This spread like wildfire around the city's five million inhabitants: 'The Germans are at the Red Gates! The Germans are at the Red Gates!' It resulted in pandemonium.

Heads of offices and businesses fled from Moscow with their families in cars and lorries loaded with their personal possessions, boxes, sacks and barrels of food. In many places in the east of the city, workers who were trying to quell the panic stopped the vehicles and took away their loads, beating up anyone who resisted them.

The authorities were all adrift. Public transport, including the metro, had stopped running. Rubbish tips and bins were piled high with portraits and busts of Bolshevik leaders, the works of Lenin and any other books in red covers, and certificates of merit and party documents. People were also burning them on bonfires and the stifling smoke was spreading around Moscow, causing even more panic.

It was 20 October before the authorities began to cope with the panic and a state of siege and curfew was announced, giving the militia and military patrols powers to take severe measures.[1] The evacuation of civilians to the east began. To boost morale, huge posters advertising the forthcoming concerts of the popular actress and singer Lyubov Orlova were put up all over the city.

A model of a three-storey building was constructed over Lenin's mausoleum as camouflage. In front of St Basil's Cathedral, the monument to Minin and Pozharsky[2] was covered with sandbags.

High in the sky, huge gas-filled barrage balloons were swinging gently in the wind to protect the city from German planes. Sometimes you could see women in military uniform hoisting up the barrage balloons like enormous sausages. At the junctions there were anti-tank 'hedgehogs' made of welded rails, and in the suburbs there were concrete anti-tank teeth. Windows were criss-crossed with strips of paper and broken windows were covered with plywood. Chimneys of temporary stoves stuck out of the windows.[3] Shop windows were covered with sandbags. All food was rationed. People looked anxious. You hardly saw any

FOR THE MOTHERLAND! FOR STALIN!

Air-raid over Moscow, 1941

Anti-tank "hedgehog" barricades, Moscow 1941

children in the streets. Bombing took place every night, sometimes several times a night. During an air raid alert, dozens of beams from searchlights would dart about in the sky. You could hear the spasmodic roar of anti-aircraft guns as they opened fire. Shrapnel from exploding shells rained down noisily on roofs, or asphalted streets. Sometimes powerful bomb explosions were heard. Many houses were destroyed. When the searchlights caught a German plane, bright tracks of tracer fire began arcing towards it. Caught in the intersecting bright beams, the plane hurtled about, diving, turning on a wing, trying to dive into the safety of the darkness below. But all in vain. It turned into a torch flaring up in the sky. The vulture was shot down. People's faces lit up with joy.

During one air raid I had to hide deep in the metro. There were thousands of people sleeping on the platform and on the rails.

The Kremlin, the Bolshoi Theatre and other distinctive buildings were painted in grey, green and black stripes—a camouflage trick. The red stars of the Kremlin were wrapped in protective covers. Nevertheless, the Kremlin was partly destroyed in bombing raids and more than 100 people died there.

I walked around the centre of Moscow. Near the Kremlin, in luxurious aristocratic mansions, lived the present-day Communist Party 'princes' and 'counts' as well as the old revolutionaries who by chance had not been killed by Stalin during the Terror of 1937–38.

Podolsk Artillery School

At the artillery school in Podolsk I was told that I had to wait until I was seventeen before I could enlist (my birthday was on 31 December 1941). Meanwhile I was admitted as a voluntary Red Army soldier in an administrative platoon at the school.

FOR THE MOTHERLAND! FOR STALIN!

German troops had breached the defensive line on the western front, surrounded four of our armies and, unopposed, moved towards Moscow. There was nobody left to stop them. So the army's 'gold reserve' was sent to Mozhaysk—that is, the cadets from the infantry and artillery schools in Podolsk, just a step away from qualifying as officers. The cadets fought courageously and selflessly at the towns of Maloyaroslavets and Naro Fominsk against an enemy who very much outnumbered them.

In his memoirs Marshal Zhukov wrote: 'When I am asked what I remember best about the war, I always answer: the battle for Moscow.' Zhukov held in high esteem the feat of 3,000 Podolsk cadets who held back a mechanised German corps for ten days at a river crossing. While they did this an infantry division of 15,000 arrived from Siberia, who were well trained, well equipped and dressed in warm winter uniforms. They took up positions in the fortifications prepared by civilians on the outskirts of Moscow and fought off the Germans. The enemy never moved beyond those defences. In the fierce fighting 2,500 Podolsk cadets died.

My military service as a volunteer started on 3 November 1941. My duties included being a sentry at the ration depot and other relatively unimportant sites; acting as messenger for the duty officer; loading ammunition into the lorries which were taking supplies to the front where the Podolsk cadets were fighting; looking after the lightly wounded in the infirmary; chopping wood; peeling potatoes; cleaning the barracks; learning about the design of rifles and how to use them; and, generally, learning the ins and outs of military service. These were not very onerous duties.

I was very proud of being a sentry. I held a real rifle in my hands and had the right to shoot anyone who approached me without my permission. When my immediate superior, the corporal of the guard, approached with the relief sentry, I would

JOINING THE ARMY

Boris as a Red Army volunteer, Poldolsk artillery school, December 1941

shout: 'Halt! Who goes there? Relief sentry, one step forward march! Others stay in line!' Many times, when there was nobody nearby, I would pretend to come under attack, raise my rifle and take aim at an imaginary enemy.

Two weeks later, our school was evacuated to Central Asia, to the ancient city of Bukhara in Uzbekistan. Among us were new cadets who were being admitted to the school every day for intensive training as anti-tank artillery officers—these were badly needed on the front. We went on a troop train and arrived on New Year's Eve. Our artillery battalion was housed in the building of a former teaching college. The rest of the school was housed in other parts of the city.

As our train passed the Uzbek town of Tashkent, I had no idea that my father was there. He had been posted to Tashkent, after being injured by a falling wall during the siege of Odessa, which had lasted seventy-three days. He was working in the personnel department of the military district of Tashkent.

3

TRAINING IN BUKHARA

I AM A CADET

On New Year's Eve, 31 December 1941, I turned seventeen and on that very day I was admitted to the artillery school in the 3rd platoon of the 9th battery of the 3rd battalion.

To celebrate New Year's Eve, each of us was given a small bun and an apple. Our commanders said 'Happy New Year' to us and wished us good health, success and happiness, then the rest of that evening passed by like any other: there was no drinking, dancing or friendly chat.

And so the year of 1942 began. The first thing I saw at the school was a huge poster in our barracks: 'More sweat in learning—less blood in battle.' In our battery everyone was either from Moscow or the Moscow region and was either a university or college student, or a secondary school (tenth form) leaver. I

FOR THE MOTHERLAND! FOR STALIN!

The Kalyan minaret, Bukhara

was the only one with just eight school years behind me. I was also the youngest, and the only cadet to have stayed down in the eighth form for two years.

My situation was also unusual in that all the other cadets in my battery had already studied for two months before I joined them. So I had to learn very intensively in four months the entire two-year peacetime curriculum of a conventional artillery school. I had to make a real effort to learn the difficult laws of military science and become part of the army fraternity.

My period of intensive study started. I worked to a very tight schedule. My daily routine provides proof:

- Reveille 6.00
- Grooming, mucking out and feeding the horses 6.15–7.05
- Washing 7.15–7.25
- Morning inspection 7.30–7.45
- Breakfast 7.55–8.15

TRAINING IN BUKHARA

- Classes 8.30–1.40
- Artillery training 1.55–2.10
- Lunch 2.15–2.45
- Feeding the horses 2.55–3.50
- Classes 4.05–5.50
- Study period 5.55–7.35
- Supper 7.50–8.10
- Grooming, mucking out and feeding the horses 8.30–9.20
- Political education 9.30–10.20
- Evening inspection and weapons-cleaning 10.25–11.00
- Lights out 11.00

We studied in classrooms, at the stables and out on the range for ten hours a day. At daybreak, when the narrow streets of Bukhara were still empty, we would walk to the range. We passed clay-walled huts, built up close to each other, numerous mosques, minarets and madrasas (religious schools). The Kalyan minaret towered in the distance, seventy metres high. In the old days it had been used as a wartime observation point: during times of peace it was called the 'death minaret', as those who had been sentenced to death and wives accused of adultery were thrown off the top.

To enter the range we had to walk through the gateway in the city wall. What an impressive sight it was! The clay wall had been built a thousand years ago. It was seven metres high (it used to be much higher) and seventeen metres thick. The town of Bukhara itself was founded 2,500 years ago.

The winter of 1941–42 in Bukhara was horrible. The temperature was 5–6°C, but we only had light summer clothes: light underwear, a cotton tunic and trousers, a cap, shoes, *portyanki* (foot cloths) and puttees.[1] We did not have scarves, sweaters or gloves.

Most of our classes were held outside on the range where we would shiver in the strong cold wind. Where was this subtropical

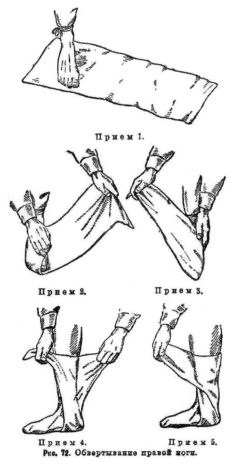

Пряем 1.

Пряем 2.   Пряем 3.

Пряем 4.   Пряем 5.
Рис. 72. Обвертывание правой ноги.

How to put on *portyanki* (foot cloths)

Central Asia with its famous watermelons? There was no romance about it at all. Three times a day we would go to the stables to look after the horses: each time to give them food and water, twice to groom them and muck out the stables. All the time we were kept hard at work, all the time we were in the public eye: there was no opportunity to relax. Crowding and lack of privacy had a strong impact on the teenage psyche. We were allowed only thirty minutes free time a day (to wash, shave, sew, polish shoes, write letters and so on). Everything was done by command, even in the mess: we were commanded to go to the mess, to sit down at our tables, to start eating and to leave our tables.

Our whole existence was mapped out to the finest detail in order to turn us into professional military commanders within the shortest space of time. The service regulations and timetable stipulated every aspect of our life. All our days were exactly the same. There were no entertainments at all. We only went out as a military formation, singing a song as a rule.

A song is a powerful weapon for morale that brings people together, creating a healthy community and making it a single entity. Imagine: a battery (120 men) or a battalion (360 men) is marching along the streets of a town. Everyone is singing: you are singing but your voice can't be heard in the joint male choir and a special feeling of friendship and comradeship inspires you. Dear reader, just imagine: you are eighteen to twenty years old (your whole life is ahead of you) and you are marching in a military formation and you can hear the soloist's clear voice, then the chorus of a hundred cadets accompanied by the heavy beat of their metal capped boots. At the time, there were about half a dozen popular military songs that we used to sing.

And whenever a pretty girl looked out of a window the sergeant major would yell, 'Eyes right!' (to the window, of course) and all 120 (or 360) cadets turned their heads simultaneously to the right and stamped on the road so hard that the glass would shake in the window frame.

For a long time we would sing airmen's songs. Owing to an over-supply of air technicians and a shortage of anti-tank specialists in the army, our battalion was joined by sixty cadets from Kharkov air technical school and 235 cadets from Chardzhou (now Turkmenabat) air mechanics school. They were the ones who set the new fashion in our musical repertoire.

At school our ration was the same as that for civilians, that is to say very little, with many fewer calories than those on the front. We were all young, our bodies were growing and we were always hungry. The most desirable duty for us was that of kitchen assistant (during peacetime it was the most menial duty). In the kitchen you could eat until you were full and you could also take away a pot of barley or rice *kasha* to eat in the morning. To stop your comrades stealing your *kasha*, you would tie it up in a cloth under your bed. But they even managed to steal it from there. All in all, such a life couldn't be called easy.

At school I ate camel meat for the first time in my life. A bit tough but quite edible.

Apart from kitchen duty, I also enjoyed being an orderly in the battery, keeping an eye on the weapons, cleaning the barracks and staying in the warmth. And the best thing was that the orderly on duty had a sabre. When nobody was around, I took it out of its sheath, swung it fiercely and killed my imaginary enemy.

My first blood is spilt in the war

At the artillery school I, like the other cadets, was assigned a carbine (a short rifle) and a cavalry horse. My horse's name was Ovod, or Gadfly. Apart from cavalry horses, the army used artillery horses and carthorses. Looking after a horse took a lot of time, energy and skill. I was a town boy and I had never handled horses before.

A horse had to be fed and given water three times a day. The daily ration was: five kilos of oats, seven kilos of hay, five kilos of vegetables, twenty-five grams of salt and sixty grams of chalk.

Twice a day we had to groom our horses using round brushes with loops for your hand, and combs, wiping their eyes with a clean cloth and cleaning out their hooves with a hoof pick, and once a day our horses had to be walked around the stable yard for exercise.

Gadfly was finely built, tall, with big fiery eyes and slim legs. In short, he was a beauty of a horse. A cavalryman's dream. Actually a horse is a very clever animal and, I would say, a noble one. He takes away all his rider's negative feelings and fills him with the joy of life. He is a true friend—he would rather maim himself than step on a person deliberately.

Once on a range in the desert near Bukhara, we were doing firing practice and I was sent to form a cordon to keep outsiders away from the firing zone. While I was riding up to my position, Gadfly, who had been cooped up too long in the stable, broke into a gallop and bolted. Conscious of my inexperience, he went faster and faster.

I started to worry. I was pulling on the reins like mad to slow him down, but it had no effect. It could have resulted in tragedy: it is so easy to lose your way in the vast desert, as there are absolutely no landmarks. He had been galloping for about five kilometres and I could no longer see our battery's firing position. But at last Gadfly decided that he'd had enough exercise and that he'd taught silly me a good lesson, showing me that he was also a personality to be reckoned with, so he slowed down and I was able to turn him back. Dealing with Gadfly three times a day every day, I came to love him and he would greet me as a friend.

I spilt my first blood in the war at the same stable. It was like this. Among the artillery horses who hauled the heavy guns into battle, a beastly-looking stallion stood out on account of his size. He was the size of two ordinary horses. He would sometimes snap his halter rope which tethered him to his manger in the stall, then stride over to the haystack in the corner of the stable and calmly tuck in. Soldiers on duty were afraid to beat him with a whip because he kicked fiercely with his hind feet and his hooves were thirty centimetres in diameter.

They tried beating him with a long pole, but this did not work either. The blows had no effect other than irritating him, and eventually he would kick the pole so hard that it was thrown up high into the air. Having eaten his fill, he would stride back to his stall where he drank his water; at that moment he was tied down.

One time the stallion was tethered next to my Gadfly. Brandishing my whip at him, I pushed him aside, then began cleaning Gadfly's belly with a brush. I was bending over in such a way that my bottom was quite near the stallion. I was concentrating so hard that I forgot about the danger. Suddenly the stallion snatched at my bottom with his huge yellow teeth. I cried blue murder and was so shocked that I lurched heavily into Gadfly. The latter, being caught off guard, was frightened and started kicking, which started the other horses off.

Escaping from that madhouse, I pulled down my trousers and asked my comrades if they could see anything. 'You're bleeding,' they said. 'Go to the medical unit quickly or you might get blood poisoning.' At the medical unit they put some iodine and a plaster on the wound and said: 'Off you go! You've spilt your first blood of the war.'

Every other day we were taught advanced riding techniques which seemed more like stunts. We had to jump on the horse while it was moving; ride, sitting back to front; pick up a handkerchief from the ground while on horseback (I never succeeded in that); trot over jumps; form a column; keep in line; and, the most difficult of all, stand up on the saddle and jump over the horse's head. I could never manage to do this. For a start, the saddle was one and a half metres from the ground, but from there you had to jump up about half a metre to clear the horse's head. But the horse is alive, it can move, and it can waggle its head. No matter how hard the commander of the platoon, spruce Lieutenant Antonenko, tried to teach me this trick, I could never jump over the horse's head. But the others could. Cavalry was definitely not my cup of tea.

The best riders could shoot targets on the move and ride back to front, or lying across the saddle, or standing up on the saddle, or even on the horse's head—but we were not supposed to do that, thank goodness.

I made friends with Alexander Barkov who came from Krasnodar region in southern Russia. He was six months older than me, a head taller, lean, and wore size 45 boots. In our platoon dormitory of thirty men, his bed was next to mine. Later we went to the front together as junior lieutenants and served in the same rifle regiment. How could I possibly know then that he would be killed in battle on 1 August 1942, the day after I was wounded? After the war I sent an inquiry to the Podolsk archive only to learn that the rifle regiment had no record of where he had been buried or of his parents' address. That is that.

Another person who was at Podolsk artillery school at the same time as me was Captain Alexander Chapayev, the son of Vasiliy Chapayev, the legendary hero of the Civil War. Alexander Chapayev was the commander of the trainee anti-tank battery. After the war, Chapayev, then commander of an artillery brigade with the rank of major general, was present at the nuclear test at the Totskoye range, under the command of Marshal Zhukov.[2] He was exposed to a large quantity of radiation and died shortly afterwards.

While I was at artillery school another rifle brigade was being formed in Bukhara, which included in its ranks the soon-to-be-famous war hero Alexander Matrosov. Later, at the front, he covered a German machine gun embrasure with his body so his platoon could mount an attack. He was the same age as me, and I might have come across him when I was on patrol in the town checking the documents of soldiers passing through.

Matrosov's heroic feat as depicted on a Soviet stamp, 1944

My studies come to an end

The time came for the end of our studies. We passed our inspection. Oh, what a fool I made of myself during the inspection! We
had spent about three days preparing for it. We had cleaned the
barracks, the stable and the yard. We had washed the horses with
soap, cleaning and brushing their tails and manes, and polishing
their hooves. At last our battalion—360 cadets with their
horses—aligned themselves into a square formation. The inspection was headed by a general. The general was highly distinguished, with stripes on his trousers, medals on his chest and
shining boots with spurs. Behind him and the principal marched
an entourage of about fifteen colonels and lieutenant colonels.
When the general approached me, I, like any other cadet should
have said: 'Bogachev, cadet; Gadfly, horse.' But I, like many others, was so excited and nervous that I mixed everything up and
said instead: 'Gadfly, cadet; Bogachev, horse.' Luckily the general

didn't seem to notice. He wiped Gadfly's neck with a white hand-kerchief: his neck was clean. The general said nothing and moved on, then I started coming to my senses.

I was in a lot of trouble from my superiors for that mistake and my comrades kept laughing at me for a long time, giving me the nickname of 'Gadfly'. But now the time had come for me to part with my horse. Having dealt with each other on a daily basis for four months, we had become attached to each other. And besides, as a teenager who was not quite used to being independent, I needed Gadfly's friendship and companionship.

There were 468 cadets in our class of graduates. Several cadets had been expelled for academic failure, bad or only 'satisfactory' marks, or misbehaviour. As far as I was concerned, I did well, although I had studied for only four months, not six like the rest of the cadets.

Here are my final results:

Political studies	good
Chemical warfare training	good
Tactics	good
Communications	good
Artillery	good
Weapons training	excellent
Gun maintenance	excellent
Physical education	excellent
Marksmanship	good
Drill	excellent
Military engineering	excellent
Cavalry training	satisfactory
Topography	good
First aid	good
Military regulations	good
Veterinary training	good

FOR THE MOTHERLAND! FOR STALIN!

Junior Lieutenant Boris Bogachev

Our intensive training prepared us well for our roles as junior lieutenants, platoon commanders of anti-tank artillery, although, as a matter of fact, we used to shoot rifle cartridges from our guns instead of shells because of the shortage of the latter.

At the leaving ceremony, the principal said something which I would remember well: 'Not every lieutenant makes a marshal but every marshal starts as a lieutenant.' However, cadets who were older than me had a different saying: 'We sacrificed our youth for our lieutenants' stars.'

I served in the rank of junior lieutenant for nine and a half months. When I look at eighteen-year-old soldiers in their first year of service now, almost children, I think: 'Was it possible that I was like them when I was expected to lead thirty soldiers into battle, some of whom were twice or three times my age?'

4

TO THE KALININ FRONT

ON THE BORDER OF ASIA AND EUROPE

In mid-May we boarded a passenger train to join our division,
just ten of us. As we all had surnames starting with B, it was
most likely that we had been distributed in alphabetical order.
The chief of our group was Budilin, the commander of our
detachment at artillery school. He was a professional soldier,
born in 1914, and had entered the school with three triangles on
his collar patches denoting his rank of sergeant major.

For several days our train travelled across the empty steppes of
Central Asia. In the beginning we could see magnificent mountains which were fifty kilometres away but seemed quite near. It
was the effect of the pure mountain air which makes distances
seem smaller.

FOR THE MOTHERLAND! FOR STALIN!

'We're going to the front in our thousands, young and healthy. Will we return?' From a newspaper cutting, June 1941

For about 500 kilometres the railway ran along the bank of a great river in Central Asia—the Syr-Darya. It was May and still spring but it was hot and stuffy in the carriage. Some of us, including me, climbed onto the roof of the carriage. Up there a light cool breeze was blowing and we could see the countryside very clearly. Old hands in the group advised us to tie ourselves to a chimney with a belt otherwise we might fall asleep, fall off the roof and not make it to the front. I heeded their advice and, indeed, fell asleep. I woke up because of the rattle—the train was going over a bridge across the river. The iron beams of the bridge were rushing right overhead.

We went along the Aral Sea coast, past the station and town of Aralsk.[1] We were going slowly, stopping at many stations to give way to military trains hurrying west. Eventually we arrived at a station which was on the bank of the River Ural.

Everyone ran to plunge into the river. Some swam quite far away from the bank. I certainly swam the furthest. I was from Odessa, wasn't I? I used to swim in the Black Sea itself. I swam as far as 200 metres from the bank, to the middle of the river— the border between Asia and Europe. Suddenly I heard the train hoot. Everyone started swimming towards the bank, dashing out of the water, putting on clothes and running to the train which was 300 metres away.

I began swimming very fast but I overrated my strength and soon weakened. In the end I was swimming very slowly, with great effort. When I emerged on the bank the last swimmers were running up to the train. I started putting on my long underpants (we did not have drawers or swimming trunks then). With my hands shaking, I could not pull the underpants over my wet legs. At that moment the train began slowly moving off. Panic gripped me. I gave up with my underpants and started putting on my trousers. But for the same reason I could not put them on either.

There was one single horrible thought in my head: I would be separated from my group. The travel order which identified me was part of a group document, which Budilin held as head of our group. Without documents I could be regarded as a deserter and punished by tribunal.

Having snatched my clothes, belt, foot cloths and shoes, I started running naked towards the train which was gathering speed. As I ran up to the platform, the last carriage was just in front of me. At that time the local people from the nearest village had no other entertainment but to come to the station to learn the latest news and gossip, so there were quite a few people on the platform. I nearly died with embarrassment!

The men were shaking with laughter, the girls were modestly turning away. By the skin of my teeth I caught up with the last carriage where two soldiers grabbed my hands and pulled me on board. For five minutes, I lay prostrate on the floor. Once I had recovered my breath, I put on my clothes and went to my carriage. When I had been running along the platform, all the passengers had hung out of the windows, watching me. And now, as I was going through the carriages, they were laughing and greeting me.

For some time people from the front carriages came to look at me. Burning with shame, I hid myself on the upper third berth behind some suitcases. So that was how I rushed to the front. Had I preserved my modesty and put on my clothes I would have certainly been late for the train and my future would have been very different...

From Vologda to Bezhetsk

Everyone except me came from Moscow or Moscow region. Our route to the 2nd reserve army HQ at Vologda was via Moscow. As we approached Moscow the others decided to go and see their families before meeting at a rendezvous in two days' time. I, however, had nowhere to go, having no relatives in Moscow: my mother and brother, as I knew from their letters, were now with my father in Karaganda in Kazakhstan, where he was a regional military commissar with the rank of general.

I spent those two days walking around Moscow and sleeping at Budilin's flat. He lived in Taganka, in Bolshoy Fakelny Lane. My future wife, Nina, lived just across the road. We might have come across each other in the street but she was only fifteen then and I would certainly not have paid attention to a young girl like her. Two days later we all got together and left for Vologda.

By the way, a few words about Budilin's fate. He went through the whole war: he was wounded, then awarded a medal, then promoted to the rank of captain. It was after the war, when he was teaching young soldiers to throw grenades, that a grenade happened to explode in his hands. He was killed instantly. The army personnel department sent us to the 111th rifle division. The division comprised 11,634 men, sixty guns, 153 mortars, 255 machine guns, 8,977 rifles and 2,740 horses. There were three rifle regiments and an artillery regiment. In each rifle regiment there were three rifle battalions, a company of submachine gunners, a company of anti-tank rifles, a battery of 76-mm guns, an anti-tank battery of 45-mm guns, a company of engineers, a company of communications personnel, a platoon of chemical defence specialists, a platoon of musicians and medical and logistical detachments (services and storage depots). In the artillery regiment there were twenty-four guns. There were separate battalions in the division, each with its area of responsibility: reconnaissance; mine-clearance; communications; training; medical and ambulance; anti-tank; and anti-aircraft.

In addition the division had a chemical defence section, a counter intelligence SMERSH-type subdivision[2] which comprised twenty-five officers (one KGB officer per battalion or battery), a military prosecution department, a military tribunal, editorial staff and a printing office for *Vpyeryod* (*Forward* newspaper), a field post office staffed by the department of military censorship which censored personal letters, a field branch of the state bank, a field bakery, a veterinary clinic and an infirmary. The division's HQ and the political department were situated in Bezhetsk, while the regiments, battalions, batteries and platoons were stationed in nearby villages.

The 532nd rifle regiment

The military personnel for our division, both officers and soldiers, were mainly drawn from the reserves, although some came from hospital after recovering from their injuries. They arrived both in groups and individually. There were very few professional military men who had served in the army before the war. Supplies of weapons, equipment, ammunition, carts, horses, food and forage also made their way to the division.

I was sent to the 532nd rifle regiment. For some time I held the post of platoon commander of a 45-mm anti-tank gun battery—and encountered horses again. All the guns in the battery were horse-drawn, with each gun drawn by two horses. But the horses were Mongolian and hadn't been broken in: they were wild, fierce and very difficult to handle.

Whenever you approached them they used to show their teeth and try to bite you. They would rear, buck, kick and roll around on the ground, lashing out in white-hot fury. I was afraid to go near them: I wouldn't have touched them with a barge pole but I couldn't do anything about it as there was a shortage of Russian horses. Only the battery officers had Russian cavalry horses. I

Horse-drawn guns in the rifle regiment

Firing mortars

also had a cavalry horse but because it was so long ago I can't remember much about it at all.

The officers of the anti-tank artillery were privileged. They were paid a high salary and on their left sleeve they had a diamond-shaped badge of black felt with a red trim, on which two crossed gun barrels were embroidered in gold.

Later, I became commander of an 82-mm mortar firing platoon and finally I was appointed commander of the 50-mm mortar platoon of the 2nd company of the 1st rifle battalion.

So by a twist of circumstance and fate I ended up in infantry. Our mortars weighed nine kilogrammes and soldiers carried them on their backs on shoulder straps. Their range was one kilometre and their shells each weighed 800 grams. Each mortar had an ammunition load of six boxes of shells with six shells in each box.

The funny thing was that at Podolsk artillery school we had not studied mortars at all and when I joined the regiment it was the first time I had seen a mortar. What is more, when I came to the regiment the platoon sergeant told me that there were thirty soldiers and four mortars, but two of the mortars were out of order. Good grief! How on earth could we fight with only half our firepower?

We formed detachments and started our combat training. We did our training mainly in the field in any weather from dawn till dusk, fifteen to sixteen hours a day.

We would crawl on our bellies through woodland clearings, charge forwards, dig in, use camouflage and study the structure of guns, grenades, weapons, mortars and gas masks; we learned how to locate our position on the map. We also had political studies, drill, midnight alerts, marches in full kit and guard duty.

By the end of the day we were exhausted. To make matters worse, we had insufficient rations. But nobody grumbled: everyone understood that the conditions at the front were even harder and that we had to prepare ourselves for overcoming hardships while in the rear. The only thing we did not have was live ammunition. Ammunition stocks were low and they were badly needed at the front. So we were to learn about mortars in theory rather than practice.

To tell the truth, we did have one opportunity to use live ammunition. My platoon was on sentry duty. Among the supplies we were guarding was an ammunition store belonging to the regiment. I was the officer of the guard. The sentry of the store, my subordinate, suggested stealing a box with 50-mm bombs and using them for mortar practice. I agreed.

We took a box containing six bombs out of the store and hid it in the forest. The next day I took my platoon for training five kilometres away from the village where we were stationed. That's where we did our mortar practice. We deliberately aimed at the river. Several bombs hit the target. We picked up fish stunned by the blasts and made fish soup to everyone's delight. There were plenty of experts and advisers on how to make the best fish soup.

By that time our country was on the edge of catastrophe. The Germans had shot the daylights out of our professional army. In the second half of 1941 they had captured four million of our soldiers and officers. They occupied the most important 'European' part of the country, west of the Urals, with the best agricultural land and the main industrial cities. We were desperately forming a new army. Total mobilization was under way. Military enlistment offices were conscripting even those deemed unfit for service on health or other grounds.

Thus in our division, which had been formed in a hurry, there was a platoon of former heads of collective farms who had been stripped of their exemption from active duty. In our company there was also a small unit of soldiers who suffered from night blindness. They could not see anything in the dark. The company commander thought they were faking it. During a training exercise at dusk he ordered them to run into attack with their guns at the ready, shouting 'Oorah!' There was a lake with a gently sloping shore ahead. So all those shouting soldiers plunged into the lake. It's a wonder that they didn't stab each other with their bayonets. Only then did the company commander believe that they really could not see in the dark. This is a symptom of a disease caused by malnutrition and over-fatigue.

In our company we also had a soldier with six fingers on his hand and a few soldiers who were cross-eyed. A dozen soldiers were criminals released from prison on condition that they went to the front. Another soldier had a crazy expression in his eyes: he was probably mentally ill and the company commander warned the soldier on duty to keep an eye on him lest he tried to strangle the officers at night. There was also a gypsy who was suspected of having untreated syphilis. Everyone tried to stay away from him.

I used to dream that after finishing artillery school I would be wearing a squeaky-clean, shiny leather belt complete with whistle and pistol holster. I wore nothing of the kind. Instead of being issued with a woollen uniform, a peaked cap, high leather boots and a leather belt, we, the commanders of the Workers and Peasants' Red Army (the word 'officer' was not used then), were given, to my profound regret, a rank-and-file uniform consisting of a pair of soldiers' boots, a second-hand cotton tunic, trousers and a soft *pilotka* cap.

There was a carelessly mended hole on the left side of my tunic. It must have belonged to a soldier wounded in the stomach. Instead of high boots I wore soldiers' ankle boots with one-metre long foot cloths. My belt was made of canvas. I sewed the insignia of junior lieutenant—a red angle bracket with a gold chevron—on the sleeves of my tunic and attached a square cut out of tin to the buttonhole of each sleeve. There were no pre-war ruby squares with a golden trim. But that was not the whole story. Instead of the TT pistol that I was entitled to (issued in 1930 and every cadet's dream), I was given a carbine. Our company commander had a revolver: only a battalion commander with 700 soldiers under his command had a TT pistol. The soldiers in my platoon had rifles designed in 1891.

Before we went to the front, each of us was given a plastic container with a screw-on lid. Inside was a piece of paper with our surname, given name and patronymic, the year and place of our birth, and our rank, as well as our family addresses—the notification data in the event of our death.[3] We kept the container in a small trouser pocket.

It was now time for us to go to the front. Eighteen trains, each with thirty carriages, were needed to transport our rifle division.

TO THE KALININ FRONT

We were going in goods carriages with the notice '20 men—8 horses' on them. Men and horses travelled in closed carriages, while guns and carts were carried in open carriages. Our route went from Bezhetsk to Selizharovo, in Kalinin (now Tver) region. There were anti-aircraft machine guns on the roofs of the front, middle and rear carriages. Inside, on both sides of each carriages, were two tiers of bunks. Following the advice of experienced soldiers, we six company officers took the lower bunks and put all our ammunition and equipment—mortars, rifles, spades, binoculars and gas masks—on the upper bunks. These would act as a protective barrier if we were fired on by machine guns from enemy aircraft.

More than half a century has passed, but I still can see this picture in my memory. Our train had stopped at a railway halt. The door of our carriages was open. In the yard of a house fifty metres away a young man and a girl were larking around, splashing each other with water and laughing. Finally the young man caught hold of the girl and started kissing her. As I looked at them I felt a dull pain in my heart—I was going to the front where I could be killed or maimed and I had never yet hugged or kissed a girl. I certainly did not share those thoughts with anyone.

The forced march

We got off the train at Selizharovo. Our division column marched along a forest road to the south, towards Rzhev.

Preparations were underway for what would turn out to be the first Rzhev-Sychevka offensive operation. We were moving quickly. It was hot and we were covering forty to forty-five kilometres a day. There were young eighteen-year-olds and old forty-five-year-olds. They walked on, covered with dust, sweaty and tired. The sun had bleached their eyebrows and tunics. They were not seeking rest but marching to deadly battle. What was each soldier thinking about as he trudged on? About the coming battle and his fate? Or about how good it would be to sit down and have a nap for thirty minutes or so? About a gulp of cold water? About his children left at home? But he had to carry on: he mustn't stop—he could hear the commanders shouting, the typewriters clattering at the tribunal... So he forced himself to keep walking under his heavy burden of arms and ammunition.

It is only in the films which drew on the advice of colonels and generals who never fought in the war that soldiers are shown marching in columns, in step, wearing high boots and peaked caps, carrying only a rifle and nothing more.

In reality it was all different. Soldiers wearing short boots with foot wrappings and soft caps just walked along the road—there were no formations and no one kept in step. It was easier to cover long distances that way.

At the beginning of the war there were few vehicles so infantrymen had to carry everything on their shoulders. Our company had only one cart drawn by a couple of horses which carried all the company equipment—a cauldron for cooking food and dry wood for the fire (we did not have field kitchens), reserves of food and ammunition, boots and lots of other things—as well as those who fell ill on the way and could not go on foot.

Most people who had been conscripted from the reserves were not used to walking long distances. Their feet were chafed and blistered. Foot wrappings were also a problem—if you wrapped them too tight your calves would ache, but if you loosened them too much they would droop.

During the war an infantryman would carry a rifle and thirty cartridges in two pouches on his belt, an RGD grenade (for attacks) and an F-1 grenade (for defensive operations—it was known as a lemon or *limonka*),[4] a folded coat, a steel helmet, a gas mask, an entrenching tool, a mess tin and a water bottle. In a rucksack on his back he carried his emergency ration, first aid kit, personal belongings and shaving equipment. In his pocket there was a handkerchief, a spoon, a penknife, and a flint and steel. He would hit the steel with the flint to produce a spark, which was used to light his roll-up cigarette (only officers had Russian cigarettes and matches). In addition to their full pack soldiers would carry the parts of a medium machine gun or a light machine gun, together with metal boxes of cartridges, an anti-tank gun (this was usually carried by two soldiers), a large entrenching shovel, a pick-axe, an axe, a cross cut saw and a heavy bar with a pointed end for breaking up frozen earth.

When digging a full-size trench (1.2 metres deep) the first two spade depths are easy to dig out, but digging deeper through compacted soil, let alone stony soil, is possible only using a pick-axe or pointed bar.[5]

On the second day of the march some soldiers succumbed: some were sleeping while walking, some would faint. Some had chafed their feet and were limping. Commanders of all ranks were nervous; they were shouting and swearing. After a short halt for fifteen minutes' rest one soldier was reluctant to get up in spite of both his company leader's and platoon commander's orders. Then his company commander came up to him with a revolver and shot twice into the earth near his ear. The soldier turned pale, got up silently and joined the others.

During the war I frequently had to march along roads to the front, but that first march was the most difficult and strained. We were walking silently, concentrating hard. I peered at my soldiers' faces. There was extreme fatigue and indifference close to unconsciousness. One of them, a Muscovite, a Komsomol[6] member born in 1922, started chanting a revolutionary song of the German communists loudly and solemnly in time with his steps.

Booed by the soldiers behind him, he stopped singing. Such bravado was fine on the stage, but in reality and under such circumstances it seemed out of place.

FOR THE MOTHERLAND! FOR STALIN!

I was carrying my carbine as well as another, weaker soldier's rifle. I walked along, surprised: how come I, a city boy, was stronger than a village lad used to physical labour since childhood? It could be explained by the fact that I was a commander and it was this responsibility that made me stronger than others because we have many latent inner qualities which don't become apparent under ordinary circumstances.

Things were even more difficult for the soldiers of my mortar platoon than they were for the riflemen. In addition to rifles and other equipment, my men carried mortars (each weighing nine kilos) and boxes of bombs (seven kilos).[7]

In the infantry, a lieutenant platoon commander with thirty to forty soldiers under his command was in the most difficult and dangerous situation. The lieutenant was the first to lead the attack towards the deadly swarm of bullets and shrapnel, and he was the one who urged the others to go over the top.

After a battle or march soldiers used to sleep huddled against each other to get warm, but the lieutenant would be running around, checking up on ammunition supplies and the sick and wounded, attending briefings and talks, and so on. At night he did not get any sleep as a rule, as he would be either checking the platoon sentries on duty, or be on company or battalion duty himself.

Infantry lieutenants underwent severe physical and psychological stress, more so than anybody else, which is why many of them passed away just after the war without leaving any record of what they had gone through. And now hardly any of them are still alive.

On the way to the front we waded across the great Volga river. At our crossing point, it was ten metres wide. Its estuary is more than two kilometres wide—its length is 3,530 kilometres.

TO THE KALININ FRONT

The windows of heaven opened (Genesis 7: 11–12)

We were spending the night in the forest, in incessant drizzle, having spread twigs from trees and bushes under ourselves. It is bad, really bad when, all night long, cold rain drips under your collar. Our overcoats became heavy, our caps soaking wet. Later, sodden, we had to walk through the slippery mud with our legs wide apart to avoid falling over. Our heads were heavy because of lack of sleep. Will our descendants pay tribute to us for our ordeals?

Soldiers fording a river

5

THE FRONT NEAR RZHEV

AT THE FRONT

We were approaching the front. At night we could see the fearful glow of fires on the horizon. We heard the heavy boom of the artillery cannonade more and more clearly. It was Moloch himself in action, devouring his victims.

A few kilometres short of the front, we started coming across the lightly wounded. They were walking towards us in an endless line along the side of the road. Some were limping, leaning on the shoulders of their comrades whose arms were in slings; some used their rifles with the barrels down as supports. Some were walking with their torsos in bloodstained bandages, others had their heads covered in bandages with a narrow slit for an eye. They were not looking at us. To them everything was clear—the danger was all over. At times I would look at my soldiers walking

57

beside me and see the growing concern on their faces. What did the future hold in store for each of us?

At night our rifle regiment relieved another rifle regiment from duty. In the morning I looked around. The ground in front of us sloped down to a stream then rose again and there, about a kilometre away, we could dimly see a frontline German trench.

We learned from the scouts that the German defensive line was very strong. Along each kilometre, the Germans had three to four tanks dug into the ground, small-calibre quick-firing guns in camouflaged trenches, five to six machine-gun earth-and-timber emplacements, and four to five dugouts with roofs made of three layers of timber for soldiers and officers to shelter from gunfire. The frontline trenches and communication trenches were dug to full size, and there were three rows of barbed wire and minefields in front of them. Behind the first trench there was a second and then a third one, each fortified in the same way.

Our trench was only chest-high and during the day we had to stoop when moving because the Germans kept shooting at us with machine guns except when they were eating. There were no minefields or barbed wire in front of our trenches. Under cover of night, seven to eight soldiers headed by a sergeant stood sentry with a lightweight machine gun about 100 metres in front of our trench.

The inadequate technical equipment supplied for our defence was due to Stalin's insistence that our troops maintain a non-stop offensive on Rzhev, which was about five kilometres away.

Although it was only a small town, Rzhev became very important strategically due to its bridge across the high steep banks of the Volga. Rzhev was the convergence point of the Moscow-Riga highway and railway, and the closest town to Moscow, which was 250 kilometres away. It took six hours to get from Rzhev to Moscow by tank and twenty-five minutes by plane. German planes took off from Rzhev's airfields to bomb Moscow when Stalin was still there. Hitler himself visited Rzhev to encourage his troops to repel Russian attacks. He told them: 'Rzhev is the springboard to Moscow. We must hold Rzhev at any cost. Losing Rzhev equals losing half of Berlin.'

Here was I, a platoon commander, the lowest officer rank or, as they used to call us, *Van'ka vzvodniy* (platoon Jack). The joke went: 'You can't get less than a platoon, you can't be sent further than the front.'[1] It meant you shared everything with your soldiers. It also meant you came under command of all the other senior officers: you were the first to carry out decisions made by the Supreme Commander, the front commander and the army commander, as well as the commanders of the corps, division, regiment, battalion and company. You had to be in front of your soldiers when mounting an attack and you were the most vulnerable link in the army.

Having become platoon commander at seventeen and a half, I had power over thirty men, all of whom were older than me and some twice as old. One of my men, a twenty-two-year-old soldier, was married and had two children.

What does such power involve at the front? I had power over men's lives and deaths. Normally if, for example, I didn't like what a soldier did or said, I could reprimand him and I had the right to make him redo a task or correct it. If it was a more serious misdemeanour, I had the right to make him carry out compulsory labour, say, five extra duties, or I could have him imprisoned for five days in the punishment cell. According to military regulations, a subordinate must carry out his commander's orders without question, to the letter and promptly. If he failed to carry out an order, he could be brought before the military tribunal.

During a battle I had unlimited power over my soldiers. If anyone failed to carry out an order, I had the right to shoot them on the spot without warning, interrogation or trial. My commanders could do the same to me as well. Fortunately, I never had to take such a measure, but there were several cases when I could have.

Being so young made my life very difficult because the psychological and physical perception of yourself as an adult develops from the age of twenty-one. Before the revolution, conscription started at this age. In the Red Army it was slightly lower, at twenty; only those who had passed their end of school exam were conscripted at eighteen. As for me, I managed to join the army before coming of age at all.

During the war, both back in the rear and also at the front, our rations were insufficient in quantity as well as in quality. But it is exactly at this age that your body is developing physically. Just add to this permanent sleep deprivation, psychological and physical stress, constant exposure to the elements and a total lack of privacy, and it is easy to imagine the physical and psychological state my colleagues and I found ourselves in.

Even now, many decades later, I can't help feeling moved when I see eighteen-year-old conscripts. In each of them I see myself in my unforgettable youth during the war.

At the front we all were young as a rule, and eager to fire all kinds of weapons—a gun, a rifle, a machine gun. Whether it was useful or not, we tried to shoot at a target whenever we had an opportunity and often we simply shot without targets. Countless cartridges were wasted in shooting at a *rama*, a German scout plane.[2] Our entire frontline was firing at the plane as well as those who were in behind us. But it was like water off a duck's back for the pilot, as the bottom of his plane was armour-clad.

We particularly enjoyed firing machine guns with tracer bullets at night, watching the dotted lines rushing up into the sky. There was always a pile of spent cartridges at the bottom of a trench near a machine gun.

The words 'Lenin-Stalin-Communism' were picked out in spent cartridges in the earth wall of the trench. At night flares went up from the German trench, one after another. The Germans had plenty of flares as the whole of Western Europe was working for them. Their deathly pale, unnatural light illuminated a terrain pitted with shell craters, a destroyed tank with its gun drooping and rows of barbed wire. We knew that in front of the wire there was a minefield ominously waiting ahead.

Experienced soldiers who had fought in the Civil War and the Finnish War, and taken part in the battles of Lake Khasan and Khalkhin Gol, instructed us: 'If you hear a bullet whistle, don't be afraid—it's not yours. You can't hear the bullet that is aimed at you.'[3]

They also advised:

- If a shell explodes, be brave and lie down in the newly formed crater—it will never be hit by another shell.
- If you have a stomach wound, don't tell the field hospital doctor that you were wounded more than six hours ago, because

Focke-Wulf Fw189, or *rama*

after six hours stomach wounds get infected and the doctors can't fight the infection, so they won't treat you because there's no point.

- Put on clean underwear before an attack. If your underwear is dirty and you are wounded, bullets or shrapnel will pull dirty bits of fabric into the wound and you can get a potentially lethal infection.

Stalin's Order No. 227

There were many signs to show us that we would start the offensive any day now. That topic was being discussed at commanders' meetings, during briefings, and at Communist Party and Komsomol meetings. Frequent inspections were carried out. Stalin's new Order No. 227 'Not A Step Back' was read out in front of each company in our regiment.

For those who did not fight at the front, especially for young people who have only read about the war or listened to veterans' stories, it is probably difficult to understand what Order No. 227 meant to the Red Army troops at that time.

All the more so because most books about the war dating from the Soviet era are written in line with the doctrine of socialist realism, which meant writing not about what life was really like but about how it should have been, and describing our actions only in a positive light, never in a negative one.

In the summer of 1942 (into the second year of the war) our troops were constantly retreating to the east, especially the troops on the southern front who were coming under violent German assault. Some detachments were resisting, but the others were just running away in disarray, leaving their weapons and vehicles behind. The Germans had reached the Don river, occupied Rostov-on-Don, Voronezh and the Crimea, and were moving towards the Volga and Stalingrad.

THE FRONT NEAR RZHEV

The situation required decisive measures. A harsh and uncompromising order with a point-blank conclusion was issued to the troops: 'To retreat further will bring ruin to our motherland. Our resistance must be deadly! Those who retreat without an order will be shot on the spot!'

Our commanders and political commissars spoke to the companies about the role of discipline in battle, and about the necessity to deal mercilessly with cowards and panic-mongers: they would not be handled with kid gloves—they would immediately be shot. Anyone who tried to desert or run away from battle would be detained and shot without trial by a retreat-blocking detachment which would stand in a cordon behind our division.

Our daily routine at the front

We got into a daily routine at the front. The days would pass slowly and monotonously. At night it was only the platoon commander who would not sleep: he was on duty—inspecting the sentries and machine gun crews. Once or twice a night the company commander or his deputy would inspect the sentries. You were always on edge, though it was not outwardly noticeable. You were constantly aware that you were in a very dangerous place. You had to be on alert and never drop your guard.

Suddenly an unexpected bombardment of our trenches began. The enemy must have suspected that we were preparing for the offensive. Shells were exploding around us. Somebody was wounded. He was shouting for help. The medical orderly sergeant went out of our dugout to give him first aid.

The roof of our dugout was quite flimsy: it was only made of two layers of thin logs. The ground shook with each explosion and there was spattering from above. Suddenly we smelled a strong, chemical smell. We were bewildered and struck by fear... Not just fear but terror. Overwhelming, animal terror. My body was shaking, my lips were dry, my heart thumped madly, my legs were wobbly.

Only one thought pierced my mind—if a German shell hit our dugout (and I knew the roof wouldn't protect us) it would not merely kill us, it would annihilate us, blowing us to pieces. And the most terrible thing, if you think about it, is that I myself had wanted to be there—and had used my initiative to volunteer.

The cannonade directed at our frontline intensified. My nerves were vibrating like stretched strings. Even now, many years later, I can remember everything I experienced then, during that first artillery cannonade, with amazing clarity. I was looking at my comrades. Their faces had turned pale, their lips were lilac. In their eyes, I could see a plea to survive. With every explosion that came close we pulled our heads into our shoulders and pressed ourselves to the earthen walls of our dugout, as if that could save us. Our helplessness was the most unbearable feeling. We really could do nothing to stop the bombardment. At last the cannonade finished, as abruptly as it had started. Thank goodness. We were alive. Our faces brightened. Life could go on.

As well as the fascists, we were also plagued by mosquitoes which were flying around in swarms, sticking to our faces and hands in that swampy place. Even the smoke from the fire did not keep them away. So many curses, mainly four-letter words, were thrown at them. 'Damn that Noah, why did he bring those bloody mosquitoes onto his Ark?' said an elderly soldier, a mortar gunner. 'Who is Noah and what is an ark?' asked a young soldier. 'In ancient times, a man by the name of Noah, having learned that soon there would be a deluge and all the world would be covered in water, built a big ship, the Ark, where he put people, animals, reptiles, birds and all the creatures on earth in couples, mosquitoes included. That Ark came to rest on Mount Ararat in Turkey, where you can still find its remains. We've been suffering ever since.'

THE FRONT NEAR RZHEV

Thoughts about death

Death is the inevitable companion of war. After a while, you get used to everything. At first you are shocked when your comrade dies: only yesterday you were talking to him about what life would be like after the war, but today he has been killed. You understand that the same could happen to you. But then you get used to it and start to conceive of death as inevitable, and you even think that instantaneous death will be better than becoming a helpless cripple.

On the other hand, the war taught us to have a good understanding of people's character, to separate truth from falsehood. And, most important—it taught us to value life, every moment of it.

Like most of us, I was convinced that I would not be killed in the war. I don't know why, but I firmly believed that others could be killed, but not me. Sometimes people ask me whether we felt fear during the war. Certainly we did. The poet Yulia Drunina answered this question very well: 'Those who declare they fear not to fight know nothing of war.'

Fear, especially fear of death, has a very strong effect on an ordinary person. It hinders their ability to think and act, their breath becomes uneven, their heart starts beating more rapidly, they become helpless and, if they can't overcome this state, they die. Every person fears death. The fear can be suppressed for some time but it cannot be overcome entirely.

Like everyone else, I feared death, but my sense of duty and my responsibility as a commander helped me to overcome it. Frankly speaking, during quiet minutes, when I pictured myself in hand-to-hand combat and somebody's bayonet stabbing my body, I must admit that I felt an icy chill. Death by bullet or shrapnel scared me less.

They say: 'How awful it was to die in May 1945.' Of course it was. To die on the eve of the victory would be awful, certainly.

FOR THE MOTHERLAND! FOR STALIN!

Nevertheless, to die near Rzhev in a swamp was probably even worse because you would never know what happened to our motherland.

6

MY FIRST BATTLE

THE ATTACK

I have remembered my first battle all my life, in every detail.
There is probably no one who took part in the war who could
not remember all the details of their first battle.

At 10 pm on 29 July 1942 we were told that we were starting
the offensive at 5 am the next day. Our division's objective was to
give a supplementary thrust in the direction of two villages. We
were to be supported by a tank brigade.

Stalin's Order No. 227 was read out to every platoon. It
emphasised that severe punishments would be issued for loss of
weapons and warned that even the wounded who arrived at the
field hospital without their weapon would be severely punished.

Then our company commander took the floor: 'Tomorrow we
are going into battle. All together. Some of you will die. But if

we act in a concerted, brave and determined way, there will be fewer casualties. Remember the infantry rule—to run up to the German trench as soon as possible and kill a German. If you fail to kill him, he will kill you. It is all very simple. In war everything is simple.'

Before that, we, the platoon and company commanders, had been instructed to go ahead of our soldiers. We were warned to instruct our deputy commanders, the leaders of the party cells, the Komsomol cell, party members, party propagandists, stretcher bearers and orderlies to be ready to stop soldiers shooting their commanders from the rear.

By that time, about a million criminals who had been recently released from prison had joined the army. Quite a few secret enemies of the Soviet state were among them. During an assault they preferred to shoot their commanders in the back and frustrate the attack. Such cases became notorious.

Eventually, after the Rzhev battle, on 8 October 1942 the Ministry of Defence issued Order No. 3060 which directed commanders to go into attack behind their subordinates, and sergeants to go into attack alongside their soldiers.

The first battle! We all anticipated that moment with excitement. What would it be like? Would my nerves let me down? I can't say I was calm. How can you be calm before a decisive battle? It was the 394th day of the greatest war in the history of mankind. Nobody knew that there would be another 1,024 days before the desired Victory, with thousands of intense and deadly battles, millions of deaths, and millions of cripples, widows and orphans.

Early morning, 30 July. Poorly disguised worry could be seen on every face awaiting the command. The most difficult minute for a soldier in war is the last minute before the onslaught of the attack, the beginning of the battle. Every muscle is tense with expectation and you wish that time would stop: wait, let me gather myself together. But we can't stop time.

MY FIRST BATTLE

Preliminary bombardment

At 5 am on 30 July our relative peace ended as the silence was shattered by the powerful preliminary bombardment of our offensive. Guns and mortars of all calibres hurled an avalanche of deadly metal onto the enemy's position. Clouds of projectiles whistled overhead. Thousands of shells and bullets battered the enemy's defence line.

The ground was convulsed and the air trembled with the salvo fire of our artillery. Around us everything was roaring and moaning, merging into the sole, horrible din of war. Its hurricane was raging above our heads.

You could see with your naked eye a solid wall of fire and smoke on the enemy side, as the explosions continued, non-stop. Splintered fragments of logs and boards from bunkers and dugouts, stakes from wire fencing, clods of long-suffering earth were flying up. All this was accompanied by the roar of dozens of our bombers throwing their deadly load down on the heads of those who imagined themselves masters of the whole world.

FOR THE MOTHERLAND! FOR STALIN!

When they exploded, the shells threw up black cones of earth along with flashes of fire. It was then that I understood why there are black and orange stripes on the ribbons of pre-revolutionary orders and medals, and on our Order of Glory. These are the colours of fire and smoke. The sign of battle.

Then everything was screened by solid smoke, fire and dust. The tension of the battle was growing with every minute.

I was exultant over the incredible sight. Here it was, our steamroller! Forty minutes of drenching artillery and mortar fire never known before in the history of all wars on earth. I was proud of my country.

At the end of the preliminary bombardment, we heard a sudden strange and horrifying roar which shook everything around us. The sky was pierced by a continuous shrill howl and an extraordinary rasping noise, and we saw flying rockets with tails of fire. These were Katyusha rockets, our secret weapon, up to that time unknown to us ordinary soldiers and officers. We were astounded to see this new type of weapon in action.

Katyusha rockets

About fifteen or twenty seconds later we heard powerful explosions accompanied by dazzling fire and smoke. Those were the Katyusha salvos. We could see eight formidable military lorries standing in a row, with raised metal carriers which held sixteen unusually elongated mortars shaped like rockets, fixed in two rows. From each lorry a mortar, or rocket, was launched every half second from left and right sides alternatively. As all the eight lorries were firing simultaneously, the rockets were being launched non-stop during eight to ten seconds as if in one salvo.

Woe to our enemies who would be pressing themselves to the ground, whispering prayers, damning the war and those who had started it. It was impossible to imagine that there was anybody who could have survived that inferno.

The company commander's order 'Prepare for attack!' was heard. We repeated the order to our subordinates. The commanders of the sections repeated it to the soldiers.

Before, when I tried to imagine an attack, I thought it would be like this: on hearing the order you had to put your toe on the step cut into the wall of the trench and then, on hearing the command 'Forward!', leap out of the trench. You would urge on soldiers who were lagging behind, getting them to hurry or crawl into position, then, on hearing the command 'To the attack!', run as fast as you could towards the enemy trenches, frantically shouting 'Oorah!' At that moment you would be the centre of the universe. Blood would be hammering in your temples, your heart pulsing with excitement. All you had to do was to run ahead and to kill the enemy, or die with nine grams of hot lead.

In reality it turned out not to be quite like that. Red rockets shot up like arrows into the sky. On hearing the command, 'To the attack! Forward!', we raised ourselves out from our trenches and began walking at first, our guns and bayonets at the ready. It was still quite dark and the Germans were possibly unable to see us.

FOR THE MOTHERLAND! FOR STALIN!

It resembled a Japanese banzai attack.[1] My mind was clear. Only one thought remained—to fulfil the order at any cost. As we approached the enemy trenches, bullets started singing and we were running bent over, in silence. The Germans launched a series of red rockets in our direction and opened a powerful, destructive wave of mortar, machine and automatic gunfire.

The enemy's dense fire made us move ahead first at a run and then at a commando crawl, pressing ourselves closely to the ground. The ground was so wet as a result of recent showers that it was impossible to dig ourselves in. In some places we were moving knee-deep in water.

The clatter of machine guns, automatic guns and rifles, bullets whistling overhead, shells and mines exploding, the cries and groans of the wounded, shouts of 'Oorah!', swearing—all those noises merged into the terrible rumble of battle. We could not hear our commands above the uproar.

Our regiment was carrying out the banzai charge in three waves, each between 150 and 200 metres away from the other. The purpose was to frighten the enemy, to suppress their will and psyche. But the Germans were experienced fighters and it did not affect them.

At that time, the situation at the front was so complicated, tense and unpredictable that each attacking battalion of our division was followed by a T-34 tank to control cowards and panic-mongers. The tank commanders were appointed by the military council of the 30th army and their task was to shoot any soldiers and officers who were retreating against orders.

I could see a wounded soldier from the rifle platoon crawling back in my direction. He had a minor wound. The bullet must have ricocheted and, having lost its killing power, only half-entered his forehead. It could easily have been pulled out by hand. A thin plume of blood was running down his forehead. There was an expression of suffering and fear of death in his eyes.

I said: 'Let me pull out the bullet.' He refused and continued crawling past me. Only later did it occur to me that if he had the bullet in his forehead, it would prove to the medical staff that he had been wounded during the battle. Medical staff and doctors were under strict instructions from the military prosecutor and counter intelligence to look out for fake injuries and for those who deliberately injured themselves: those with minor cuts, scratches, aches and bruises were to be returned to the frontline immediately. That requirement was met to the letter.

Above the clamour of battle, one of my sergeants shouted: 'Lieutenant![2] There's a German crawling behind us!' I looked back. Indeed, about fifty metres away from us, between our line and the second line, was a soldier in a German helmet. Nobody in our division had a helmet. Besides, a German helmet is a very different shape from ours.

I rose to my knees and shot at the German three times, but missed. He was still crawling. At artillery school I had always got excellent marks for shooting and, with a target at fifty metres range, I could shoot thirty out of thirty, getting all three bullets within the ten point zone of the target. But the tension of the battle made my hands tremble. The next second, someone cried that it was not a German but a messenger working for the platoon commander nearby; he had simply found the German helmet on the battlefield and put it on. I stopped shooting.

Another sergeant shouted to me that a Tatar soldier bringing the shells from his section (one box strapped on his back, the other in his left hand, with his rifle in his right hand) had stopped and, despite orders, was refusing to move on.

There were six Tatars in my platoon who could hardly understand Russian: they only knew about a dozen Russian words, not counting swear words. I crawled up to the soldier and shouted at him to move forward, using a couple of swear words. He shouted back something in Tatar, his face frozen with horror. I could not understand him. Then I shot my gun near his ear. With a look of terror, he started crawling forward.

The company commander's messenger crawled up to me. He shouted in my ear: 'The company commander orders you to direct fire at the bushes 200 metres away from us on the left. There is a disguised German sniper there. A lieutenant, a rifle platoon commander and two of his sergeants, the section commanders, have already been killed. All were shot in the left side of the head.'

I ordered the section commanders to direct fire at the bushes. Four mortars shot six rounds each. When the shooting finished, we made a series of short runs to catch up with the line of gunners crawling ahead.

I saw a freshly made crater and jumped in, inadvertently jabbing the muzzle of my rifle into the side so it got clogged with earth. I had nothing to unblock it so I fired the rifle. It could have blown up, but this did not happen. Our Russian steel was hard. In front of me was a small hill which was being fired on by a German large-calibre machine gun. I could see lumps of soil flying up. Two motionless human bodies were lying there.

By now we were crawling. I did not want to keep going ahead and meet certain death so I commanded the soldiers to go to the left and the right of the hill. At that moment I heard somebody behind me shouting: 'Stop that! Move on straight ahead!' I turned and saw the company deputy political officer, a senior lieutenant (I do not remember his name), with a gun in his hand. He shouted and swore at me, accusing me of being a coward. 'I'll shoot you!' he ended.

I had to retract my order and the soldiers started again to crawl straight towards the hill which was under fire from the enemy machine gun. The deputy political officer was sending us to certain, futile death either out of fear or stupidity. A minute later he disappeared and I ordered the soldiers again to bypass that deadly and dangerous place.

After that episode, I began to understand Marshal Zhukov's antipathy towards political officers in the army. There was too much control over the battle commanders who were under the supervision of higher rank commanders and political commissars, as well as the surveillance of the secret police (NKVD-KGB).[3]

Again we saw red rockets spiralling up into the sky. This was the battalion commander's signal to the gunners that we were ready for the assault on the enemy's first trench, which was about seventy metres away. The artillery started firing on the enemy's second trench. On the company commander's order, all the soldiers raised themselves from the ground and frantically shouting 'Oorah!' rushed towards the enemy trench, firing from every kind of weapon to hand.

When we reached the trench we did not find Germans there, only corpses. The survivors had seen no point in resisting and had run through the deep communication trenches to the second trench from where they opened fire on us.

We crossed the first trench. It was an impressive sight. The ground was pitted with craters and fires were burning here and there. Nothing was left undamaged: the trench was smashed by explosions; dugouts had collapsed and weapons, helmets, gas masks, backpacks and bloodstained corpses were strewn everywhere.

We did not linger. We had to move on. We knew that the Germans would have measured the distance between their trenches and their guns, and when necessary could open fire on their own trench without preliminary adjustment.

Indeed, a number of explosions hit the trench just after we left and those who had stayed behind to loot the German dugouts found themselves in a predicament. Usually in German dugouts you could find French brandy, Dutch butter, Swiss cheese, Spanish fruit and so on.

Nowadays certain wartime photos of soldiers mounting an assault make me grimace. For example, there is a famous photo

FOR THE MOTHERLAND! FOR STALIN!

Soviet officer (probably A. G. Yeremenko, Company political officer of the 220th Rifle Regiment, 4th Rifle Division, killed in action in 1942) leading his soldiers to the assault. Voroshilovgrad region, Ukraine, USSR

taken in summer of a political officer ordering the soldiers crawling behind him into attack. This photo often appears in newspapers, magazines and books, not to mention on postcards and badges. The political officer is not wearing his helmet. He has a gas mask case at his side and a gun is attached to the holster on his belt with a leather strap. He also has binoculars on a leather strap around his neck. Behind him soldiers in helmets are crawling on the ground, guns at the ready, with gas mask cases strapped to their sides, backpacks on their backs and rolled coats across their shoulders.

I wonder why the political officer is not wearing his helmet. Were they short of helmets? Most unlikely. He would be the first to get one. And why on earth would anyone going into an attack need binoculars and a gas mask? Is he expecting a gas attack or is he going to look through his binoculars at the fascists shooting at him? Why is his gun attached to his belt with a strap? During the assault he might fight the enemy hand to hand and the strap would get in the way.

A rolled coat and a backpack (in which there are usually grenades, additional cartridges, a billy can, a mug and some personal belongings) make it difficult for a soldier to move quickly—given that an assault is supposed to be a blistering attack on the enemy.

Now for the photographer, who, together with the soldiers, had run and crawled nearly a kilometre from our trenches under deadly fire from the enemy and then, when they were thirty or forty metres away from the enemy trenches, had run ahead, turned back and taken his famous photo. Is it possible? It is incredible!

In reality, as I see it, this photo must have been taken by the photographer using reserves from a regiment safely in the rear during a military exercise held by commanders with no combat experience.

When we were preparing for the assault near Rzhev in the summer of 1942 everything was different. Half an hour before the assault, we were ordered to hand in our coats, backpacks and gas masks to the company sergeant major. When a newly drafted recruit asked: 'How will I be able to find my coat later?', the experienced sergeant major answered: 'If you are lucky enough to stay alive after the battle, there will be plenty of coats to choose from.'

7

THE FIRST WOUND

MY FIRST WOUND

Our attack on the second trench was similar to that on the first one. Again, there were the short advances, shouted commands and groans from the wounded. Shells detonated with a crash, blasting the ground upwards, bullets were singing, shrapnel was flying and the caustic smell of explosives filled the air.

During the advance, a shell hit a young soldier from my platoon in the chest. The picture of the dead man remains forever in my memory: his bright red naked body torn in two halves and his protruding white ribs. (Even now, more than half a century later, when I go to the butcher's, I avoid looking at bloodied animal carcasses with protruding white ribs.)

It was under such circumstances that you had to make sound judgements, pull yourself together, and restrain your emotions and that terrible feeling of fear, so that the subordinates who were looking to you, full of their own fear, could see that you had not lost your nerve.

We had crawled as far as the second trench and were ready to rush into a bayonet attack. Suddenly my carbine received a direct hit, then I felt acute pain in my right foot. My boot was ripped. Blood was pouring out of my foot, forming a small pool on the ground. I had to act quickly. I took off my boot and unwound my foot cloth, but I didn't have time to examine the wound. I covered it with some cotton wool and a bandage from my first-aid kit. The bullet must have hit my carbine, which was level with my stomach, and glanced off into my right foot. Later I would realize that this had saved my life. I put the platoon sergeant major, my second-in-command, in charge. I gave him my carbine—'the symbol of power'—and took his rifle. His rifle was longer and I could use it as a crutch. With soldiers from my platoon glancing at me—because the battle was over for me—I started crawling back to the rear. I couldn't walk upright as bullets were relentlessly whistling overhead.

All the way back, for nearly a kilometre, I passed soldiers' bodies. There were plenty of them; they had been killed before they had even clapped eyes on a German.

As soon as I crawled out of the firing zone, I started to walk, propping myself on the rifle butt and stepping on my heel. It was very painful but I had to put up with it. I went out onto a forest road. I was walking ankle-deep in the mud. I couldn't see my bandage, as my ankles were so muddy.

Sometimes in groups, sometimes by themselves, lightly wounded soldiers in bloodied bandages were moving in the same direction. From the opposite direction came fresh reinforcements, as we had been some time ago.

I reached a small village which had been completely turned into a hospital. There were hundreds of wounded soldiers. The villagers had gone—they had all been moved sixteen kilometres away from the frontline in case of espionage. There were wounded soldiers in every peasant hut and barn. The operating theatre was in a big tent. There was a queue for dressings. Bloodied used bandages were piling up next to the tent.

I was placed on the straw on the floor in a peasant hut. There was no furniture and the wounded were lying along the walls. They were moaning continuously. A junior artillery lieutenant was groaning beside me. He had been wounded in the stomach. Then he went quiet. I did not know him. Judging by the artillery emblems on his buttonholes, I decided he must be a graduate of the Rostov anti-tank artillery officers' school. (During the war each military school had its own emblem—crossed gun barrels which might be slightly different from those in other schools.) A few hours later we realised he was dead. A nurse came in. The wounded soldiers wanted the dead man to be taken away. It would be horrible to spend a night with him in the same room.

The nurse took his documents out of his breast pocket and read them: 'Bik, Vasiliy Josiphovich, born 1922.' How could this be? Bik had been my comrade-in-arms in the 45-mm anti-tank battery in our regiment! I looked at his face again and recognised him only with difficulty. The agonizing wound in his stomach, together with death, had altered him out of all recognition.

I remembered staying with him in a village hut when our regiment was being formed. Once he came galloping up on his horse and tethered it by the door. (Our battery used horses and every officer had his own horse.) While Bik went into the hut, I jumped on his horse and rode it to the end of the village and back. There were only twenty houses in the village. When I returned, Bik was furious and started punching me. The other soldiers had difficulty breaking us up. I was surprised. I wouldn't have minded if he rode my horse: we were comrades-in-arms and friends, and the horses were not our personal property.

In spite of that, we became friends: we slept together on one coat, covering ourselves with the other; we shared our rationed bread; we ate from one pot; and, after drinking a glass of vodka, we would sing together—he sang his favourite old Siberian folk song and I joined in (this didn't happen often, as there was a shortage of alcohol at that time). And now he was dead... He had not yet turned twenty...

Two days later, when the road had started to dry up, I was among ten lightly wounded men who were taken away in the back of a lorry accompanied by a nurse. During a stop each of us was given a small piece of rye bread and a small piece of herring. I had not eaten for two days. A pale soldier stood next to me holding a sandwich which he was not eating. I asked him why he was not eating it. He said he could not. Then I suggested that he should give it to me. He gave it to me. It was a small insignificant episode in my life, but the fact that I remember it reveals a lot about the atmosphere of that time.

The rain started pouring down again, but by then we had already come to a small village where there was a clearing station. It was impossible to go further. The forest road was too muddy. All the vehicles had come to a halt. There weren't any asphalted roads in that marshy area. Deliveries of food and medicine had stopped. All the huts and barns were full of wounded soldiers. There were thousands of them. I was put in a barn where there were about thirty wounded men lying on plank beds. We were given one meal a day, which was a small portion of watery por-ridge. Our bandages were not changed because there were no fresh supplies. Some people had wounds that had pus in them, even maggots. Those in plaster casts suffered the most. The cast was not taken off and the sufferer could feel swarming maggots eating his body. Some died without getting medical attention, then the orderlies would take them away. I lay in the barn for three or four days. A nurse kept coming but she did nothing other than change the colour-coded tags on the chests of the wounded. A red tag meant 'badly wounded' to be evacuated as a matter of urgency, a yellow one meant the case was less urgent, and a green one denoted low priority. I had a green tag and I could walk a little, resting on my rifle.

The whirring of planes could be heard nearby. I saw small PO-2 biplanes (named after their designer, Polikarpov) landing and taking off on a grassy meadow on the outskirts of the village. Out of curiosity, I limped slowly over to the meadow to look at them. I had never seen planes at close range. It turned out that they were evacuating the wounded, with two casualties on each plane. Three planes arrived. While the pilots went to have lunch, the orderlies started loading stretchers of wounded soldiers onto the planes. Without much ado I got on a plane, climbed into a stretcher container and closed the lid. A minute or so later, the orderlies opened the lid. 'Oh, there's somebody here already,' they said, shutting the lid. They put a wounded man into the container next to me. There

A wounded soldier being loaded on to a PO-2 biplane

was a partition between us with a small round window. I asked my companion: 'What shall I do? I don't have a certificate for food. Will they accept me at the next place?' 'They will,' he answered. I didn't have my rifle with me and I later regretted leaving my rucksack behind in the barn. It contained two packs of pre-cooked millet *kasha*. But the rifle and *kasha* were unimportant, unlike my artillery textbook, which was also in the rucksack. This was a vital book for any artillery officer.

For the first time in my life, I was flying by plane: nowadays everybody is used to it, but back then it was a real event. There was a constant risk of being hit by a German fighter. Our PO-2 was an unarmed, slow-moving plane and German planes were dominating the air. We were flying at an altitude of 200 metres. Below there was endless forest. Fortunately everything went well.

When we landed, nurses took me out of the plane and carried me to the field hospital on a stretcher. A nurse who was following my stretcher looked at me as I lay there, thin and pale with loss of blood, and asked my age. I answered: 'Seventeen.' She shed a tear: 'Oh dear! Such young people are sent to the front.'

At hospital, in the operating theatre, I was given a glass of red wine instead of anaesthesia. It was incredibly painful when they tore off my bandages which had stuck to the wound. The doctor asked me: 'What made the wound?' 'A bullet,' I answered. (There had been no shell or mine explosions when I was wounded.) The doctor took a thin metal probe with a small ball at the end and used it to search my wound for the bullet. The pain was intolerable. I was writhing and moaning in agony.

There were other wounded men writhing, groaning and crying on two other tables. Later, such was my fear of the probe, I told doctors at other hospitals that I hadn't got an embedded bullet and that it was a flesh wound, so that my foot wouldn't be probed again.

Initial surgical treatment was provided by the regiment's medical detachment or by the medical battalion. They used chloramine to bathe the wound. It was only after the war that scientists found out that chloramine contained dioxins, a class of toxic chemical compounds. Also, according to post-war scientific research, a bullet or a fragment of a shell in a human body changes its genetic code and damages its adaptation to stress.

According to the official data, the number of wounded and sick troops who returned to the front after medical treatment came to a total of about seventeen million. When this figure is compared to the total number of our troops during the war—which rose from 3.4 million in December 1942 to 6.7 million by 1 January 1945—it is clear that the war was won mainly by soldiers and officers who returned to the front after being treated for wounds.

On account of gross errors in the organisation of medical services for troops in the Rzhev-Sychevka military operation, Stalin, as People's Defence Commissar of the USSR, issued Order No. 701 on 19 September 1942: 'About the Defects in the Work of Medical Service and the Ways of Eliminating Them'. This stated that 'military councils of the fronts and the armies should pay more attention to the management of the troops' medical service'.

A young Jewish man, Junior Lieutenant Bekker, arrived at our division to be a member of our team. He was taken on as an interpreter at the division HQ as he could speak German very well. We envied him. It was much safer serving at the HQ than leading a platoon into an attack or directing battery fire from the frontline.

But man proposes, God disposes. On the third day of our assault on the village of Polunino, all the officers were either killed or wounded by enemy fire, leaving the soldiers without a commander. By that time no other commanders were left at HQ, so the commander of the division ordered Bekker to head the assault team and attack the enemy. Half an hour later, Bekker died the death of a hero while leading his soldiers into the attack.

FOR THE MOTHERLAND! FOR STALIN!

Anna Kern's estate

I went to the town of Torzhok on an ambulance train and was taken to a frontline hospital for the lightly wounded. The hospital was about five kilometres from the town. It was housed in the single storey buildings of a former collective pig farm. The pigs were slaughtered at the beginning of the war, but their smell still remained.

When you arrive at a frontline hospital, you follow the same set of procedures—it is like an assembly line: a bath, a visit to the bandaging room, a meal at the canteen and then to bed. For a fighter from the front, after a world of soggy, muddy trenches and constant hunger, it is bliss to lie quietly and peacefully in a bed with clean sheets and a soft pillow. At hospital I came across a regimental comrade of mine, who was a rank-and-file soldier and former philosophy lecturer at Moscow University. He had been wounded in the same battle as me. He told me the following:

After the command 'To the attack!', I crossed myself as many others did, although I'm an atheist, then jumped out of the trench and, holding my gun at the ready with its bayonet attached, advanced in a line of 700 soldiers from the rifle battalion. We kept close together, only about a metre apart. There were two lines of soldiers from two other battalions in our regiment in front of us. The Germans opened intensive automatic and machine gun fire. Shells and mines were exploding all around us. We saw soldiers from the two front lines falling as they were hit by bullets and shrapnel. At first we stepped around the corpses and the wounded soldiers who were crawling back, their faces distorted with pain. Then, during the attack, we started running, jumping over the corpses like athletes in a cross country race. All around us, Death was howling and rattling horribly. Death had let all hell loose. As for us, with our teeth clenched and grasping our guns, we were hurrying forward to kill people, the enemy. We were walking, now running towards certain death, but none of us lost his nerve or lagged behind. This was not a place for the faint of heart...

THE FIRST WOUND

As he finished his story, he added: 'I didn't think of it in that way at the time—it is only now that I think of it in these terms.'

The village of Mitino was near the hospital, on the other side of the River Tvertsa (which flows into the Volga). Three or four days later, having caught up on sleep, I started walking around, leaning on my crutch and enjoying the quiet and beautiful Russian scenery which is second to none in the world.

Not far from the hospital, on the river bank, I came across a derelict chapel and some neglected tombstones. There was an inscription on one of them:

> I remember the wonderful moment
> You appeared before me
> Like a fleeting vision
> Like a spirit of pure beauty.

I asked an old man who was passing by: 'Why is this epitaph here?' 'Anna Kern is buried here—Pushkin's muse,' he answered. 'Mitino was her estate.'[1]

When she was seventeen Anna was married off to a fifty-two-year-old general whom she did not love. Soon he died, and Anna lived in Torzhok where she met Pushkin, who was passing through the town.

At the hospital, for the first time in my life, I went to an adult party: it was held to commemorate the twenty-fifth anniversary of the Great October Socialist Revolution. There were six officers and four nurses, all of us young, with our whole life before us. We mustered a few small snacks, drank some alcohol and started singing Civil War songs.

In the hospital we were on short rations and we were always hungry. We had money, but we could not buy food anywhere. We could not barter for food with the villagers because we had nothing to barter with. There was an old people's home across the river. The elderly residents grew mangelwurzels. Day and night, these old people would guard their vegetable garden from thieves. But we outwitted them. At night we would crawl on our stomachs to the vegetable beds, pull out the mangelwurzels, then eat them raw back at our barracks. I can't say they were tasty, but at least we managed to quell our hunger.

During war, as in peace, life can have its amusing moments. One day, while walking along the river bank, I came across poachers who were blasting fish with pellets of TNT. They were throwing the burning pellets into the water. The pellets exploded, then fish came floating up to the surface, ready to be caught and thrown into a basket.

I started to help the poachers by stringing the fish on a line, secretly hoping that they would give me some fish. While trying to string a forty-centimetre long pike, I struggled to open its jaws in order to thread the string through its mouth and gills. At last its jaws opened and I tried to prop them apart with a stick. But the stick came out and my fingers on both hands were caught between the pike's sharp teeth. The pain was intolerable and I could not take my fingers out by myself. The fish seemed to gloat in retaliation. The poachers released me from my fishy captivity with laughter. But my hopes of getting some fish came to nothing. Poachers will be poachers.

The road to Torzhok

Once the wound on my foot began to heal, I could walk without my crutch. But while walking, I felt as if I was constantly stepping on a stone. I guessed that I still had the bullet in my foot. A doctor examined me and confirmed my suspicions. He said that the bullet should be extracted.

Together with the other wounded troops, I went by lorry to the hospital in Torzhok where there was x-ray equipment. I had heard a lot about the ancient Russian town, so I looked forward to visiting it.

THE FIRST WOUND

There can hardly be another town on earth which has been sacked and burnt by enemies so frequently (25 times!) by Lithuanians, Poles and even by the Zaporozhian Cossacks who were serving in the Polish army in the sixteenth century. In 1237 the Mongolian ruler Batu Khan besieged Torzhok for two weeks, eventually taking it by assault, killing all its inhabitants and setting the town on fire. However, weakened by their losses during the assault, the Mongols gave up their intention to attack Novgorod and went south.

Torzhok was sacked and burnt to ashes by Oz Beg Khan, ruler of the Golden Horde; by Ivan the Terrible; by the Novgorod troops; and by the princes of Smolensk, Moscow, Tver, Vladimir and Suzdal during internecine wars. Unlucky Torzhok.

Near Torzhok a prominent military leader, Skopin-Shuisky, defeated the army of the imposter, False Dmitri II, in 1609, then liberated Moscow from Polish invaders.[2]

Glorious Torzhok (it dates back to 1139) was once a rich, bustling merchant town with numerous fairs and taverns. Boats sailing down the Tvertsa river carried foreign goods from Novgorod. The forty gold domes of its cathedrals and churches shone in the sun. Pushkin chose the name of a Torzhok merchant, Eugene Onegin, which he saw on the sign of a tavern, as the name of the protagonist of his famous novel.

But now back to my x-ray trip. The road went along the top of a hill. From here we could see Torzhok clearly below. Suddenly, faraway in the sky, we heard a chilling, discontinuous wolfish howling 'OO-OO-OO'. It was an armada of about thirty German Junkers 87 Stukas, two-engine bombers with black swastikas on the sides. They were flying so low that we could see the pilots' heads in helmets and goggles which made them look like insects.

Our lorry stopped. We all jumped out and hid in the ditch by the road. Pulling my head into my shoulders, I felt as if an evil iron force was bearing down on me. We were afraid that they would bomb us. But we escaped this fate: they were not interested in an empty lorry.

We could see the bombers, with their sirens on, making a heart-stopping howl, diving and each dropping a number of bombs. Black and red plumes of explosions rose up over Torzhok. The anti-aircraft shells which exploded around the planes formed small black clouds in the sky. Below, in the town, something horrible was going on: we saw smoke, flames, dust, objects spiralling up high into the air, fires raging in some places.

The engine noise of the German planes sounded like: 'VIZZOO, VIZZOO, VIZZOO, VIZZOO...' (CARRYING, CARRYING, CARRYING, CARRYING). The clear and frequent shots from the anti-aircraft guns on the ground sounded like: 'KAMOO? KAMOO? KAMOO? KAMOO?' (TO WHOM? TO WHOM? TO WHOM? TO WHOM?). To which the powerful bomb explosions seemed to answer: 'VAM! VAM! VAM! VAM!' (TO YOU! TO YOU! TO YOU! TO YOU!).

When the planes flew away, we drove into Torzhok. There were ruined buildings and fires everywhere. A lorry drove past us, loaded with bodies of people killed in the bombing. A leg of a corpse was hanging over the side, swinging; the hair on the head of another corpse was stirring in the wind. It was a terrible sight.

Torzhok hospital was also ruined and we returned to our frontline hospital without being x-rayed. The bullet was extracted from my foot by hand. I asked the doctor to give it to me as a souvenir and I sewed it into the hem of my handkerchief for safekeeping.

Once my foot had healed after surgery, I was transferred to the convalescent unit where those who were recovering from their wounds and were still too weak for military service could recuperate for a week or two. During that time the head of the hospital ordered me to accompany four fully recovered political officers to the reserve section of the Kalinin front's political HQ in the village of Kuvshinovo, about 100 kilometres away.

At that time, the totalitarian regime was so strict that officers, political ones included, were not trusted to arrive at their new posts, either alone or even as a group, without being accompanied. I had to accompany the political officers, get the signatures of the officers at their HQ when they arrived, then bring the signed document back to hospital.

On our way (walking and hitch-hiking), we spent our nights in the villages. In order to stay the night, we had to get the written permission of the chairman of the village council or of a military commandant, if he was in the village. We had to show our written permission to a house owner before she could let us into her house for the night. Local people had to inform the authorities about any outsiders who came to their house. I still have a permission of this kind in my files.

I brought the political officers safely to their destination, obtained the relevant signatures, then went to the centre of the village where there was a pond to wash my face and hands. I also washed my handkerchief, which had the bullet sewn into the hem. I had dreamed that when the war was over I would put the bullet under a glass dome on a black piano and show it to my guests as a curiosity, because the bullet was unusual, larger than our rifle bullets. Experts had told me that it was an Austrian bullet. But my dream would never come true. I hung the handkerchief on a bush to dry and had a nap. When I woke up I completely forgot about the handkerchief, remembering it only once I had walked ten kilometres out of the village. I did not want to go back (how I regret this), as I thought that the war would last for a long time and that the bullet would not be my last. Future events would prove me right on both counts.

8

MY THOUGHTS ON RZHEV

THE RZHEV-SYCHEVKA OPERATION

In hospital I had an opportunity to think over my recent experiences. I noticed an interesting fact: near the frontline I had come across wounded soldiers from my regiment, then, further away, wounded soldiers from our division, then further still, the wounded from our army, and then those from several armies. This meant that vast numbers of military reserves had been deployed near Rzhev.

The aim of the Rzhev-Sychevka operation was not achieved: Rzhev was not liberated. The only positive result was that the Germans decided that the main Soviet defensive campaign was taking place near Rzhev and concentrated their great reserves there, overlooking the fact that Soviet troops were concentrated near Stalingrad. Once the German army under the command of

Field Marshal Paulus was surrounded near Stalingrad, the Germans could not transfer any of their divisions from Moscow.[1]

The Rzhev campaign was the Red Army's first significant summer offensive. The Germans had to transfer twelve infantry divisions to Rzhev, including those from the south which could have been sent to Stalingrad. Following fierce battles, the Germans were pushed back to Rzhev but our troops did not manage to liberate the town.

Our losses near Rzhev were enormous. During the assaults on fortified enemy territory, most infantry soldiers were wounded or killed within a week, and platoon and company commanders lasted three to seven days. On average, among the casualties there were three wounded to one death; for every twenty soldiers wounded, one died in hospital. For every seven men killed, one was missing in action. The corpses were dumped into common graves. It was very hot in July and

A woman and two girls look at the ruins of their house

August, and the corpses were decomposing rapidly, so it was impossible to remove documents or identity capsules from the thousands of bodies on the battlefields. As a result, thousands of the dead were categorized as missing in action and their families were not eligible for any pensions or benefits. Many mothers and wives of the dead hoped in vain until their dying day that their sons and husbands would turn up sooner or later. Most houses in Rzhev were burnt to ashes and dozens of villages nearby suffered the same fate as Khatyn.[2]

Rzhev had been occupied by the Germans for nearly seventeen months. During all that time battles were taking place, day in, day out. After the war, dozens of memorials were erected on the common graves.

Our historians, as well as our famous commanders, do not like to remember this tragic period in the history of the war. There, near Rzhev, Marshal Konev's operation failed, as did that of Marshal Zhukov himself. What I am going to say below is hard to believe; I myself would not believe it, had I not been an eyewitness and participant in what was going on.

In order to liberate two villages, Gory Kazeki and Polunino, just five kilometres outside Rzhev, we deployed thirty-two rifle battalions (including my 3rd rifle battalion), eleven rifle brigades, fifteen tank brigades and many other military units with different specialisations (aircraft, artillery, cavalry, sappers and others). These were engaged in eighteen months of unbroken fierce fighting. Over 10,000 of our dead could be identified and buried, but who knows how many died who were never identified? I had thought there could not be more deaths in a campaign to liberate a village. I turned out to be wrong. According to the data given in *Krasnaya Zvezda* (*The Red Star* wartime newspaper), there were villages where between 20,000 and 30,000 people died during fighting. As cadets at the Military Law Academy after the war, we were told that our commanders had displayed great military skill during the defeat of the Germans at Rzhev. Knowing the high death toll as I do now, this sounds bitterly ironic.

The village of Sinyavino near Leningrad was assaulted by our troops from September 1941 to January 1943, with short breaks in the fighting. According to official figures, 130,000 soldiers and officers were buried there—an estimate derived from the number of burials. How many died who were not buried or who were reported as missing in action?

The battles for Polunino are even mentioned in *Velikaya Otechestvennaya Voyna 1941–45* (*The Great Patriotic War 1941–45*), an encyclopaedia published in 1985 by the Institute of War History attached to the USSR Ministry of Defence. Usually battles for villages of barely twenty houses are not mentioned in such tomes.

After the war, an English journalist, Alexander Werth, who spent the war on the Soviet-German front, wrote: '...the battles for Rzhev were some of the hardest ones the Soviet troops had ever fought. They were so fierce that there were very few who were captured alive.'

At the site of the common graves in Polunino, there is a monument with a soldier in a military coat, his head bent, holding his helmet in one hand and an automatic gun in the other. On the monument is an inscription:

> Here lie the soldiers and officers of the military units which took part in the battles for the village of Polunino:
>
> Rifle battalions: 3, 10, 16, 20, 24, 32, 37, 43, 52, 78, 107, 111, 114, 143, 178, 182, 210, 243, 246, 247, 248, 250, 348, 357, 359, 369, 371, 375, 379, 413, 415;
>
> Rifle brigades: 4, 35, 36, 119, 130, 132, 136, 153, 156, 238;
>
> Tank brigades: 18, 25, 28, 38, 55, 85, 115, 119, 144, 153, 238, 249, 255, 270, 298.

The truth about the huge losses near Rzhev was never disclosed. They must have been incredibly high. On account of that, the commander of the Kalinin front, Marshal I.S. Konev, was dismissed. (He had previously been dismissed as commander of our western front for his failure to stem the German advance towards Moscow in October 1941.)

Fifty years later, after I visited the battlefield near Gory Kazeki and Polunino, and read authentic documents about the Rzhev offensive operation in the central archive of the USSR Ministry of Defence in Podolsk, I learned that the fierce battles for Rzhev lasted from October 1941 to March 1943.

To win Rzhev back, two Rzhev-Vyazma offensives and one Rzhev-Sychevka offensive were launched on the Kalinin and western fronts. In the Rzhev-Sychevka offensive, which lasted from 30 July to 23 August, our forces comprised six combined armies (including our division), one aircraft army, two tank corps and one cavalry corps. Nevertheless we failed to regain Rzhev.

I know I may tire my readers, but I must record the numbers of the combined armies which were fighting to win Rzhev back: 1st, 5th, 10th, 16th, 20th, 22nd, 29th, 30th, 31st, 33rd, 41st, 43rd, 49th, 50th; as well as the 1st and 2nd rifle corps and the 11th cavalry corps.

I cannot help contrasting the Rzhev operation with the campaign to take back Kiev, the capital of Ukraine, in November 1943. This operation took just ten days, even though it involved having to cross the Dnieper river (which is very wide), with our forces comprising the 38th combined army, the 3rd tank army, a tank corps and a cavalry corps.

So we could not win back Rzhev. In March 1943 the Germans left of their own accord to avoid being besieged by our forces which had made advances to their rear.

General D. Lelushenko was in charge of the 30th army for a year near Moscow and Rzhev. He published his memoirs, *Moskva-Stalingrad-Berlin-Praga* (*Moscow-Stalingrad-Berlin-Prague*), and sent me his book in response to my letter in which

I congratulated him on the thirtieth anniversary of our victory. The book has 450 pages, but only nine lines are devoted to Rzhev. We don't like to write about our failures.

When our troops started the first Rzhev-Sychevka offensive on 30 July 1942, 20,000 Soviet prisoners of war were being kept in terrible conditions in a concentration camp at Rzhev. Among them was a former cadet of the Moscow infantry school, Konstantin Vorobyov, who later became a famous writer. He wrote that the prisoners would hear the commotion of battle nearby, full of joy and hope that they would be liberated soon, but this all was to be in vain. It would take seventeen months of relentless fighting to win Rzhev back.

Here is an entry in the diary of G. Rzhevskaya, an interpreter at 30th army HQ:

> Today a [German] captive showed us the text of the oath which every German soldier fighting against us near Rzhev has to swear in Hitler's name. They swear not to leave their positions near Rzhev. The Führer said: 'To surrender Rzhev means to open the road to Berlin for the Russians.'

As a result Rzhev was completely destroyed. Out of 5,434 houses only 297 survived. Before the war Rzhev had a population of 60,000: when the town was liberated there were only 362 inhabitants left. On a bank high above the Volga river is a monument to 90,000 soldiers who died during the liberation of Rzhev. A total of 120,000 soldiers were buried (these were the recorded dead) in the Rzhev region, and 342 villages and settlements were destroyed. Here is the inscription on the monument:

> We did not ask for medals,
> We expected no reward—
> For us the communal glory
> Of Russia was our reward

The following poem by Alexander Tvardovsky was very popular:

MY THOUGHTS ON RZHEV

I was killed near Rzhev
In a nameless bog,
In fifth company,
On the Left flank,
In a cruel air raid

I didn't hear explosions
And did not see the flash
Down to an abyss from a cliff
No start, no end

And in this whole world
To the end of its days—
Neither patches, nor badges
From my tunic you'll find

During the war Stalin only visited the front once. This was in August 1943 when he went to Khoroshevo, a village near Rzhev fifty kilometres from the frontline, where he met the two heads of the armies and made a decision to hold artillery fireworks in honour of our troops winning back the towns of Oryol and Belgorod.

By order of the Supreme Commander, J.V. Stalin, on 23 February 1943, it was written:

> Our people will always keep in their memory the heroic defence of Sevastopol and Odessa, the last-ditch battles near Moscow, on the foothills of the Caucasus, near Rzhev and near Leningrad, and the battle of Stalingrad, the greatest one in the history of war.

As far as I know, this is the only time that the battles for Rzhev have been ranked equal to the greatest battles of the Second World War. Rzhev represents only a Pyrrhic victory, however. Seventeen months of fighting with innumerable casualties resulted in the enemy retreating just twenty kilometres. That is why the battles near Rzhev were subsequently hardly ever mentioned and never researched. We do not like defeats.

FOR THE MOTHERLAND! FOR STALIN!

Our huge losses

At the Podolsk military archive I browsed through the records kept by the officers of my division in 1943. In the course of one year, between five and seven commanders were replaced in each rifle platoon, as were three to four commanders in each mortar platoon, four to five commanders in each company, three commanders in each anti-tank gun platoon, and two to three commanders of each battalion or regiment. Their predecessors had been either killed, wounded, declared missing or transferred.

During the four years of the Great Patriotic War, the military personnel (both soldiers and officers) of infantry companies, battalions and regiments were completely replaced between ten and twelve times. Each day an average of 12,000 people were killed.

Sergey Smirnov, the poet and researcher of the Second World War who wrote a book about the defenders of the Brest Fortress, was right when he once said in a television programme: 'Every soldier who went through the horrors of attacks and defensive battles is a hero.'

Our enormous casualties were caused by our senior commanders' incompetence: countless frontal attacks with the enemy's defences being insufficiently weakened in advance; the tendency to concentrate on taking control of high ground regardless of its tactical importance; trying to ensure that cities were recaptured before public holidays, and so on.

During this period, the Soviet generals could only achieve victory by shedding rivers of soldiers' blood. The pointless cruelty and senselessness of some of our attacks were mentioned in a letter written by a German officer who had been captured by our scouts:

> In summer we were fighting off Russian attacks. We opened fire from a distance of 600 metres and in the first wave of the attack whole subdivisions fell to the ground... Those few who survived were continuing to advance. It was uncanny, incredible, inhuman. None of our soldiers

A cavalry charge

would have moved forwards. The second wave also suffered casualties, but closed ranks over the corpses of their comrades who had been killed in the first wave. Then, as if under command, lines of soldiers started running towards us. As they were approaching, a discordant, reverberating cry of 'Oor-a-a-ah!' was heard. The first three waves were annihilated by our fire... The onslaught of the fourth was slower: the troops were making their way through the corpses. Our machine guns were hot from constant fire and we had to stop shooting to change the barrels. The number, length and virulence of the attacks depleted our energy and left us exhausted. Frankly speaking, they frightened us. If the Soviets can afford to lose so many people in an attempt to take back even the insignificant gains of our offensive, then how often and with what amount of people will they attack if a target is really important?

In a German logbook of military operations, a writer from the 4th German tank army mentions the attacks of the 17th and 44th Russian cavalry divisions on German positions:

FOR THE MOTHERLAND! FOR STALIN!

We could not believe that the enemy was going to attack our tanks on that wide field more suitable for holding parades... But three lines of cavalry started moving towards us. Across the snow, which sparkled in the sun, the riders were galloping boldly with their sabres drawn, pressing themselves to the necks of their horses. The first shells blew up in the midst of the attackers. Pieces of men and horses flew up in the air... We were puzzled when after the first attack the Russian horsemen started attacking again. It was impossible to believe that after the slaughter of the first squadrons the horrible performance would be repeated... The target was already fixed by our guns and the second wave of the cavalry was slaughtered even more quickly than the first. Nearly everyone in the 44th division and three quarters of the 17th were killed.

Attacks like the one described, which were meant to exhaust the Germans, were quite common in 1941 and 1942. We overwhelmed them with our corpses.

The lines of the pre-war song, 'with minimal bloodshed and a powerful blow', turned out to be a delusion. The proof lies in numerous episodes in both the Finnish and the Great Patriotic Wars when, 'near an unknown village on a nameless height', infantry companies and battalions were slaughtered up to the last man. What was the life of a peasant in a military coat worth, when marshals and army commanders had been executed?[3]

Marshal Zhukov wrote in his book *Vospominaniya i Razmishleniya* (*Reminiscences and Thoughts*):

So many times I saw soldiers rising to attack. It is not easy to stand when the air is full of deadly metal. But they did! Many of them had hardly tasted life. The best age in your life is 19–20, when everything is ahead of you. But for most of them, there was only a German dugout blazing with machine gun fire. A Soviet soldier had a hard life back then. Today their old wounds ache, their health is fragile. A veteran of the front won't complain; it is not in his character. Please, be considerate to them without damaging their pride, and treat them with tact and respect. It is a small price after what they did for you in 1941–1945.

MY THOUGHTS ON RZHEV

Sometimes I ask myself if it is really necessary to write about our weaknesses and errors in a war which we eventually won. After all, we were the victors and you don't usually criticise success. But I think it is necessary, otherwise history will blame us for covering up our faults and then reveal what really happened. So it is better now, while we, the war veterans, are still alive, to show our children and grandchildren that, in spite of our weaknesses and errors, our troops at the front and those in the rear showed such incredible heroism, courage, stamina, willpower, skill and endurance which amazed humanity when we finally defeated the most powerful army in the world.

Nowadays, when I talk about the war to young people, they ask me how the veterans still keep their energy and stamina in spite of their terrible experiences during the war. I usually answer as follows: as true soldiers who experienced all the horrors of the war, they appreciate life and want to enjoy it with dignity.

After I resigned from the army, I tracked down a 111th division veterans' council in Moscow and attended several veterans' meetings on Victory Day (9 May) in Gorky Park on the bank of the Moscow river, where they are usually held. I visited the battle sites at Polunino and Gory Kazeki, near Rzhev, where the soldiers from our division had fought bravely and where thousands had remained forever young, lying in the ground. No trace of the fierce battles remained.

In Gory Kazeki, there is a small war museum which has a display of exhibits associated with the battles for the village. The museum director asked me for my photograph. As for the village of Novo Semyonovo, it no longer exists. The stream which we had crossed chest-deep during an attack had become a large lake, two kilometres long. Life goes on!

There were three Heroes of the Soviet Union in our division. One of them, Lieutenant Alexei Shemigon, born in 1916, repeated the heroic deed of Alexander Matrosov, who blocked a machine gun emplacement with his body. Shemigon had been fighting at the front since the beginning of the war in June 1941. On 20 August 1944, during a battle near the town of Yassy in Romania, after an opening salvo of artillery fire he prepared his company for attack. However, the soldiers could not advance owing to machine gun fire from a German earth-and-timber emplacement, so Shemigon crawled up to the machine gun and positioned himself in front of its barrel. He was posthumously awarded the title of Hero of the Soviet Union and a street in Kharkov was named after him.

Another Hero of the Soviet Union, Sergeant Yuzef Balabukh, born in 1921, was the deputy commander of a rifle platoon. When the platoon commander was killed, Balabukh assumed command and singlehandedly blew up a German tank, an armoured vehicle and a dozen German soldiers. He was wounded, but continued fighting. When the war was over he left the army and worked on a collective farm.

Vasil Bykov, who later became a famous writer, was the commander of the 45-mm anti-tank guns in the 399th regiment which was in our division. In a battle near Kirovograd he was badly wounded and left lying in a peasant hut in a village. During a German counterattack, a German tank destroyed the hut and Bykov lay hidden under the debris for two days until the Germans were kicked out of the village. He was found by chance.

Of the soldiers born in 1922, 1923 and 1924, only 3 per cent survived the war. This is a real statistic. Of the eighty cadets from Vasil Bykov's old military school, only four survived. Almost all his peers would remain eternally young, either killed near Moscow or Rzhev, or during the first hours of the war on the border, or during the last minutes of the war in Berlin and Prague, or some other time in the war when each of its 1,418 days took away lives.

MY THOUGHTS ON RZHEV

Vasil Bykov

Their soldiers' shoulder straps, their wounds, the hospitals where they were rescued from death, their last fatal wounds and finally their nameless graves under turf hastily thrown on top of them...

Vasil Bykov's career at the front is summed up in these brief lines: although his name was inscribed for a long time on the obelisk which marks a common grave near Kirovograd, he had survived by sheer chance, which is such a powerful factor in war.

Looking through the papers on the history of the 111th rifle division, I came across a report by the head of the division HQ which I must mention as I have sworn to write only the truth about the war. The report was about a battalion which had been attacked and surrounded by German tanks accompanied by troops with submachine guns. The tanks destroyed the battalion's two 45-mm guns, and the knee-deep trenches could not protect our soldiers. Their rifles and machine guns were useless against the armoured tanks. Everything was over in thirty minutes. The brutal Germans finished off the wounded with submachine guns and disfigured their faces with spades.

Three days later, another Soviet division drove the Germans away from their position. On account of the unbearable stench of their decomposing corpses, nobody bothered to take the dead soldiers' notification documents and they were hastily buried in the shallow trenches. In order to conceal the truth, the head of the 111th division HQ reported to the superior HQ that all 180 men were missing. This meant that their families would be stripped of the benefits due to frontline soldiers and officers. They would be always looked upon with suspicion by their neighbours and colleagues, and they would be under surveillance by the local branches of the state security apparatus (NKVD, MGB, KGB): what if your husband or son had defected to the Germans and had been sent back to spy on our country?

At the archive I could only write down any interesting information in a notebook which I had been given, with all the pages numbered and the last page stamped. When I had finished I had to give the notebook to an official who sent it to my local military office where it was kept in a secret department. I could only look at it in the presence of the head of the secret department and when I had finished I had to give it back to him.

So my notes about the tragic death of 180 people were crossed out with black ink in the archive, because it was forbidden to write anything negative about the war let alone to publish it. When the head of the secret department wasn't watching, I turned the page to the light; with some difficulty I could make out what I'd written about that tragic event near Kharkov, so I copied it down into my own notebook.

Even the head of the Institute of Military History (part of the USSR Ministry of Defence), General Colonel D. Volkogonov, could not get permission to read some of the top secret documents which were kept in the military archive.

They shouted (and are shouting now) that you must write the truth and only the truth about the Great Patriotic War, but in reality the opposite has happened. Later, when I visited the archive I used a stratagem. Whenever the documents stated, for example, that eight Russian soldiers were captured by Germans, I wrote down that eight German soldiers were captured by us. At home I rewrote everything the correct way round.

9

THE MORTAR REGIMENT
AT VYSHNY VOLOCHYOK

VYSHNY VOLOCHYOK

When I recovered, I was sent to the personnel department of the Kalinin front in Kalinin (now Tver) where I spent several days and from there I went to the division of the officers' front reserve force.[1] The division was stationed in Vyshny Volochyok (*voloch* is to pull in Russian: in ancient times boats carrying goods between Scandinavia and Greece were pulled overland from the River Tsna to the Tversta, which flows into the Volga).

While I was off-duty, I wandered along the streets and numerous canals of that ancient, typically provincial town, admiring the architecture of its old houses. Vyshny Volochyok is known as the 'Venice of Russia'. Its canals had been dug during the reign of

Peter the Great so that boats and ships no longer had to be hauled overland.

I stayed in the reserve force for a month doing military studies, including the use of cannons and mortars. During this time, in November 1942, I became a Komsomol member. I was aged seventeen years and ten months, but I was considered to be a battle-seasoned veteran because I had fought in battles and been wounded.

Lieutenant Mikhail Garifullin was in the same reserve force, together with Sergeant Uvenaliy Semionov, who was a record-clerk in a battery of the division. Twenty-five years later we would meet again as colleagues on the Odessa military tribunal. Garifullin became a lieutenant colonel of justice, a military assistant judge advocate general of the military tribunal; as for Semionov, he became a colonel of justice, a member of the same military tribunal.

Soon I was appointed commander of a platoon in a mortar regiment which was being formed in Vyshny Volochyok. My military title was now senior lieutenant. There were two scout departments and two field cable-laying departments: in total, there were thirty-five people in my platoon. But I did not hold my position for long.[2]

I had a problem: in our regiment we used horse-drawn vehicles, but the carts of hay for our horses had been destroyed in bombardments, so we had nothing to feed them with as all the fields were under snow. There were eighty horses in our regiment.

Among the scouts in my platoon were several former criminals who had been released from prison on parole and sent to the front. As far as I remember, one of them was a thief and another had killed a person in revenge. In 1941–42, 900,000 inmates—the equivalent of ninety conventional divisions—had been sent to the front from prisons and prison camps.

The criminals suggested stealing a stack of hay from a field belonging to the collective farm. I stupidly agreed, hoping to be praised by our regiment commander. We stole the hay, but the farmers found it by following the tracks left by our sledges. They complained to the secretary of the regional party committee, who passed the complaint on to a member of the military council of the front. As a result, both the regiment commander and I were punished. I was demoted to the post of commander of the battery platoon (the rank was junior lieutenant) and the hay had to be given back to the collective farm.

I remember another incident. Telephone engineers who had already fought at the front told me that it was necessary to have a supply of extra telephone cable. During fighting a spool of cable would sometimes have to be abandoned because there was not enough time to unreel it: as a result a commander could be left without a telephone connection and in battle this was equivalent to being blind. This prompted me to find a solution by looking for cable in Vyshny Volochyok's factories.

At a glass factory I found plenty of rolls of iron wire rusting under a covering of snow. I asked the factory director to give us some of them, as we would be shortly going to the front. To my surprise he refused flatly, and all my appeals to his conscience and patriotism were of no use. What could I do? My criminals found a solution again.

In the morning, six soldiers marched past an armed guard at the factory checkpoint. Without stopping, I said quickly to the guard: 'We are going to work in the factory, by order of your director.' She did not stop us. Having thrown five or six reels of wire over the fence onto our waiting sledges, we marched back past the guard, saying: 'There is no work for us today.' That time we got away with it.

In my platoon there was a scout from Moscow called Novikov who was the same age as me. He had volunteered for the front in August 1941 when he was seventeen. The division he joined was formed of volunteers. There were fifteen such divisions in

Moscow at that time, each from a district in the city. Each division had 10,000 soldiers—former workers, students, professors and others, all of them ineligible for conscription for various reasons. All the volunteer divisions were destroyed by German tank and motorised divisions, and all the soldiers were taken prisoner or killed.

Novikov was among those who were captured. He told us:

> Several hundred of us were being taken to the west by German guards. We came across a tank column moving in the opposite direction. We were herded to the side of the road, but the tank column stopped. The commander leaned out of the front tank's hatch and issued a command. The guards quickly ran across the road and opened fire on us. Machine guns from the tanks also began firing at us. We all started running, but only a few people were able to escape. I hid myself under a steep river bank. German troops with submachine guns were finishing off the wounded, but they did not find me. Two months later I crossed the frontline, exhausted and malnourished.

He hated the fascists and instilled his hatred in his comrades-in-arms.

My father-in-law, Dmitriy Krupin, also fought in one of Moscow's volunteer divisions. His division was encircled, but he managed to escape and came home half-dead. His health was ruined and six years later he died, aged sixty.

To the front again

When our regiment was completely formed, it was time for us to go to the front. Although the precise hour of our departure had been kept secret, we were accompanied on our two-kilometre journey to the railway station by girls, young women and old women and men from the village where we had stayed, as well as by the village band of five musicians, who played all the way. As our train moved off, the band began playing an old traditional military march, 'Proshanie Slavyanki' ('The Slavic Woman's Farewell').[3] It was an emotional parting. During our month in the village, three or four men had stayed in each house, and many of them had developed relationships with local girls and women. When parting, those in love and those not so much in love hugged and kissed, exchanged addresses, promised not to forget each other and to write, and implored each other to return alive and healthy.

As for me, my girlfriend surprised everyone: she gave me a big loaf of rye bread. I was the only one of the thirty soldiers from my platoon who had been given such a generous gift. It really was an excellent present during those hungry times and I remembered it for the rest of my life. Later my soldiers talked and laughed a lot about it.

So off we went to the front by train. Our regiment was composed of:

Officers	61
Sergeants	157
Rank-and-file soldiers	343
Total	561
Mortars (there were six batteries and each had six mortars)	36
Mounted machine guns	6
Hand-held machine guns	53
Vehicles comprising:	64
Dodge 3/4 ton	12
Studebaker	3
Willis	1
GAZ AA	48

To this day my conscience has bothered me over something I did on that train. There was an iron wood burning heater in every carriage. These heaters had round cast-iron lids. My criminal scouts talked me into taking a lid for the artillery controller to use as a shield when he was up a tree (these were used as observation points). For some time the lid was used as a shield, but later, in a hurry, we left it behind, attached to a tree. As a result the heater in our carriage was left without a lid, so no one could use the heater.

On our way to the front, we had to cross the frozen River Lovat, which is about 150 metres wide.[4] There was a thaw, so we were walking through ten centimetres of water above the ice. We were all wearing *valenki*, traditional felt boots, which got soaked, but none of us caught a cold. Indeed nobody seemed to suffer from illness at the front. It was as if illnesses had ceased to exist.

Soldiers in *valenki* with a POW in giant *lapti*

THE MORTAR REGIMENT AT VYSHNY VOLOCHYOK

It is a well-known fact that war has an impact on the human psyche: it focuses our minds and metabolism on outer dangers and does not let us concentrate on our inner maladies. During the battles in the Crimea, people who were being treated there for tuberculosis became partisans. They went through terrible ordeals, and great psychological and physical stress. Incredibly, they recovered from tuberculosis. Something similar happened to us on the River Lovat.

We were moving along a country road, the soldiers on foot, the mortars on sleighs pulled by two horses. We went through thick forest surrounded by marshes. On both sides of the road the snow lay knee-deep. The nearest railway station was 120 kilometres away. There were small villages twenty or thirty kilometres away from each other, all of them burnt to ashes. Nothing was left but blackened chimneys: a lonely cat sat on one of them, hopelessly waiting for its owner.

By January 1943 the front stretched for more than 6,000 kilometres. All along the front, blood was being shed—theirs and ours. We had been sent to the area of uninterrupted forest and marshes where fighter ace Captain A. Maresyev had carried out his legendary feat. After being badly wounded he managed to land his fighter plane in a field, then crawl for eighteen days and nights until he reached the nearest Russian settlement. Both his lower legs were frost-bitten, but he showed tremendous stamina and willpower. Although his lower legs were amputated he continued to fly his fighter plane and added seven more German planes to the four he had brought down before his accident. For his heroic feats he was awarded the title of Hero of the Soviet Union.

In early January 1943 our regiment reached the front near the town of Kholm in the Novgorod region and joined the 3rd shock army of the north-western front. The famous scouts Yegorov and Kantaria were in a division in that army. Towards the end of the war they would hoist the Victory flag on the roof of the

Reichstag in Berlin and become Heroes of the Soviet Union. The personnel of the shock army had certain privileges including higher salaries and the right to return to their unit following discharge from hospital. The battle near Kholm was part of the Velikiye Luki offensive operation.[5]

Boris, a platoon commander in the mortar regiment, Kholm, February 1943

10

THE NORTH-WESTERN FRONT NEAR KHOLM

AT THE FRONT

After arriving at the front some of us started making shelters of fir branches, while others gathered dry wood for a fire and springy fir twigs for our 'feather beds'. Soon the fire was burning cheerfully: soup bubbled away in one cauldron while tea brewed in the other. A soldier on duty was responsible for the fire. If you lay with your face to the fire, your face and chest got hot while your back was cold. If you turned over, your face, chest and knees became cold. If you stretched out your legs in your sleep, your felt boots or your knees were liable to be burnt. As the pine needles were warmed by the fire they emitted the fresh, invigorating smell of resin. But the air also smelled of tobacco, sweat and drying clothes. We lived for two months in winter like this: in shelters at night, out on the snow during the day.

During the day I would watch the enemy from an observation point. I would phone the battery commander to report everything I'd noticed and also enter it in the logbook. As a rule the battery commander directed the firing, but several times I directed the shooting at targets which the battery commander could not see from his observation point. On one occasion I managed to annihilate a German machine-gun earth-and-timber emplacement.

There was no solid frontline. Five or six riflemen and their sergeant lay all day behind an icy parapet of snow, armed with an automatic rifle. They were changed over at the end of each week. Similar groups were spread out at 100–150-metre intervals along the entire frontline. Both our scouts and German scouts wore white camouflage smocks and went behind the enemy line to capture *yazik* or 'tongues'—prisoners who would talk. The fact that there was no solid frontline made the scouts' life easier. Night and day we had to be on alert for German scouts and snipers.

An incident took place in our regiment. A battery commander was watching the Germans from a tree. He had three scouts below. Germans wearing white smocks crept up and tried to capture the scouts, who noticed them in good time and opened fire. The battery commander leapt off the tree and they fled from the Germans, shooting all the time. One of the scouts was killed and the commander, in his panic, left his short sheepskin coat behind together with a bag containing a map with information about Soviet and German defence lines. All of these, as well as the dead scout's documents, fell into German hands. The commander was interrogated by special agents for a whole month, but all ended well for him.

Preparing for attack

On 22 February our regiment was urgently transferred to another part of the front about ten kilometres north of Kholm. An attack was being planned on a German fortified defence line along the road from Kholm to Staraya Russa. The Germans had been there for a year and during that time they had fortified their defences fairly well. Everything indicated that we would take part in the attack. The soldiers playfully wrote in their letters to their next of kin: 'We are staying in light "barracks", with the horizon as our walls and the starry sky as our ceiling.'

The regiment commander announced that we would support the lines of infantry from the 8th guards division who were mounting the attack with mortar fire. This division was famous for its role in a decisive battle near Dubosekovo, outside Moscow, in November 1941. During that battle twenty-eight soldiers destroyed sixteen German tanks with just one 45-mm anti-tank gun and managed to hold back the German advance on Moscow for four hours. They were all awarded the title of Hero of the Soviet Union, twenty-four of them posthumously, including the commander of the division, I.V. Panfilov, who was killed in the battle. Later the division was named after him—the 8th guards rifle Panfilov division.

After the call we all went to the dugouts and huts which had been constructed before our arrival. Everyone was serious. No jokes were made. We were already old hands. We knew that huge losses were inevitable during an attack on a fortified defence line. In the dugout I started to shave. My mirror fell down and broke. Everyone stared silently at me. A broken mirror is considered a bad omen.

In the evening all the officers were invited into the regiment commander's tent. He told us that at 6 am the next day the regiment and the division would launch an offensive with the aim of overwhelming the enemy's defences. My immediate task was to go to the frontline at night, set up the telephone connection with the battery and establish an observation point. During battle my platoon was to support the rifle company with mortar fire: I was to be near the rifle company commander and the battery commander was to be near the rifle battalion commander. Our defence line was not continuous but consisted of separate posts which were 100–200 metres apart. That is why, when making your way to the frontline in the dark, you had to look out for Germans.

The briefing meeting was over. I quickly returned to my platoon and told my soldiers about the offensive. They prepared their rifles and checked their machine guns, then tightened their belts which had pouches of cartridges and grenades attached. Their faces were grave: they could not conceal their deep worry. I knew that by tomorrow some of them would be missing. But who? I looked from one man to another and my heart sank. War is ruthless. My soldiers would have to attack a strong, experienced and well-armed enemy. Not all of them were experienced. Would they be able to carry out their mission?

I took three scouts and three soldiers to lay cables, and we went into a thick wood. The location of my observation post was indicated on my map. I was using my compass and we counted our steps. The post was about a kilometre away. Every twenty or thirty paces I checked the bearing with my compass by torchlight. There was no path and the snow was above our knees, so it was very difficult to walk. From time to time we swapped places in the line, with the first man going to the end so it was easier for him to make his way through the snow.

We finally succeeded in finding the observation post. Five or six soldiers and their sergeant lay inside a round snow parapet with a machine gun. There were no trenches or communication trenches, no cables nor a toilet. It was impossible to dig a trench, as this was a swamp. Once you dug away the snow, you just hit water.

Early in the morning, when it was still dark, the rifle company arrived. I introduced myself to the company commander: from that moment I would be near him all the time. Both the rifle company and my platoon wore white camouflage suits (a smock and trousers). We had white strips on our caps. Some soldiers had wound white bandages around their machine guns so they would not be noticeable against the snow. I asked why they did not have gas masks. They answered that they had thrown them away on the way to the front and their commanders had not objected.

When putting your life in danger, a rifle company does not differ from a penal company.[1] Frankly speaking, very, very few rifle platoon or company commanders who fought through the war managed to survive. Their chance of survival was like that of a man who is being hanged, whose rope might break.

On 23 February we started with a weak artillery bombardment which lasted twenty minutes. There were not enough guns and mortars, let alone ammunition. We did not have tanks or aircraft to provide back-up in our part of the front. Our artillery preparation turned out to be ineffective. The enemy's numerous and well-disguised firing units—its cannons and machine guns—were not destroyed.

Into battle

At last the rockets were set off. Three red stripes crossed the sky to signal the attack! On the command, the soldiers rushed forward after their commanders, leaving their footprints behind in the deep snow. Bullets started whistling around us, sending up small fountains of snow; bursts of machine-gun fire sounded clear in the frosty air; an automatic weapon started barking. After running thirty or forty metres the soldiers had to lie down and crawl, tunnelling their way through the snow. Metre after metre, the line of soldiers moved steadily onwards. Platoon and company commanders kept cheering them on: 'Company (or platoon) advance! Follow me, fuck you, for the motherland, fuck you, for Stalin, fuck you!' Or, alternatively: 'I'll shoot you! Fuck you!'

Here and there the wounded started crying and moaning; behind them the dead lay motionless. The lightly wounded were crawling back by themselves. The badly wounded were crying: 'Help! I need a stretcher! Over here!' The stretcher bearers crawled over to bandage them and transport them to the rear before they were shot by German snipers.

The Germans were repelling our attack with machine-gun and mortar fire. Sometimes you heard shots from a quick-firing small-calibre 20-mm Erlicon-type gun. Soldiers called that gun a *sobaka* or dog. Both this gun and the machine guns were well disguised. To find them you had to rise up on your knees or stand up. I stood up for a split second but I couldn't see a thing. The battery commander was almost continuously directing the firing; he was about 200 metres behind me and slightly to my left.

At last we were 100 metres from the German trench. On the command, the soldiers rose up to attack in a series of short runs. Because of the dense, multi-layered fire our attack was frustrated. The lines of men lay down again. My mortar gunners and I did not stand up to attack but kept crawling through the snow, pulling the telephone wire along with us. The division, regiment and battery commanders were demanding that we should attack, pouring out a stream of furious expletives.

But how can you raise your body from the ground under the enemy's fire of annihilating lead? You would like to dig yourself deeper into the snow, but you are lying as if you were on a plate and the Germans seem to be directing their aim solely at you. Yet the example of the company commander and that subconscious thought, 'I must...', make you jump to your feet and run forward. But again in vain. The enemy fire is so dense that after running ten steps, men fall on the spot. And you can't run alone without them. The attack was frustrated.

The soldiers were digging themselves into the snow, hiding themselves in the shell craters, dying in vain. There were large bloodstains on the snow; you could see them in the distance. It was impossible to tell who was alive and who was dead. It was horrible for our comrades growing numb with cold.

The short winter day, which seemed very long to us, finally drew to a close. Heaven-sent darkness came. Our nervous tension subsided a little. But there was no command to withdraw. Throughout the entire winter night we lay on the snow, illuminated by the deadly pale light of German rocket flares winging their way one by one through the darkness. Bright dotted lines of tracer bullets crossed the black sky. By the colour of the tracer bullets you could locate both the Russian and German positions. The Russian tracer bullets were red and the German ones were electric blue.

On no man's land you could see the frozen corpses of those who had died in the futile attacks and in previous battles, half covered by the snow. They lay in the poses in which death had caught them—this was a horrible sight, and not for the faint-hearted, especially in moonlight—one man had his hand raised, another lay with his leg sticking up.

The weather, as bad luck would have it, conspired against us. By day it was always cloudy. Grey clouds blowing in from the west nearly touching the tops of the trees. Cold gusty wind hit our faces. Wet snow turned into drizzle. It became increasingly difficult to see where the enemy's guns and machine guns were firing from.

The shell craters where we hid from German snipers filled up with water and icy slush during the day. Our greatcoats, short sheepskin jackets, wadded trousers, felt boots and mittens never dried. We dried our spare foot wraps by wrapping them around our naked bodies beneath our clothes.

The fact that we could warm ourselves with vodka at night helped a bit. It was our company commander, or rather his orderly, who had vodka in abundance. Realising that our attacks were futile, our experienced company commander resorted to cunning—he led a mock attack. On his signal, we opened intense fire from our rifles, submachine guns and machine guns, threw grenades and shouted a prolonged 'Oorah!' at the top of our voices, but we did not rise from the ground. Then our company commander reported to the battery commander and the latter reported to his superiors that 'the attack was frustrated because of the enemy's dense fire and heavy losses of personnel'.

The explosions of mortar bombs and shells put us under constant nervous strain. Mortar bombs are more dangerous than shells. When exploding, a shell sinks into the ground making a small crater, so the fragments fly up at an angle. A mortar bomb explodes instantly on touching the ground without making a crater, so the fragments fly parallel to the ground and hit anyone lying nearby.

Lying on the snow (and during the day we had to remain motionless because of the sniper who was 100 metres away from us), we all cursed the awful weather and Hitler a thousand times. It was because of him, I thought, that we had to go through these unbearable torments. Since we had to fight anyway it would be much better to fight in the south, where it was warmer and drier. I did not know then that this wish would come true. I also dreamed of getting enough sleep in a warm, dry bed with clean sheets, without cold water dripping under my collar.

The enemy's rifle and machine-gun fire would kill anything that stirred. Now and then I thought that my life would end here. Many of us would remain lying on the snow forever. Why did we have to die in such an undignified way? How could our infantry attack the enemy's strongly fortified position without destroying their guns and machine guns beforehand? Why were we advancing to the German frontline in such a ludicrous manner? It is awful to die foolishly, senselessly on account of your own or someone else's idiocy. Experienced soldiers said: 'It is not war: it is slaughter.' I tried not to think about it. My life had taught me not to give way to difficulties, but to overcome them, and not to yield to death, but to fight until the end while I still had strength. Maybe this enabled me to survive.

On the snow for three days and nights

The night on the snow in the cold, under enemy fire, seemed endless. It was beyond the limits of human endurance. And I had to lie on the snow for three days and three nights in a row. During the whole world history of mankind there were only a few who had to go through the experiences of a soldier in the Great Patriotic War.

If anybody doubts it or wants to experience at least a thousandth part of what we had to go through, I would advise them to lie for at least an hour on snow without moving. I am sure that even in fine, sunny weather this hour would seem like an eternity to them and they would look differently at a decrepit old man with a stick and a soldier's medal 'For Merit in Combat' pinned on his chest. When old soldiers remember those cruel days, and the immeasurable losses they experienced and suffered during the war, they can't stop tears coming to their eyes, and young people who did not experience this look at them in bewilderment.

Those without inner strength could not endure such ordeals and committed suicide or injured themselves (by shooting themselves in the foot or hand, or in the side), or they deserted, defected to the enemy, went mad or simulated illness. They may have been few in number, but they existed. I doubt that they are mentioned in films and books about the war.

While working for the Military Collegium of the Supreme Court of the USSR in the 1950s I found out that 157,000 soldiers (the equivalent of fifteen rifle divisions) were sentenced by military tribunals to be executed for high treason and desertion in front of their units. In total, 994,000 members of the armed forces were convicted by military tribunals.

However, such ordeals could also lead to desperate acts of heroism, as demonstrated by Alexander Matrosov's world famous feat. It happened during the same Velikiye Luki offensive, thirty kilometres south of the village of Chernushki, on the River Lovat on 26 February 1943. Matrosov was the same age as me, born in 1924. He lost his parents as a small child and was brought up in an orphanage, he then worked as a teacher's assistant at a reformatory. So his life had been rather tough.

It was Matrosov's first battle. His company was lying in front of the German trench under heavy fire. They had been lying in the snow for six hours. Their commanders kept repeating the order: 'No retreat. Just advance.' So many of his men had been killed already, their ammunition was running out, and the German snipers were on the alert, especially the machine gunners in an earth-and-timber emplacement. Damn it all, death is better than such a life! Matrosov crawled up to the emplacement and covered the machine gun with his body. The machine gun went silent. The company then rose and took the German trench. A high ranking, narrow-minded commander decided to change the date of this brave deed to coincide with Red Army Day on 23 February, for propaganda purposes. But sooner or later every lie is revealed and so it came to pass.

I was an eye witness of the unrecorded death of a neighbouring company commander who, when very drunk, ordered his soldiers to mount an attack. They were reluctant, so the commander and his orderly ran among them, kicking them and swearing; he was shot dead by a sniper's bullet.

On the third day of our offensive, early in the morning while it was still dark, the gunners hauled a 45-mm gun into position to open fire on the enemy at daybreak. The frontline soldiers, or *frontoviki*, called that gun 'Farewell, motherland'. So we started crawling twenty to thirty metres away from the gun, heading in different directions. Experienced fighters knew that as soon as the gun opened fire it would be the target of all kinds of enemy fire, and this is exactly what happened. At daybreak the gunners managed ten to twelve shots before they were killed and the gun was destroyed by enemy fire.

We were confronting a German anti-aircraft field division. The personnel from several German anti-aircraft units had been merged with infantry. These divisions were supplied with a large quantity of anti-aircraft artillery which opened direct fire on ground targets. There were twelve 88-mm and forty 28-mm anti-aircraft guns. For the greater part of the day a German Focke-Wulf scout plane or *rama* used to fly in circles high in the sky. Eventually we became used to its monotonous buzz. For fun, the Nazi pilot would drop a barrel pierced in several places, or perhaps a piece of rail. These made an infernal howling or singing sound as they came hurtling through the air towards us— this was truly intimidating. We would all shoot back, but we did not know that the bottom of the plane was iron clad and all our shots were in vain.

During the three days and nights that we spent lying in the snow there were no hot meals. We had forgotten what they tasted like. We were hungry. We ate nothing but dry bread. Deliveries of food and ammunition had become almost impossible because of the heavy mud on the roads. Before the offensive we had all been given a loaf of bread as our ration, so at night we used to crawl up to the dead soldiers, cut their rucksacks open with a knife and take their bread.

11

THE SECOND WOUND

HOW I WAS THREATENED WITH EXECUTION AGAIN—AND THE SECOND WOUND

After the third day of lying in the snow I had to do something. A damaged telephone cable provided me with an excuse. Instead of finding a field engineer, I went to mend it myself at night without asking for my commander's permission. Later I went to see the division commander. A paraffin lamp lit up his tent, where he was drinking with other officers; he was very drunk.

When he saw me he was so angry that I had left my position without permission that he did not bother to hear me out and, shouting four-letter words at me, snatched a pistol from its holster, released the safety catch, loaded it and then, aiming it at me, ordered me to return to my post. And so, facing the drunken commander, I could have been shot—such incidents did take place in the front, but, as they say, there but for the grace of God...

Back in my position, I spotted the enemy firing position through my binoculars—a machine gun on an earth-and-timber emplacement which was showering our infantry with bullets. After phoning the battery commander for his permission to open fire I passed on the command to the firing post of our 120-mm mortar battery.

The battery opened fire with twelve rounds. All the mortar bombs hit the target. When the smoke from the explosions cleared only a dark patch was left to mark the site of the emplacement and there was silence. Many years later I was reading a book about the Heroes of the Soviet Union: among them was a platoon commander in charge of a mortar battery who had destroyed an enemy machine gun in battle. He was awarded the title of Hero of the Soviet Union, but as for me, I was not even given a medal.

It was my first 'achievement', as they used to call it—the destruction of a firing position. The glory did not matter: what counted was the moral satisfaction in knowing that one small action had contributed to the common cause of defeating the enemy—it was one step towards Victory.

Then came the fourth day of lying in the snow 100 metres away from the enemy trench. Only our youth and sense of sacred military duty made us bear that ordeal. I was lying hidden behind a small tree stump looking through my binoculars when I spotted a German quick-firing gun which was repeatedly shooting at our infantry. I rolled over onto my back (I was numb after lying for so long on my stomach) and started to calculate the firing data for our battery. Suddenly I felt a terrible blow on my right shoulder as if a strong man had hit me with a heavy cudgel. At first I thought I had been hit by a shell from the quick-firing gun—if so, I would have been torn to pieces, but I was not.

THE SECOND WOUND

I must have been shot by a sniper who had noticed my movement behind the stump through his telescopic sight. My white smock turned red on my chest. I was not frightened. My mind was working clearly. Blood was pouring out of my mouth, nose, my right shoulder (where the bullet had entered) and the left side of my neck (where the bullet had exited). For a moment I felt overcome by weakness and was oblivious to everything around me.

I was saying to the scouts and wireless operators who were lying next to me: 'Bandage me quickly,' but they couldn't hear me because my words were coming out as a hiss. They were looking at me in bewilderment, trying to understand what had happened—a moment ago the commander had been safe and sound, and now he was bleeding everywhere. On the left side of my neck was a large hole. Later, the doctors who examined me were surprised that I survived.

The bullet was one millimetre away from my carotid artery and spinal cord. I could neither eat, speak nor turn my neck. My right arm was paralyzed (the nerve was damaged). My hand and fingers were paralyzed too. 'Four steps separated me from death' were the lyrics of a famous song during wartime: as far as I was concerned, it was one millimetre.

I could not be bandaged on the spot as we were in the sniper's range. Two men put me on a cape and dragged me fifty metres to a hollow which could not be seen from the German side. I left a trail of blood. They started bandaging me, but it was very difficult to dress the wound because of its location and the contents of my first aid pack were not enough, so they had to open a second pack, but blood still oozed through the bandages and cotton wool.

A passage one metre wide and sixty to seventy centimetres deep had been made in the snow from the frontline to the rear. They dragged me on the cape along that passage. Every time a shell or mortar bomb landed nearby they would throw themselves to the ground. I was eventually brought to the regiment commander's tent. The female commander of the regiment's medical service was frying potato chips in a pan on a primus stove. They offered me some chips but although I was hungry I could not eat—I could not even swallow my saliva because of the acute pain in my neck.

The regiment commander, Major Barabanov, told me that on 19 February 1943 I had been given the title of full lieutenant by the order of the commander of the Kalinin front, Lieutenant General Konev. I was eighteen years and two months old. Due to my great loss of blood I did not react at all to this joyful news.

As our four-day offensive on German positions proved to be a failure it was called off. We incurred heavy losses. The 8th rifle division alone lost 611 men, with 1,115 wounded, and this is without taking into account losses in the units attached to the division. In our regiment a battery commander, a platoon commander and several soldiers 'died the death of the brave', as they wrote in the official letters to the next of kin. Several horses were also killed and others were wounded. Newspapers reported the following about our offensive: 'Battles of local importance were taking place on the north-western front'. Kholm was only liberated from Germans a year later—on 21 February 1944—and the 561st mortar regiment, which had fought alongside us, was given the honorific title of *Kholmsky* (of Kholm).

For two days and nights I was carried 120 kilometres along a forest road to the nearest railway station on a peasant's sleigh. As well as me and the sleigh driver there were two other seriously wounded soldiers. I was very weak: I had lost a lot of blood and I couldn't eat anything. All the way all three of us were groaning with terrible pain. Each time the sleigh hit the edge of the slippery road and tilted, I fainted.

One night we stayed in a village, in a big house that may have been a school. In one room there were about twenty wounded men lying on the floor which was covered with straw. The air smelled of disinfectant. Nearby someone asked for water in a weak voice, while another was muttering away to himself, evidently in a state of delirium. Many were groaning. One man kept shouting: 'I'm choking! I'm choking!' He was wounded in the chest. His chest was in a plaster cast which had tightened as it dried out, preventing him from breathing. Of course, everyone else was suffering and they had to endure his heart-breaking cries on top of everything else. Somebody couldn't bear it any longer and shouted: 'So choke then, damn you!' It was eerie.

Three days later I was taken to a mobile field hospital where they changed my bandages. By that time my bloodied bandages had dried and stuck fast to the wounds. Tearing the bandages off was incredibly painful.

So, after I was wounded I was taken to the medical battalion, to the mobile field hospital and then to a medical evacuation hospital.

At last I came to Ivanovo on the hospital train for my final treatment. At that time there were twenty-five military hospitals in Ivanovo, with different specialist areas. Some treated head wounds; others, stomach wounds; others, chest wounds; others, wounded limbs and so on.

I was among thirty people being taken from the railway station to the hospital which specialised in head wounds. Like all the others, I had my medical report tucked in my jacket. The medical report was a document that confirmed that you had been wounded at the front and that you were not a deserter. Suddenly I had an idea: now that I had my medical report I could go and see my father, mother and brother who were currently living in Petropavlovsk (now Petropavl) in the Kazakh Republic (now Kazakhstan). I hadn't seen my family since I left them two years previously when I was sixteen.

At eighteen it's not easy to bear the cruellest aspects of life when you are so far away from your family. For everyone there comes a time when the yearning for your kith and kin, for your roots, becomes so unbearable that it gives you heartache. Such was my yearning for the special world of my youth which I had voluntarily left behind in 1941.

At that time my health was very poor because of my injury. I had a perforated wound in my throat and it was aching intolerably. I could only swallow three or four mouthfuls of mashed food with water a day; I dared not have any more because of the terrible pain. Due to malnutrition and heavy blood loss I became very weak and could hardly walk.

My right arm had atrophied—I couldn't bend my elbow or my wrist, or move my fingers which were still bent. I couldn't put my arm into the sleeve of my short sheepskin coat so I had to wear it thrown over my shoulders. I had to do everything with my left arm. My vocal cords were also damaged and I could only just manage to speak in a husky voice.

In spite of all that I decided to run away! As far as I was concerned it was a case of nothing ventured nothing gained. I would have to steal a ride as I had neither documents nor money with me. After leaving the hospital backyard unnoticed, I plodded to the railway station and boarded a passenger train heading for the east. I had to travel 2,000 kilometres across the Ural Mountains and through Siberia to Petropavlovsk.

How much unexplored energy there is in a human being! I managed to travel in a terrible state of health, changing trains several times, during ten days in winter. Jack London was right—lust for life is a great force. The military patrols were my main danger: they were checking every train for deserters. They showed no mercy. The men in these patrols who spent the war in the rear were well-fed, fat-faced and plump: they slept in warm beds, wore clean uniforms and clung tightly to their posts. They dreaded being sent to the front, which is why they tried to gain promotion by detaining travelling soldiers for the slightest reason and taking them to the commandant's office from where there was only one exit—to the tribunal.

Since then, like many other front veterans, I have hated those who stayed in the rear for the whole war. I'm sure they feel the same about us, but try not to show it. After the war the veterans, who had been wounded more than once, who had suffered severe psychological and physical stress and numerous illnesses, couldn't compete with those who had spent their entire war in the rear in reserve regiments, military schools, commandants' offices, military enlistment offices, warehouses and so on. Those who had previously carried out back-up roles started gaining better positions and obtaining promotions. In particular, many of them joined our troops abroad where their salaries were five to ten times bigger than those of the people who served in Russia. Well... it's all right for some!

During my train journey I spent most of my time lying on the floor under the bottom berth (in the dirt and dust), or hiding behind suitcases and bundles on the upper berth. My fellow travellers did their best in helping to conceal me from the military patrols.

I arrived in Petropavlovsk at 2 am. The station was two kilometres away from the town. There was a frost and the temperature was–30°C. My impatience to see my family was so great that I did not wait until morning but headed straight into town even though I had never been there before. I knew the address: Kirova Street, House 116. After much searching I finally stood in a dark, empty street outside the door of my family's house. Now, more than half a century later, even I can hardly believe that this actually happened.

I was knocking at the door. A long time passed. At last the door opened slightly and through a narrow crack a woman asked me what I wanted. I hissed my reply, but she didn't understand and pushed me away so I fell into the snowdrift outside. And now, having reached my goal, my spiritual and physical strength were completely exhausted. I remained lying in the snow, likely to freeze to death, but the door opened again and a man bent over me. It was my father.

As it turned out, my aunt Vera (my mother's sister) had recently been evacuated from Kiev and had come to stay at my parents' house with her two children. My parents hadn't had time to tell me about it. She had started working as a waitress in a restaurant and had got used to dealing firmly with drunken customers, so she had assumed I was a drunk.

When my father had asked her what was going on, she had answered that it was a drunken soldier. My father was the military commissar of Petropavlovsk and he had decided to find out for himself who this drunk was, knocking at his door in the middle of the night.

Of course everyone got up and didn't go to sleep until the morning: my father, my mother, my brother Anatoliy, Vera with her children, Luda and Nikolai. The first thing my father asked was had I come legally, to check that I was not a deserter. But when I silently took off my short sheepskin coat and everyone saw my neck and shoulder in dirty bandages and my right arm in a sling, there was no doubt.

In the morning I was taken to hospital where I was treated for three months. My wounds healed but the fingers of my atrophied hand still couldn't flex. More than fifty years have passed since then, but the fingers in my right hand are still not completely mobile.

When I was discharged from hospital I asked my father to try and get a post for me in the rear, because he had the power to do this. According to the law, you are conscripted once you are eighteen, but I had already been in the army for eighteen months and I had been wounded twice at the front, and after I was discharged from hospital the medical commission declared me fit for light duties, but my father, being a highly principled party member, did nothing.

THE SECOND WOUND

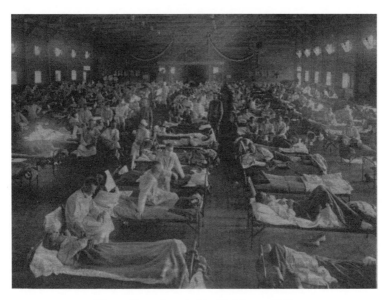

The military hospital in Tashkent, 1943

12

IN THE REAR IN TASHKENT

THE 25TH ARTILLERY REGIMENT OF OFFICERS

In June 1943 the Petropavlovsk garrison's medical commission considered me fit for light duties. Those fit for light duties serve in the rear, not at the front, so I was sent to the artillery reserve division HQ in Tashkent. The division was stationed in a military camp near Chirchik, forty kilometres from Tashkent. We were next to the Kharkov tank school.

I stayed there for about a week before I was summoned to the HQ's personnel section, along with some other officers. I was appointed platoon commander at the heavy artillery school in Ryazan, where I would be using 203- and 280-mm calibre weapons.

I was delighted! It had always been my dream to be a real artilleryman. Heavy artillery was what I had been taught about at Podolsk artillery school: 45- and 76-mm direct fire anti-tank guns were not considered to be real artillery by many artillerymen. But I had made an annoying mistake. Before my appointment, the inspector of personnel section had tested us. I was asked a very simple question. How many union republics were there in the USSR? I was nervous and thought that until recently we had sixteen republics and then three Baltic republics had joined us (!), so I answered: 'Nineteen.'[1] 'You're wrong,' the inspector said. 'You may go back to your division.' Only when I closed the door did I remember in horror that we had a total of sixteen republics including the Baltic republics, but it was too late, so my chance to join the real artillery never materialised. Life is not a bed of roses—you can't escape bad luck.

So now I was appointed platoon commander in the 25th artillery regiment of officers, with forty officers under me ranging in rank from junior lieutenant up to captain. When you are eighteen it's quite an honour to be a commander of such a platoon. The regiment was stationed in Tashkent.

From 6 am to 10 pm I was busy with my work: reveille, inspections, fatigues, dealing with personnel, grooming and feeding horses, servicing artillery guns and many more duties. Full-time regimental instructors, some of whom were veterans from the 1918–20 Civil War, taught the cadet officers artillery tactics and firing, engineering, chemical and veterinary studies, topography and communications. My task was to teach them weapon handling and firing, political ideology, riding, drill and PE. Sunday was our day off. No leave was granted for officers or rank-and-file soldiers during wartime.

In our platoon there were two 122-mm M1910/30 guns,[2] twelve artillery horses (six horses for each gun), and two carts for carrying artillery shells. I had my own horse and when I had free time, I often rode him along the avenues of Tashkent. I wore spurs on my high boots and on my left sleeve was the badge of

IN THE REAR IN TASHKENT

Boris, platoon commander in the officers' artillery regiment, Tashkent, March 1944

an anti-tank officer—a black velvet diamond with red edging and two crossed guns in the centre. There were two stripes on the left side of my shirt: a gold stripe to denote a heavy wound and a white one for a light wound. On my shoulders I had golden epaulettes with two silver stars. I looked very smart and lots of passers-by stopped to watch me riding up the main streets of the capital of Uzbekistan. I really enjoyed the attention.

There were five battalions in the regiment and five batteries in each battalion, with four platoons in each battery. There was a total of 3,200 cadets. I received my first disciplinary penalty in this regiment. It happened like this. I had been appointed commander of one of the batteries and I was to be part of the guard of honour escorting the cortege of a general to the cemetery. There were four 122-mm guns in the escort; each gun was drawn by three pairs of horses. Before firing the gun salute, the horses were unharnessed and led some distance away from the grave. The horses had never been at the battlefront so they were not used to gunfire, and their drivers were inexperienced.

When the four guns were fired, some of the horses panicked and started to rear. Their frightened drivers let go of them and the horses bolted around the cemetery, breaking monuments and tombs. For this incident, the regiment commander sentenced me to five days and nights in the glasshouse, or military prison, which I never served for reasons I will never know and the affair was never mentioned in my records.

While I was in Tashkent my mother was ill, so my father sent me a doctor's certificate and I was granted ten days of leave to visit my parents in Petropavlovsk. I went by train on the Turkestan-Siberian railway, built in 1930. I had a TT pistol with me; at Barnaul I left the coach to walk along the platform. I was detained by a military patrol and taken to the station commandant. He confiscated my gun and gave me a certificate. It turned out that the Defence Ministry had just issued an edict which forbade military personnel from having weapons with them while on leave. When I returned to my regiment I was reprimanded by my seniors for having given away the gun.

At this time, I came across a girl who had been my classmate in Dnepropetrovsk with the surname of Falkenstein and I visited her several times on my horse. Once when I called on her, she was having a party and a drunken guest offered to sell me an Order of the Red Banner, with a certificate confirming that I had been awarded it. I was astounded by his cynicism and refused.

When I had toothache I was treated by a dentist who was an Armenian woman. She had an eighteen-year-old daughter, a pretty girl who worked as a nurse in our medical unit. When the woman got to know me better she pleaded with me to marry her daughter, promising me that if I did I wouldn't be sent back to the front. I was very young and I didn't have any thoughts about getting married. I imagined myself married in the far future, but only to a Russian girl. Even the possibility of spending the rest of the war in the rear didn't attract me. I was more committed to going to the front than getting married.

Near Tashkent the Uzbeks were building one of the USSR's many canals. The first secretary of the central committee of the Communist Party of Uzbekistan had promised Comrade Stalin that the canal would be finished by a certain deadline. But they couldn't manage it and it was impossible to break their promise to Comrade Stalin—no one would dream of it. So they took the whole officers' regiment of 3,200 men off their course and sent them to dig the canal for two weeks. And that is how I did my bit for canal building in Uzbekistan.

When I learned that the military academy of the rear in Tashkent was seeking admissions I was eager to apply. I wasn't embarrassed by the fact that the academy was training officers as quartermasters who would be dealing with food and uniform supplies, ammunition and fuel, as I was desperate to get a higher education, even if it was a military one. I must admit that by now I had become sick and tired of being a platoon commander. I wasn't promoted as I was considered too young. After preparing the necessary documents I applied to the academy but I was not accepted as I had not served long enough as an officer, less than the two years required—my service was only one year and eight months.

I remained in my regiment until May 1944. While serving in the deep rear I was surprised by the vast numbers of officers who had never been to the front at all even though the war had already been going on for three years. In our regiment, 60 per cent of the officers hadn't been to the front. Only a few applied to be sent there, and they were all front veterans as a rule. As for the 'rear veterans', they did their best to avoid being sent to the front. At the end of the war they would all claim that they had kept applying to be sent to the front but the commanders had refused. It was about them that front veterans would say, as a joke: 'He fought gloriously with the 5th Ukrainian front on the Tashkent line.' (During the war there were only four Ukrainian fronts, the 1st, 2nd, 3rd and 4th.)

But a specific number of people had to be sent to the front and I became one of them. They took no account of my objections—the fact that I had already been there twice, that I had been wounded twice and that the military commission had declared me fit for light duties as a result of my heavy wound (my right hand being weaker than my left)—and sent me to the front again.

I must say that I was a little reluctant to return for the third time to this human meat grinder of a war, but I wasn't unhappy about it. As a front veteran, it's difficult to adapt to life in the rear and you feel out of place. At the front you have more freedom, camaraderie, mutual help, honesty and decency—and the food is much better! In the rear there is only bureaucratic paperwork. I soon became fed up with it all. I had to write plans for each lesson, then give three to four such lessons to my cadets every day except Sundays. I would come back tired to my flat (like all officers I rented a flat) at 10 or 11 pm, then I would end up writing these hateful lesson plans until midnight.

13

HOW I JOINED THE SAPPERS

I AM ORDERED TO JOIN THE SAPPERS

In May 1944 I left for Moscow to report to the head of the main command of the Red Army artillery. I was temporarily accepted by the artillery division of the reserve, which was based at Iksha railway station, near Moscow.

Here again, as at Podolsk military school in 1942, I acted as a sentry at the division's HQ and ammunition stores. It's hard to stand guard for four hours. All kinds of thoughts go through your mind while you stand guard, a rifle in your hand. You think about your life, and all your family and friends, but most of all you look at the black sky with the silver tracks of the Milky Way, our galaxy with millions of stars.

After I had been in the reserve for ten days I was summoned to the artillery personnel department where I was told that I would be sent to the 1st Ukrainian front to be a platoon commander in a sapper battalion. When I said that I didn't know anything about sappers, the head of personnel (a man who had spent his life in the rear, by all appearances) told me that there were too many artillery officers and they needed officers in the engineering corps. I was to be appointed to this position because I had studied engineering at military school. I would have the same rank that I had previously held at the front—platoon commander—but this time in charge of reconnaissance and communications.

The head of personnel told me that this was an order and orders must be obeyed, and that this order had been underwritten by the Supreme Commander of the Red Army and Marshal of the Soviet Union, Comrade Stalin, and, for a military man, such an order was sacred and could not be open to discussion. Of course I couldn't object to Comrade Stalin, so I had no choice other than to obey.

I had to go to my destination via Kiev, where my numerous maternal relatives were living. My cap was stolen on the train to Kiev so my relatives gave me a black Astrakhan hat of the type worn by the cavalry. Thus I would join the sapper battalion looking like a member of the cavalry in my new hat, with spurs on my high boots.

I had come by my spurs earlier that spring while I was still in Tashkent. As horses were used by our artillery regiment, I had the right to wear spurs but I didn't own any. It happened that I fell ill and had to go to hospital: in the huge hall there must have been about 100 sick and wounded people lying on the beds. The noise was terrible, with constant cries of pain, groaning, swearing and snoring. The light was on all night. It was a horrible scene. Next to me lay a teenager whose father was a general at the front. The boy had cavalry officer's spurs and I pleaded with him for a long time to give them to me. I finally talked him into it and when I came out of hospital my new spurs became the envy of the officers in my regiment. I used to wear them at work and in my spare time, whether I was riding or just strolling around Tashkent. But I didn't wear my spurs for long in the sapper battalion. They only had draught horses and nobody else wore spurs, so I soon took them off.

While I was in Kiev I went to look at the main street—Kreschatik. It had been the most famous street in Kiev, almost one and a half kilometres long, flanked with elegant buildings, houses and apartments standing seven to nine storeys high. But now it was all in ruins. It turned out that as the Germans approached Kiev in July 1941 the buildings in Kreschatik had been mined with hundreds of tonnes of explosives. Three days after the Germans occupied Kiev there was a tremendous explosion and the whole of Kreschatik went up in the air.[1] Not a single German died. The Red Army had assumed that the Germans were fools, but they were wrong. The Germans had learned that

Kreschatik, Kiev after liberation, November 1943

147

Kreschatik had been mined and they hadn't moved into the buildings. After the war it cost us thousands of millions of roubles to rebuild Kreschatik.

Sometime later another marvel of Russian architecture, the Cathedral of the Ascension in the Kiev Pechersk Lavra (Kiev monastery of the caves), was blown up in a similar fashion. The cathedral was built in 1078 and had stood for 850 years. For a long time Soviet propaganda spread rumours that the cathedral had been destroyed by the German vandals. In 1932 the Soviet authorities had blown up St Michael's Golden-Domed Cathedral, built in 1113. It was subsequently rebuilt in the 1990s.

Here, near Kiev, the worst defeat in the history of all wars took place. In September 1941 the Germans surrounded our four combined armies, and 665,000 soldiers and officers were captured, including my aunt's husband who was a major (he died in captivity). But our rulers were very good at making victory out of defeat: when Khrushchev was head of state a medal was issued for the defence of Kiev.

I am not an entrepreneur: I tried to make money two times in my life and on both occasions I ended up making a loss. In May 1942, when I was fresh out of military school and on my way to join my division, I bought a big sack of salt for 100 roubles at Arys railway station in Central Asia. I had learned that salt could be sold for double that price further on in the region of Mordovia. After reaching a deal with a woman at a station in Mordovia I began untying my sack, but there was a knot in the rope, which made it difficult to pour the salt into her sack. Meanwhile the train started to move off. The salt was still trickling out of my sack into her sack while the train was beginning to accelerate. At last I finished and the woman paid, but she only gave me half her money. I took it anyway, only just managing to jump into my carriage in time. When I counted the money it was exactly the sum that I had paid for the salt at Arys!

HOW I JOINED THE SAPPERS

My second money-making venture took place on my way to join the sappers. My family had moved to the town of Dubno, where I was heading, so I decided to pay them a visit. My relatives in Kiev had advised me to buy yeast in Kiev to sell for a profit in Dubno where there was a shortage, so I followed their advice and bought a whole suitcase of yeast. But when I arrived in Dubno it turned out that a yeast factory had recently been built there and there was plenty in the shops. My mother barely managed to sell it at half price in the market. That was my last business venture. It really was not my cup of tea!

Dubno and Mlinov

In May 1944 I joined the 16th assault engineering sapper brigade in Dubno. There was a total of twenty-three assault engineering sapper brigades in the reserve, of which three were mechanised. The brigade's role was to storm fortified enemy positions where infantry with engineering and technical skills were needed. The brigade's soldiers were trained for all kinds of battle in the most difficult and unusual situations, and also for storming complex defensive structures on the enemy frontline and in its rear. The brigade commander was forty-four-year-old Colonel Boris Kordukov, who already had four medals. In the first years of the USSR, when he was twenty-three, he was appointed minister of health in the Tatar republic before becoming a military engineer; it was not unusual to change roles in our complicated times. He died in Moscow, aged fifty-six.

Dubno is an ancient Ukrainian town. It was first mentioned in the chronicles in 1100, so it is fifty years older than Moscow. There is an old castle in the town. In his historical novel *Taras Bulba*, Gogol describes the siege of Dubno, then in Polish hands, by the Zaporozhian Cossacks. Andriy, the son of the Cossack leader, Taras Bulba, has fallen in love with a Polish girl from a noble family. He sees her on the wall of Dubno Castle, changes side and betrays his motherland. During the ensuing battle Taras Bulba kills Andriy, saying: 'I was the one who gave you life and I am the one who will take it away.'

From Dubno I was sent to Mlinov (Mlyniv) where the 78th assault engineering sapper battalion was stationed. I was allocated a platoon and appointed platoon commander. I was in charge of reconnaissance and communications. We had two communication units—radio and telephone—and two reconnaissance units. In the radio communication unit there were two female operators; one woman carried a radio on her back while the other carried the batteries. The commander of the battalion HQ was in overall charge of communications.

Assault sappers were in the front row during an offensive. They had to build bridges for vehicles and small assault bridges across rivers, clear paths through enemy minefields, destroy for-

A T-34 tank hit by Faustpatrone

tifications including batteries, pillboxes, concrete teeth and anti-tank ditches, and dismantle barricades and barbed wire entanglements before the attack. They were also the last to retreat, blowing up bridges and other strategic structures behind them. Very often they had to do this under enemy fire.

During an offensive sappers with automatic weapons sat on the tanks to protect them from German Faustpatrone. These anti-tank weapons could penetrate the metal casing of the tank, detonating all fifty shells inside. Of the tank crew, only their twisted medals would remain. The Germans tried to shoot the sappers, knowing that without them the tanks would be an easy target, especially in towns, forests and marshes.

Assault sappers were armed with automatic guns, machine rifles, sniper rifles (one per platoon), anti-tank weapons (one per platoon), grenades (each sapper had two: anti-personnel and anti-tank) and captured Faustpatrone, and they carried explosives in their backpacks. They wore steel helmets and bulletproof vests and had a knife attached to their belt. They were equipped with mines (anti-personnel, anti-tank and anti-vehicle), mine detectors, shortened iron mine detectors made of thick wire and grappling hooks on long ropes, which were used to detonate mines which could not be safely deactivated, for example in winter. Sappers also carried flame-throwers and smoke grenades to create a smokescreen while detonating mines during daytime.

There is a well-known saying that sappers can only make one mistake: the sappers say they actually make two mistakes—the first is to join the sappers and the second is to detonate a mine... The sappers' motto is: 'If you are enrolled as a sapper, be proud; if you failed to make it, be happy.' In the Imperial Russian army, the sappers were called pioneers. Another sapper joke: the average sapper's life expectancy when removing a mine at night is nine minutes.

While the infantry soldier goes into attack next to his comrades who can help him if need be, the sapper is always left to clear

Sappers at work

mines alone, face-to-face with death. This is the strict rule of the job. A sapper must be courageous and cautious, resolute and patient, strong and dexterous. Many famous people were once sappers: Field Marshal Mikhail Kutuzov, famous for his role during the Napoleonic Wars, started his career as a military engineer; writer Feodor Dostoevsky graduated from Nikolayev Military Engineering Institute in St Petersburg; the composer of the French national anthem, *La Marseillaise*, Claude Joseph Rouget de Lisle, was an engineer, later a captain in the French Revolutionary Army; and regiment engineer Nikolai Ogarkov became Chief of the General Staff and Marshal of the Soviet Union.

14

ADVANCING INTO POLAND

THE 78TH ASSAULT ENGINEERING SAPPER BATTALION

By spring 1943 the Red Army had carried out a number of successful offensives. Our troops now had to break through strongly fortified enemy defences, so there was a need for specialised engineers who could destroy reinforced concrete structures and wire barricades. In May 1943 the head of the engineering troops, Lieutenant General Vorobyev, suggested to Stalin that 'shock engineering units' should be created. Stalin agreed, but he specified that they would be called 'assault engineering sapper brigades'. The 16th assault engineering sapper brigade of the reserve was formed in the town of Zagorsk (now Sergiev Posad), twenty-five kilometres from Moscow. My career at the front would be closely connected with this brigade.

FOR THE MOTHERLAND! FOR STALIN!

Our battalion never stayed in one place for long. Once we had carried out our mission (mining, demining, building roads and bridges) we would be transferred to another location, and so it would continue, over and over again.

In the summer of 1944 we were moving west through Polish territory. This area was rich in history. We passed the town of Zamość, where Colonel Maxim Krivonos, a member of Bogdan Khmelnytsky's army, was buried 300 years ago.[1] In the town of Krasnik a great battle took place in 1916 in which General Brusilov's army defeated the Austrian army during the Brusilov offensive. We entered the old town of Vladimir-Volynsky (Volodymyr-Volynsky) which, in the twelfth century, had been part of the Galitsko-Volynskoye principality that had spread as far as the Black Sea coast.

Unlike September 1939, nobody met us with flowers.[2] Local people had fully experienced what Stalinism was like: it was ten times worse than living under what was known as 'the yoke of Polish oppression'. Much later, I found out that between September 1939 and June 1941 the NKVD had deported 300,000 people from western Ukraine to Siberia (the north and the far east)—only a handful came back. Some of the houses had graffiti on their white walls: 'Hitler and Stalin out!' We were very surprised to see such words back then.

My duties involved carrying out a reconnaissance of our battalion's route and gathering information about the fortifications of enemy positions and occupied areas, together with enemy systems of defence, including barricades and obstructions, with a particular focus on minefields. I also had to assess the condition of roads, bridges and other potential obstacles, and seek out any local information that could be useful for logistics and military planning.

On our way to the west we had to carry out reconnaissance of dozens of rivers: we analysed their width, depth, the direction and speed of their flow and currents, the condition of the soil, the profile of the riverbed and the character of the banks; with this data we could assess the possibility of building a small assault bridge, or providing mooring for pontoons so that tanks and military equipment could be taken across the river. We would also search for convenient escape routes, not to mention potential building materials such as logs, boards, nails and struts.

Whenever the battalion was transferred to a new location I had to find billets for the personnel. A day before the battalion was due to arrive in a village, I would go ahead with my scouts and select the house where the commander of the battalion would stay (he stayed with the head of the medical unit, a doctor who was a pretty twenty-five-year-old Jewish woman from Odessa). Then I would commandeer huts for the HQ deputy commander and for the heads of departments responsible for the personnel of the three companies of my platoon, together with huts to store food, ammunition and medical supplies, and finally, huts for NKVD operatives.

I remember an episode when my scout and I were two kilometres ahead of our battalion conducting a reconnaissance of the area. We had reached a village where a road crossed a river and went up a hill. I met a local woman with rosy cheeks and asked her in Ukrainian what was beyond the hill and what was the road like. 'I don't know,' she answered. 'How come you don't know?' I asked. 'How long have you lived here?' 'Thirty years,' came the reply. 'And you have never gone over the hill?' 'No. What is there for me to do there?' I was amazed by her complete lack of curiosity.

Once we reached a fork in a road in Poland and didn't know whether to turn left or right. A Polish man came up to us, so I asked him in Polish: 'Which way is the village of Skarżysko?' He pointed ahead, saying, 'It's simple (*prosto*).' I grew angry. 'It may be simple for you, as you have lived here all your life, but I am here for the first—and last—time.' Later, I found out that 'it's simple' also means 'straight on' in Polish.

FOR THE MOTHERLAND! FOR STALIN!

I recall another episode... When you are nineteen, you are still growing and you are always hungry. Your ration is not enough because you are always on the move in the fresh air. You might stay in a hut or *izba* for the night. The man of the house is away in the army and only his wife is at home, with plenty of children. You know from experience that no matter how politely you ask for something to eat, the woman will not give you anything. You start your usual game: 'This boy is two years old.' 'Correct,' the woman says. 'And this girl is four years old.' 'Correct,' the woman says. And so on. Having passed hundreds of *izbas*, I became very skilled at this and could accurately guess the ages of small children. As a result you could see their mother warm to you. The next moment, she would go down to her cellar and bring up milk, cream or even eggs or bread—exactly what you needed!

If this didn't work, or if there weren't any children, you would try another tactic. You would say: 'I have travelled across half of Russia, but I have never tasted such delicious water.' The result is the same: the woman goes into the cellar and brings up food. As she goes, she is thinking: 'My goodness, we live in such a godforsaken place, yet it turns out that our water is best!' Perhaps that is why we have this military saying: 'Give me some water please, as I am so hungry that I have nowhere to spend the night.'

The battalion camel

The star of our battalion was a two-humped Bactrian camel. When the battalion was fighting near Stalingrad in 1942, it had several camels which were used instead of horses. By the time I arrived, only one camel was left. His role was to pull the battalion's kitchen wagon. So as we made our way through the villages of western Ukraine, we were accompanied by crowds of curious children and adults who had only seen a camel in an alphabet book.

When we lined up for parade the camel would proudly stand on the left with his kitchen wagon, chewing all the time, his

A Red Army camel

head raised with ears pricked, rising up above everybody. The two-humped giant looked over the soldiers with contempt and haughtiness as if ignoring them, and seemed to gaze at something hidden far beyond the horizon which only he could see from his lofty height of two and a half metres.

He used to get caught under fire and bombardment, and even received a slight shrapnel wound in his back near Lvov (Lviv), but nevertheless he never chickened out. He was not a coward and calmly carried on, chewing his cud. Unlike us, he never suffered from the July heat and burning sun.

Our camel was a useful landmark. Very often commanders and soldiers left the battalion to go off on various missions. During that time the battalion might move ahead or veer off to the side for tens of kilometres. How could you re-join the battalion? Secrecy was very strictly observed and no one would tell you where the battalion was. And here our camel was of great use. You would go back to the village where you had left the battalion and ask the children: 'Where did the camel with the kitchen wagon go?' They would tell you and then you would go in the same direction to the next village and ask the same question, and that way you would successfully and quickly catch up with the battalion.

A camel seems to walk slowly, but this is not always so. When in danger—for example, under sudden artillery fire—our camel could move at fifty kilometres per hour. He divided all people into goodies and baddies. I don't know why, but I was a baddie. Every time I came up to stroke his head in a friendly way, he raised it up high and started hissing viciously. Something started bubbling ominously in his throat. Before he could spit sticky green saliva at me, I beat a hasty retreat.

A camel is supposed to be herbivorous, eating grass, hay, leaves and thorns, but to our surprise our camel didn't mind meat, fish, or even American tinned meat.[3]

Camels pulling a wagon through a German town

He came with us as far as Germany—as far as the asphalted roads and tin roofs. Against a background of tanks, artillery weapons and innumerable American trucks (Chevrolets, Studebakers, Fords, Willys), our camel stood out in great contrast. He looked at all those vehicles with contempt and arrogance, holding his aristocratic head high. Once a very important general drove past and saw him. The general shouted at our battalion commander who was at the front of our formation: 'What a disgrace. Going into Europe with a camel! Remove it at once!' And so our camel was sent far back to the rear for good.

Nonetheless, a two-humped camel lifting his head proudly was photographed in the background of the ruined, blasted facade of the Reichstag before its walls were covered with the victors' graffiti. This photograph appeared on the cover of the magazine *Ogoniok* (*The Beacon*) and was subsequently syndicated all around the world, becoming famous. Could the camel be ours? Perhaps not...[4]

15

THE BATTLE OF GOROKHOV

THE LVOV-SANDOMIERZ OFFENSIVE[1]

At the beginning of July 1944 our battalion was hurriedly trans-ferred from one part of the front to another. It was hot—about 30°C—and our soldiers were walking along a country road under a burning sun, covered with dust, tired and sweaty. As usual, I went one kilometre ahead with my scouts to carry out a recon-naissance. I was using a topographical map which had been issued fifteen years before, so it was outdated in many respects. What had once been a tiny hamlet was now a village and what had once been a wood was now a cornfield. I came to a fork in the road, but the fork wasn't shown on the map. Where should I go? Right, or left? Quickly I returned to battalion and reported the problem to the deputy commander, Captain Petukhov. I said we would have to go to the village to find the way.

FOR THE MOTHERLAND! FOR STALIN!

The battalion (300 soldiers) came to a halt. Petukhov became angry and began swearing at me in front of the other soldiers. Then he barked an order: 'Run to the village!' I started to walk. He shouted again: 'I order you to run. I will shoot you like a dog.' He took his gun out of its holster and I heard the familiar click of the breech block as he loaded the cartridge. I can't explain what happened to me but I kept walking. I confess that the back of my head went cold, in anticipation of the bullet. Three hundred pairs of eyes were staring at me and waiting with tension to see what would happen. But no shot came.

Petukhov could easily have shot me for disobedience and there would have been no comeback. At the front, the commander is your tsar, your lord and your military boss. His order cannot be discussed and must be carried out immediately, without argument. After asking the way in the village, I returned to the battalion and the incident was over. That is how I was threatened with execution for the third time!

In the Lvov-Sandomierz offensive which began on 12 July 1944, the 1st Ukrainian front comprised seven armies, three tank armies, two mechanised and horse-drawn groups, two artillery divisions and one tank sapper army, under the command of Konev, with members of the military council Khrushchev and Kranukov. This made a total of fifteen armies. In comparison, the entire Russian force consisted of thirteen armies during the First World War.

The fifteen armies comprised eighty rifle and cavalry divisions, ten tank and mechanised corps, four separate tank and mechanised brigades, one Czechoslovakian infantry corps and ten sapper brigades. In total, there were 2,806 planes, 1,614 tanks, 13,900 guns and mortars and 843,000 personnel. As a comparison, when Napoleon invaded Russia in 1812, he had an army of 500,000. The July 1944 offensive was considered strategic in that it would have a decisive influence on the outcome of the war.

THE BATTLE OF GOROKHOV

The direction of the offensive for our battalion was the town of Gorokhov (Horokhiv) in Volyn region. This town had been liberated from the Germans on four previous occasions: in 1943 by Ukrainian nationalists; in February 1944 by partisans under the command of General Naumov; then by a battalion from the 1st Ukrainian partisan division under General Vershigora; and finally in April by the 389th Berdichev rifle division which had to leave under German attack several days later.

The fact that the 389th rifle division killed more than 2,000 Germans to win Gorokhov shows how difficult the battles were. Our losses were also great. After the war, the names of more than 2,000 soldiers and commanders were engraved on the military memorial at Gorokhov, including thirty people from our battalion.

Fire and bombing

On the evening of 13 July 1944 our assault battalion was passing through Gorokhov just after it had been won back by our troops. The centre of the town was ablaze—it was a terrifying sight. We were walking along a street thirty metres wide, and the wooden houses were burning to our left and right—the town was lit up as if it were day. The interminable heat, smoke and soot scorched our eyes; it was difficult to breathe in the hot air and we felt as if our clothes would catch fire.

The walls of the houses, their roofs and partitions came crashing down. Tongues of flames swept on with a roar, reaching our formation and nearly blinding us. Charred logs were flying through the air, scattering streams of bright sparks. Flames were shooting out of windows and doors, and veils of black smoke barred our way. Against the crackling and roaring flames and the crash of collapsing floors and walls, the sounds of battle seemed very faint.

Nobody was fighting the fire—there were no inhabitants around. Only once we had emerged from this roaring sea of fire and entered the suburbs could we heave a sigh of relief. I thought that hell must look like this.

I found myself in the central square of Gorokhov the next day while carrying out an errand for the commander. My thoughts were interrupted by a powerful roar. Suddenly nine German Junkers 87 dive bombers appeared, accompanied by Messerschmitt fighters with black crosses like spiders. Thinking there was no escape, I quickly jumped into a nearby trench, my head and body only slightly lower than the ground.

The planes started diving, their sirens emitting a bloodcurdling howl. The town square was a good target for them. Black bombs were falling. They seemed to be flying down directly towards me, hypnotising my gaze and paralysing my will. I closed my eyes and braced myself, waiting for the first explosion. Time seemed to stop. Seconds stretched out endlessly, agonisingly... my heart was pounding. The planes were literally hurling their bombs down onto my head.

The ground was shaking as if in a fever from the exploding bombs. Their detonations blended into one tremendous roar. I breathed in the sharp, pungent smell of cordite and caustic smoke while fragments hailed down on me, including balls of cindered earth. It was as if the sky had split in two, releasing an avalanche of bombs and bullets. German planes were diving down towards my head, one after another, like a flock of predatory birds.

I was preparing for death. Time stood still. There was no sun, no sky, only the feeling that the end had come. The planes were flying over the square, firing from large calibre machine guns. The bullets were flying around me, digging into the earth. No matter how much I tried I couldn't stop trembling. My mouth was dry.

And then, a ringing quietness. Here and there fires had started. The wounded were calling for help. It was a horrible picture which will prove impossible to forget. But this time again, Death, who stood close to hand, had only singed me with his breath. The bomb craters were seven metres wide and two metres deep. I knew from experience that the bombs could weigh 250 kilogrammes.

It is terrible to think that you could die during a bombing raid. It is also extremely galling—you are lying there, trying to dig yourself into the ground, while he, the damned Nazi, can see your helplessness, and, gloating, aims his bomb straight at you. It is not so bad to die in open battle. As Mikhail Lermontov wrote in his poem, *Mtsyri (The Novice)*: 'He met his death face to face as a warrior should in battle.' But to die like this is both frustrating and futile.

After the bombing you are deafened and stunned. You seem to be alive but you don't know whether you are still in one piece. A popular rhyme among officers at the front was very appropriate in this situation:

Is each limb alive and quick?
Don't forget to check your dick.

When military pensions are calculated you can understand why one month at the front is worth three in the rear. On my way back to the battalion once I had recovered I thought to myself: 'Thank goodness the danger is over! But why were those bastards bombing a town square so furiously and with impunity? There weren't any military targets, just a few passers-by like me, and one peaceful cart drawn by a horse which happened to be there by pure chance. All the military targets, the frontline of our defence, the artillery position and our strongholds are in the western suburbs. Did my presence attract their attention?' Well, I never found out the answer, but a few grey hairs appeared on my head to preserve the memory of this episode for the rest of my life.

A poet, Yulia Drunina, who had been a company nurse during the war, described my feelings in her poem:

We lay there, waiting for death
Since then I have hated those empty plains
They were firing at us from their Messerschmitts
Their minds full of medals
Carrying out target practice at point blank range

Since then I have been haunted by dreams of
Monstrous carousels of planes circling above as we
Lie motionless on the ground then
They nose dive down...

Hopelessly, we fired back
We could not die without a fight
We blasted our bullets at their cockpits, at the crosses emblazoned on
    their wings and
At the blank sky—at God's damned heaven itself.

Poor Yulia Drunina, a poet of life at the front. During *perestroika*, the transition from 'developed socialism' to wild capitalism, she took too closely to heart the accusations that 'if the Germans had defeated Stalin's state, we would be living well now and drinking Bavarian beer'. She failed to find any solace when she left the bustle of Moscow for Stary Krym, the former capital of the Crimean Tatar khanate, in a quiet corner of the Crimea.

Wounded twice during the war, she couldn't cope with the change of values for which she had led her life and spilt her blood. So she closed her garage door, turned on her car engine, drank a bottle of brandy, smoked a cigarette, fell asleep and quietly left this life. She was buried in the town cemetery next to her husband Aleksei Kapler (the famous filmmaker who was the first love of Svetlana Stalina and was consequently sent to a gulag

for ten years by Stalin) and the romantic writer, Aleksandr Grin.
May she rest in peace.

> I can't say that life passes me by
> It is too full even now
> And yet I can't escape from the war
> A war that ended so long ago...
>
> I feel dead inside. Like you
> I was blindfolded
> And now I can see. We must break with our past
> Or else we are doomed
>
> Or else despair will destroy us
> Like a black gun held to the head.
> Even my enemy
> Should not suffer this—
> I can't live with the past and I can't live with despair.

14 July: a black day for our battalion

Once I had carried out the commander's errand I returned to my
battalion which was stationed in a field to the west of Gorokhov.
The troops were in an 800-metre long trench which had probably been dug by the Germans. I sent my scouts to carry out a
reconnaissance and when they came back I was able to report to
the battalion commander, Major Kalyniuk, that the HQ of the
389th rifle division was to the right of us. The division was staying there for the night. In front of us, one kilometre away, Major
Batishev's rifle battalion had taken up position in its trenches.
This battalion was part of the 545th rifle regiment which was
due to start the offensive at dawn.

Our battalion's role was to provide technical support to the
389th rifle division during the advance on the town of Rava
Russkaya (Rava Ruska). During this offensive, the 389th rifle
division was part of the 3rd army which was on the right wing of

the 1st Ukrainian front. The 3rd army was quite a formidable military unit: it comprised ten rifle divisions, one tank brigade, two tank regiments, one artillery division of assault troops, one anti-aircraft artillery division and a separate anti-aircraft artillery regiment, three anti-tank regiments, five artillery regiments, two divisions of armoured trains, a sapper brigade and supply units.

As night fell the soldiers immediately fell asleep at the bottom of the trench, tired after a hard day. Together with two lieutenants I decided to sleep on the grass nearby, but stray bullets were flying over from the German side so we considered it was too risky and joined the others in the trench.

At dawn a soldier suddenly came running along the trench, trampling over our sleeping bodies. He was from the observation point near the road leading to our rear. In a worried voice he told the battalion commander that the Germans were heading down the road towards our rear. I looked out of the trench and saw a group of people in grey walking along the road. After discussing the situation with his deputy, Captain Gorshkov, and the head of HQ, Senior Lieutenant Veselov, the battalion commander finally gave the command: 'The enemy is on the road. Prepare for attack. Grenades at the ready. Fly the red flag! Battalion—follow me! Attack! For the motherland! Forward! Oorah!'

I can still picture this battle vividly because such things are remembered for the rest of your life. With our weapons at the ready, we jumped out of the trench and ran towards the road. The red flag was waving ahead. Solid automatic and machine gun fire suddenly poured on the enemy's formation. I heard grenades exploding and loud firing from the anti-tank guns which we had in every platoon. All those sounds merged with our deafening and continuous shout of 'Oorah!' Our 150 soldiers were running towards the Germans and shooting them at point blank range.

We shot some of the Germans on the road, while the others escaped in different directions. Then, after the command was given we started moving in a line eastwards, towards Gorokhov. However, the enemy gradually recovered and started shooting at us with automatic guns and machine guns.

Soon shells started exploding in our midst. These were coming from German tanks which were not far away. At the same time the German infantry, which had taken up position in Gorokhov, began firing at us. After we received the command we went into attack again. Two female radio operators from my platoon, Krilova and Ganina, found themselves in the heat of a real battle for the first time. One operator's legs went numb with fear and the other radio operators from her unit had to drag her by the hands across the battlefield, while the other operator lost her voice (it came back two days after the battle). They left their radio station and batteries behind.

During the attack I was running in front of my platoon. I was in a state of great nervous tension, or stress as they call it now. I was running straight towards the enemy as they fired directly back at me, at my chest, face and heart. Some soldiers just dropped down dead. The wounded were calling for stretchers. We couldn't call off this attack because if we stopped and lay down the Germans would simply shoot all of us in the open field.

I noticed that a soldier from my platoon called Chernavsky, who had joined us ten days earlier and who was already notorious for breaches of discipline and for bragging about his heroic deeds, was running away from the battle despite my shouts. Afterwards we found his body about twenty metres away from the place where he had left us.

I was running with my gun in my hand. A soldier who was running ahead of me fell down. As I ran past, he shouted: 'Shoot the German ahead! My automatic is stuck and the German is recharging his automatic.' (The soil in the trench where we had spent the night was sandy, and it had got into his automatic gun and jammed the mechanism.)

FOR THE MOTHERLAND! FOR STALIN!

About fifty metres away I saw the German lying in the grass. When you are in danger you think surprisingly quickly. I instantly shot him with all seven cartridges in my TT pistol. All seven cartridges, with my hand shaking and unsure whether I could actually hit him. As he was motionless, I immediately ran up to him. He was dead. A bullet had gone straight into the bridge of his nose. I looked at the dead man—he was young, about twenty-five years old, blond, no moustache, wearing a good quality mouse-coloured uniform, with stripes on his chest and chevrons on his sleeve, and short boots, where he had tucked spare gun parts, and he had a broad belt with a buckle on which was written 'Gott mit uns'. Next to him lay his automatic gun and a grenade with a long wooden handle.

I took his documents from his pockets together with his gun (a Schmeisser) and its spare parts, then continued to run. We broke through the German line and ran towards the outskirts of Gorokhov. Many of us were missing. Our rifle regiment and the 45-mm guns of the regiment's anti-tank battery were in the town. They were strengthening our defences.

14 July 1944. This date is etched on my memory and those of my fellow soldiers for the rest of our lives. For the first time, on that fateful day near Gorokhov, I had seen the deadly enemy face to face with his weapon in his hand. Not everyone who was at the front experienced this.

Among those who died a courageous death near Gorokhov was Colonel Piotr Stolyarchuk, born in 1906. He was head of the political department of the 150th tank brigade. On 14 July 1944 he took part in repelling an assault by fifty German tanks outside the nearby village of Pidberezzya and died in battle. He was post-humously given the award of Hero of the Soviet Union. The collective farm in his village and several streets in various towns and villages were named after him.

THE BATTLE OF GOROKHOV

The funeral

To those who pass by, may you stop at this place and show reverence. It is a sacred place, for here lie the warriors who loved the motherland and defended her honour until the end.

Stanislav Ribas

In that battle our battalion lost nearly 20 per cent of its personnel: thirty were killed, thirty-two were injured and six went missing.

Three days later, having repelled two German tank attacks, our battalion and the rifle regiment started a counter offensive. As a result the Germans retreated. The rifle regiment moved on to the west, while we remained on the battlefield to bury the dead.

It was very difficult to look at the bodies. During three days of July heat the bodies had started to decompose, and tiny grey maggots swarmed all over their mouths, noses, eyes and armpits. Injuries on the bodies showed that some badly wounded soldiers had been finished off by the Germans' bayonets and knives. There was an awful, unbearable stench.

We buried our comrades in a park in the centre of Gorokhov. We laid them in a one-metre deep common grave—a total of twenty-nine people. Only Captain Gorshkov was buried in a separate grave. We were burying them without coffins. In accordance with the order then in effect, uniforms and boots were taken from all the corpses, except those of officers. We put our comrades body to body and, as a war poet said, 'We dug them into the Earth.'

Captain Solovyov said the words of farewell: 'It's difficult for us to say farewell to you for good, friends! It won't be our tears that will assuage our grief, or our sobbing that will honour your memory. It will be the bloody tears shed by those who took your young lives. Our revenge will be merciless until the last Nazi lays down his arms or is reduced to a heap of dust on our soil. We know that you fulfilled your duty honestly and to the bitter end. Rest in peace. You shall have eternal glory: your memory shall live forever!'

Three automatic gun salvos were fired as the last military honours to the dead.

Captain Solovyov's words resounded in our minds. They were like a vow for us, the soldiers of the battalion. Each of us would carry the sacred memory of our friends who died in the battles for our motherland. They would forever remain young in our hearts. Those who were lucky to survive would wear with pride, among their other awards, the medal 'For taking Berlin'.

Although an atheist, I looked up a commemorative prayer and read the words: 'Let their purity be reflected in your deeds and let their souls rest in eternal peace; let their names be sacred.'

In France, 14 July is a national holiday, marking the fall of the Bastille prison, the ancien regime's symbol of oppression. But more happened at Gorokhov than at the Bastille on that fateful day. At the Bastille there were only seven soldiers guarding four old prisoners. At Gorokhov we lost sixty-eight people during the two-hour battle.[2]

But the Gorokhov debacle was not over yet. Our battalion's red banner was missing, together with the three sergeant majors responsible for carrying it. What had happened? And how had we ended up in the German rear in the morning, when we had been behind a line of Soviet rifles the previous evening?

It turned out that during the night scouts had told the commander of the 389th division that the Germans were massing their tanks and could attack in the morning. He then moved his line of rifles to Gorokhov's suburbs in order to repel the attack more effectively. We knew nothing about it. The Germans noticed the retreating soldiers and immediately followed them, also stopping at the suburbs. That was how we found ourselves in their rear.

According to the papers which I had taken from the soldier I killed, he was a rank-and-file submachine gunner of the 171st Cretan grenadier regiment. The regiment was named after Crete, which the Germans had occupied following an airborne assault. The grenadiers were their elite troops. I was the only person who handed over such papers to battalion HQ, although others said that they had also killed Germans during the battle.

As for the banner, its fate was as follows. Before the attack the battalion commander told his deputy, Captain Gorshkov, to lead the troops into battle with the banner held aloft by the three sergeant majors. They were to encourage the soldiers forwards with the open banner, then fold it up and move aside because under no circumstances must the banner be captured by the Germans. But when the sergeant majors moved away from the waves of furious soldiers running into attack they were ambushed and were taken captive together with the banner.

Soldiers kneel in front of their battalion's banner

FOR THE MOTHERLAND! FOR STALIN!

As we gathered our comrades' bodies we searched for the banner. Captain Gorshkov was found dead, lying to the side of our battalion's line of attack. A bullet had hit him straight in the forehead. Not far from him we found the flagstaff with a scrap of fabric attached. But neither the banner nor the bodies of the three sergeant majors were ever found.

The fate of our banner would remain a mystery. The battalion commander asked our counter intelligence agents whether it had been mentioned in any German radio communications, but they knew nothing. The most likely explanation is that the sergeant majors had managed to hide or bury the banner before they were killed or taken prisoner.

A military regulation at that time read: 'Servicemen guilty of the disgrace of losing their banner are subject to trial by tribunal and their military unit is subject to disbandment.' This was the fate of the legendary 25th Chapayev division, which had distinguished itself during the Civil War and also during the defence of Odessa and Sevastopol in 1941. During the war nearly all the officers of any military unit which lost its banner were sent to penal battalions where they had to expiate their crime with their blood or their life.

The interrogation

Three days after the battle at Gorokhov an investigating officer came to the battalion to interrogate us about the loss of the banner. He interviewed all the officers who took part in the battle as well as many sergeants and soldiers. My interrogation lasted for over an hour. I was very nervous because I thought that all the officers would be sent to a penal battalion. I even thought of leaving my battalion. I had heard that the 111th rifle division which I had fought with near Rzhev in 1942 was not far from us at the front. So I contemplated going to my former division and asking them to let me re-join them.

But it did not go that far. It was the first interrogation in my life and I remember the investigator's face very well. By an incredible coincidence, I bumped into him two years later at the Military Law Academy. I was going downstairs as a lieutenant colonel of law came upstairs (plenty of them were there, attending proficiency development courses). Being a military man, my eye was drawn to the ribbon bars on his chest which showed where he had fought. Among others he had the bars 'For the capture of Berlin' and 'For the liberation of Prague'—both medals which I had been awarded. Then I looked carefully at his face: it seemed familiar. I asked him if he had investigated the case of the missing banner of the 78th assault sapper battalion in July 1944 near Gorokhov. He answered that when he was at Gorokhov he had investigated four or five such cases and that he did not specifically remember our battalion. I thought that it must have been pure mayhem during the battle for Gorokhov if so many military units had lost their banners.

I will now return to August 1944, when we learned about another tragedy near Gorokhov. A disabled fighter plane had been landed in a forest clearing by its pilot, Senior Lieutenant Likhovidov, Hero of the Soviet Union. Likhovidov returned to his regiment before coming back to his plane with two mechanics. However, they were tracked down at night by *Banderovtsi* who ambushed them while they were asleep, tied them to the plane, poured petrol over them and burned them together with their plane.[3] It was a terrible death. Pilot Likhovidov had shot down sixteen German planes.

A week after the memorable and tragic battle for Gorokhov the banner issue was resolved. During the offensive our battalion had been at the sharp end of the main thrust of the 1st Ukrainian front's right flank. The objective had been to besiege Lvov from the north. Our battalion's role had been to provide engineering support for the advancing 389th rifle division. This had included the destruction of German minefields, building bridges across small rivers and streams, and building dikes in marshy areas.

Due to our sudden and decisive attack our battalion had succeeded in dispersing and partially annihilating the 171st Cretan grenadier regiment which was subsequently forced to start a counter offensive in the direction of our troops' main line of attack. Under such circumstances the senior command considered that the battalion's personnel and commanders had shown courage and fortitude, and were worthy of an award. Therefore we could not be blamed for the loss of our banner. Through the 'soldiers' telephone', or grapevine, we came to know that this decision had been made by none other than the Supreme Commander-in-Chief, Marshal of the Soviet Union, Josef Stalin.

Shortly afterwards, according to the decree of the Presidium of the Supreme Soviet of the USSR, our battalion was awarded the Order of the Red Banner for the heroism and courage shown by its personnel, and our battalion commander, Major Kalyniuk, was awarded the same order by decree of the commander of the 1st Ukrainian front.

One night after we had been given a new red banner with the Order of the Red Banner attached, I was sitting by the camp fire with several fellow officers, including Major Kalinyuk. We asked him why no one else in the battalion had been awarded the order for their role in the battle. He answered that after that battle an award had been the last thing on his mind. What had concerned him was the thought that his successful career was over and that he, as well as the other officers of the battalion, would have to pay for his disgrace with his blood, or, at best, a life sentence in a penal battalion.

Among those who distinguished themselves in winning back Gorokhov was the commander of the 136th rifle division, Lieutenant Colonel Mesheryakov. He skilfully organised a breakthrough of the enemy's defence. On 18 June 1944 his division forced its way across the Bug river, a tributary of the Vistula on the Ukrainian-Polish border, and by the following morning the division had widened its foothold to fifteen kilometres, enabling other military units to cross the river successfully. Mesheryakov was awarded the title of Hero of the Soviet Union.

For some time after the battle the stores for our 16th assault brigade were about 100 kilometres to the west, in Dubno, Rovno region. My father, Lieutenant Colonel Ilya Ivanovich Bogachev, was the military superintendent and commissar of Dubno. He was living there with my mother Maria and my brother Anatoliy who was now fourteen years old.

Officers coming to the stores told my father that my battalion, the 78th, had been besieged during the offensive and completely annihilated together with its red banner. My father bore the news with courage, but my mother was cast into great sadness. My father sent an enquiry to the brigade commander about my fate and a month later he received a reply informing him that I was safe and sound, and that I had been awarded the Order of the Red Banner for the assault across the River Vistula.

My generation, born in 1924–25, went through difficult times in our youth. We learned to overcome all difficulties and obstacles in our life by ourselves, without the help and advice of our parents and teachers. We suffered from hunger and cold, we had to sleep on the snow, and we did not know what the future held in store. Tomorrow would bring the same routine as the day before—the daily routine of the front and constant danger. But our youth carried us through and we went on with our lives in spite of everything.

After the battle

In Moscow in the 1990s I managed to track down the former commander of the 389th rifle division, Lieutenant General

FOR THE MOTHERLAND! FOR STALIN!

(retired) L.A. Kolobov. He told me about the circumstances under which our battalion had been besieged. Kolobov took command of the division in summer 1942 in place of Colonel Malikhin, who had defected to the German side and become deputy to General Vlasov, founder of the German-backed Russian Liberation Army (*Russkaya Osvoboditel'naya Armiya* or ROA).

Why did Malikhin turn traitor? In 1942 there was a rule: the punishment for retreating without an order to retreat was execution by firing squad. Under pressure from the Germans, Malikhin's division retreated without waiting for orders, or rather its troops fled in panic. Malikhin received a suspended death sentence and continued in his role as commander of the division. But a month later the division retreated again in similar circumstances. Malikhin knew that this time he would not be pardoned so he defected to the Germans along with his driver, and Kolobov was appointed the new commander of the 389th rifle division.

Kolobov also told me about the fate of Vlasov and his comrades-in-arms. As the Red Army approached Prague in May 1945, Vlasov, who stayed with the ROA, was captured by the 4th tank army. According to our newspapers, Vlasov and the other ROA commanders were to face an open trial. But Vlasov and his companions refused to admit that they were guilty of high treason. They said that they had been engaging in a struggle against Stalin's regime of terror and wanted to liberate their people from the rule of a dictator and tyrant. Therefore they were not traitors, but Russian patriots. They did not change their stance even when promised that they would then not be executed.

They stood their ground in spite of threats of torture, the pleas of their relatives and the blandishments of the secret agents who shared their cells. Vlasov continued to say: 'I am not a traitor and I am not going to plead guilty. I hate Stalin—I consider him to be a tyrant and I am going to say this at the trial. Yes, I am afraid now, but the time will come when people will remember us kindly.' They were tortured for a long time in the most gruesome ways, but they refused to give in. Half-dead, they faced a secret trial in the Military Collegium of the Supreme Court of the USSR, where they were sentenced to death. By Stalin's order, each of them was hanged with a guitar string.

Rava-Russkaya

The circumstances of our winning back the town of Rava-Russkaya (its name is on the banner of our 16th assault brigade) in July 1944 are of interest. Rava-Russkaya occupies a notable place in history. On his way back to Russia from England in 1698, Peter the Great made a verbal agreement in Rava Russkaya—the Rava Agreement—with the Polish king, Augustus II, laying the foundation of an anti-Swedish alliance in the Great Northern War of 1700–21.[4] It was also there that General Brusilov made his famous breakthrough of the Austro-Hungarian front in 1916.

Many important events were connected with the town during the war. On 23 June 1941 a report from general HQ stated: 'On the way to Rava-Russkaya, the enemy who drove a wedge into our territory was defeated by the counter attacks of our troops in the afternoon and pushed back behind the frontier.' For five days the soldiers of the 41st rifle division, which was stationed in Rava-Russkaya, held back the enemy in a series of bloody battles despite being outnumbered and so enabled the country to assemble its strategic resources.

In July 1944 Rava-Russkaya once more became a battleground. The powerful steel wedge of troops from the 1st Ukrainian front cut through the enemy's defence. During a battle on the night of 20 July the 6th guards rifle division, under the command of General Onoprienko, won back the town. The division was part of the 13th army, commanded by Lieutenant General Pukhov, Hero of the Soviet Union. The division was supported by the

44th guards Berdichev tank brigade under the command of Colonel Gusakovsky, twice awarded Hero of the Soviet Union. The brigade was part of the 1st guards tank army under the command of Lieutenant General Katukov, also twice awarded Hero of the Soviet Union.

The sappers of five assault battalions and a flame thrower unit from our 16th assault brigade were smashing through the enemy's defences to prepare the way for tanks and infantry. Three guards assault aircraft regiments of the 2nd air army were attacking the enemy from the air. Five military units, including our brigade, were awarded the honourable title of 'Rava-Russkaya' by the order of Supreme Commander Stalin for distinguishing themselves in battle.

16

THE VISTULA OPERATION

THE RIVER VISTULA

While on reconnaissance, our group of scouts was the first to approach the River Vistula, near Józefów nad Wisłą. This town was on the boundary between the 1st Ukrainian front and the 1st Belorussian front, putting us on the northernmost flank of the 1st Ukrainian front. As we approached the river we came under fire from the Armia Krajowa on the opposite bank.

This was the resistance army of the Polish government-in-exile based in London, which was now our enemy.[1] The bullets whizzed past our ears. We lay down on the ground, answered their fire and then, making a series of runs across the field, left this dangerous place.

Stalin had placed great importance on the assault across the Vistula, and had ordered that soldiers and commanders who distinguished themselves in action should be awarded titles including Hero of the Soviet Union.

Soon our battalion reached a point facing a small foothold occupied by our troops on the opposite bank. There was an urgent need to set up a river crossing to bring them reinforcements and ammunition. The battalion commander told me to make a technical reconnaissance of the river (measuring its depth, width and the speed of the current, and assessing the character of the riverbed) and then to construct an assault bridge. The task was extremely dangerous. Our foothold on the opposite bank was small, only about 300 metres wide and 150 metres deep, while our bank was constantly under fire from enemy snipers, rifles and machine guns.

With all the industrial plants of Western Europe to supply them, the Germans spared neither shells nor mines, bullets or bombs. Everything around us was so densely swept with fire that at times it was impossible to look out of the trench. The river was churning with explosions from German shells and mines. Lashed by fearsome orders from Berlin, the German commanders did not spare their own people in their attempts to hold back our advancing troops, or, if they were lucky, push us back to the river.

I lined up my platoon of twenty-three and explained the mission to them. I asked which of them would like to volunteer to make a reconnaissance of the river. A young soldier, Kashintsev, came forward. I was relieved: if it wasn't for Kashintsev I would have to do the job myself because nobody except Kashintsev and I could swim across the Vistula, which was 600 metres wide with a current of one and a half metres per second.

I went down to the river with Kashintsev, who had been given a two-metre ruler, and two sergeants. The water was eddying with explosions. On the bank shells and mines were exploding, their fragments shrieking and howling over our heads—a blood-curdling din.

Kashintsev was swimming across the river, struggling against the current, trying to keep a straight line. Every ten metres he measured the depth by putting the ruler into the water: one of the sergeants looked through his binoculars and counted the graduations, which the other wrote down in his notebook. We only had one thought between us—would he reach the opposite bank or not?

Kashintsev made it. For several minutes he lay on the sandy beach, recovering from his desperate swim. Then suddenly we noticed something: along the edge of the bank, shells were exploding, one by one, closer and closer to Kashintsev. He had nowhere to hide. It would be risky for him to run, as a running man is more exposed to the fragments. At last the explosions reached Kashintsev. My heart sank: the end had come; our comrade-in-arms was dead. But when the dust from the explosions dispersed we saw Kashintsev move, then crawl away from the river. We were overwhelmed with joy: Kashintsev had performed a great feat. I recommended him for a decoration, the Order of the Red Star, which he was given shortly afterwards. Now we write letters to each other and remember our glorious young years in the war.

While we were watching Kashintsev we were spotted by an enemy sniper on the opposite bank. A bullet hit the outer wall of our trench near my head. We did not pay much attention, thinking that it was just a stray bullet. But when another bullet hit the top of the trench a minute later, we realised that there was a sniper about 700 or 800 metres away, the wounding range of a bullet being 1000 metres. We decided to check. We put a soldier's cap on a rifle butt and raised it up from the trench. It was immediately hit by a bullet. For half an hour we lay low in the trench, then all three of us simultaneously jumped out and rushed in different directions up the slope away from the river. Luckily all turned out well.

Once darkness had fallen the battalion started to build the assault bridge across the river. Thick poles which had been joined in the middle with crossbars 80 centimetres long were rammed into the river bottom. Planks were laid on the crossbars, rails were put along the sides and the bridge was ready. Infantry soldiers ran across the bridge to the other bank and ammunition was brought over: at night the wounded were carried back on stretchers, or they made their own way back.

And all this was happening under constant fire, day and night. If any part of the bridge was damaged by a shell, mine or bomb, the team of sappers on duty rushed to repair it. If sappers or infantry soldiers were badly wounded on the bridge, they fell into the water and drowned. There was no way of saving them because of the swift current: no one ever tried.

During the bridge's construction and subsequent use, fifty-five individuals from our battalion were wounded or killed. Lieutenant Zhukov, a handsome twenty-year-old lad with curly hair, was one of the dead. Another twenty-year-old, Lieutenant Kuznetsov, was wounded in his hip. It was not a severe wound, but Kuznetsov suffered from haemophilia. He died from heavy blood loss in his comrades' arms. How could a man with such an illness be sent to the front?

For us it was a hard ordeal, but there was no alternative. We knew that the general, the commander of the rifle corps, whose soldiers had forced their way across the river in whatever manner they could and snatched a foothold, had ordered our battalion commander to build the assault bridge at any cost so that help could be brought to his infantry who were now bleeding to death on the opposite bank. Any non-compliance with this order would be punished by summary execution. And we knew very well that this was not a mere threat. There had been precedents.

In 1943, when a howitzer artillery regiment was four hours late for the beginning of artillery preparation, resulting in the failure of the mission and great losses among our troops, its commander, a lieutenant colonel, was shot in a summary execution carried out by order of Lieutenant General Tanaschishin of the tank troops. Tanaschishin was never punished for this: a year later, he would be killed at the front during a German air raid. It was a cruel time with cruel ways.

One evening when it was already dark, I was on the bank near the assault bridge. Suddenly shells started exploding around me. Bombardment at night when you can't see where the shells are detonating is much worse than in daytime. Nearby was a pontoon which had sunk several days before. To escape from the bombardment I jumped into the pontoon and saw two, then three bodies lying there. The situation on the bank of the Vistula was so tense that there had been no opportunity to bury the dead.

About 200 metres downstream, the 77th assault sapper battalion of our brigade was carrying out a separate operation. The battalion commander, Captain Katchalko, had been ordered to transport the landing force across the river. The river crossing was taking place in very difficult conditions: the enemy was shooting from a high bank along the whole reach of the river. The sappers put up a smokescreen, then the first detachments of storm troopers and the infantry landing force set off. Under mortar and machine-gun fire, the soldiers had to steer their boats across the 600-metre wide river.

They eventually reached the foothold with great losses, but their mission was not yet completed. They had to put together a five-tonne ferry boat to transport the regiment's artillery. The enemy fire became heavier, but the sappers carried on with their mission. As darkness fell the battle abated a little.

At night Captain Katchalko made a brave decision: to transport the troops without artillery preparation or artillery coverage. He reasoned that the Germans would hardly expect a new landing force on account of the swift current and the great width of the river. His decision proved to be right. The first party of four boats transported 100 soldiers and ammunition across the river quietly and quickly. The second party consisted of six boats. When the enemy suddenly realised what was going on, it was too late—our landing force had strong reinforcements. Over seven days and nights, the assault sappers' battalion had transported the whole guard division across the river in the most testing conditions. The foothold on the left bank of the Vistula was well and truly secured.

For their role in the Vistula operation, Captain Katchalko, Senior Lieutenant Kulik, Senior Sergeant Stepanov and Medical Orderly Katukhin from the 467th rifle regiment were awarded the title of Hero of the Soviet Union. Katukhin was one of the first to cross the river on the night of 2 August 1944. He tended to the wounded and carried more than 200 men from the battlefield.

We received an urgent order to move fifty kilometres south to the town of Sandomierz, which had been occupied by our troops. They were in the process of consolidating their position. Many years later, after I retired from the army in the 1980s, I found the documents dealing with this bridgehead in the central archive of the Ministry of Defence in Podolsk. It turned out that there had been more than ten similar footholds within the theatre of operations involving the 1st Ukrainian front. Except for Sandomierz all of them had to be abandoned and ceded to the Germans. That was the cruel reality of the war.

From the archive documents I learnt that the 81st Kalinkovichskaya division had been operating within the foothold. There were twenty-three Heroes of the Soviet Union in this division (twenty-two of them received their award for crossing the Dnieper river). The division comprised 9,887 people from the following nationalities:

Russian	5,778
Kazakh	1,272
Azerbaijani	43

Armenian	35
Moldovan	3
Polish	5
Ukrainian	730
Uzbek	679
Kirghiz	126
Jewish	125
Kalmyk	32
Mari	30
Udmurt	28
Komi	27
Greek	3
Estonian	1
Latvian	1
Karelian	1
Belorussian	122
Turkmen	10
Chuvash	79
Buryat	95
Chechen	3
Georgian	73
Mordvin	73
Bashkir	58
Tajik	44
Ingush	2
Dagestani	9
Ossetian	6
Kabardian	3
Balkarian	2
Other	45

There were 1,052 officers; 2,134 sergeants; 6,702 rank-and-file soldiers; 1,016 horses; and sixty-four vehicles.

FOR THE MOTHERLAND! FOR STALIN!

How I prayed to God

I am going to tell you about the time I prayed to God during the war. As a platoon commander I was often sent two or three times a day by the battalion commander to the other units, or to the brigade's HQ, or to the other battalions with various verbal or written messages. As a rule I went alone, without company.

Once I was walking along a path through a field on one of these errands. No one was around. Suddenly an artillery strike started and soon shells were exploding around me. There was nowhere to hide. If I was wounded, nobody would be there to help me. I pressed myself hard against the ground and covered my head, my gun in one hand and a map case in the other. Our most vulnerable parts are the head, stomach and certainly the heart.

No one who has experienced an artillery strike can ever forget it. I felt alone and helpless on that stormy field of fire. My heart was thumping. My nerves were taut. I expected death any minute. And I knew that death would not be instantaneous. You never knew where the next shell would explode. Could that shell be the one that would end your fragile existence? This anticipation was horrible!

Death hovered over me, as I lay spread on the ground. I could see insects and spiders crawling through the grass, oblivious to the war. And then a thought came into my mind: 'Good God! Can all nature in its beauty last for ever while I simply perish?'

Some believe that the soul might be immortal and the soul of a fighter killed in war will go straight to paradise, but I was not consoled by this. I had been brought up as a member of a family of an officer, a member of the Communist Party. Not only at home but wherever else I had been, no one had ever mentioned God. But at that moment, in spite of my atheist upbringing, I pleaded: 'God, if you exist, save me!' Then the artillery strike was over, and I was safe and sound. I had never prayed to God before, but in that case I had to. If anyone would like to reproach me for weakness of spirit, let them go through what I had experienced.

I stood up and walked towards the river. A forest lay ahead, screening me from the Germans. There was no living soul in the forest. Then another artillery strike started. The Germans were firing at the forest because they thought that our troops could be located there. Suddenly I heard the terrible rumble of exploding shells and the terrifying crackling noise of trees being blown apart.

Quickly I jumped into a nearby dugout. Suddenly I noticed dense black caustic smoke starting to drift in through the entrance. 'Well,' I thought, 'this is the end. They must be using shells loaded with some poisonous substance.' I did not have a gas mask: none of us had carried one for a very long time. I faced a dilemma: if I stayed put I would be poisoned with gas; if I left the dugout I could be killed by shrapnel. I preferred the second option. I quickly climbed out of the dugout, ran through the cloud of gas and fell face downwards. Then the artillery strike was over.

When I looked around I realized that the smoke had come from a smoke canister used by sappers for making smoke screens—the canister had been hit by a shell. I cheered up. I was safe! I was alive! After what had just happened I burst into nervous laughter: I had been gambling with Death too closely, all the advantages being his.

Once I completed my errand, I went back up a long, slightly sloping, sandy bank towards the forest. I was an easy target from the opposite bank of the river. Suddenly I heard the increasingly loud roar of a shell, then a plume of sand and smoke shot up in front of me with a deafening blast. The explosion reverberated through the forest, but I did not attach any significance to it. But when a second shell exploded behind me I understood what was going on. I realised that the shells were aimed at me and that the next one would explode even nearer.

I ran to the side and, indeed, the third shell exploded exactly where I had been a moment earlier. I started running towards the wood, zigzagging this way and that way like a hare, while shells exploded around me. I now saw that the German artillerymen were having a bit of fun. They could afford to, as they had plenty of shells, and so they were having a blow-out.

It was exhausting to run uphill through sand in the August heat. My heart was thumping, my temples throbbed, sweat was pouring over my eyes and my legs were unresponsive. Never before in my life had I been so exhausted. But still I kept running to the forest. Once I was there I recovered my breath and came to my senses. I was so thirsty. I felt as though I had cobwebs in my throat.

I walked through the trees and came to a farm on the edge of the forest—a house with outbuildings. A cow started mooing in the cowshed. Nobody was in the house and I could not find any water. I opened the cellar door. A Polish family was there. My torch lit up the frightened faces of adults and children, all looking at me. I asked them for water. They answered: 'We don't have water.' I asked them for milk. They answered: 'We don't have milk.' I was trembling with anger. The cow had been mooing, so there had to be milk in the house and they did not want to give it to me. I had already discovered, not just once, that the Poles treated us Russians in different ways: some were friendly, but others were not.

I snatched a grenade from my belt, put in the fuse and took out the ring. I wanted to hurl the grenade into the cellar and kill them all. I had just suffered so much, yet they wouldn't spare me a drop of milk! But when I saw the stiff faces of the children I changed my mind. I closed the cellar door and continued on my way back to my battalion. That was how I passed one of the many days of war. There were many days of war, so many...

Another day, I was making my way to the frontline with several soldiers from my platoon as darkness fell. As a rule, sappers on the frontline work at night. Suddenly an artillery raid started—whether it was targeted, or random, it was difficult to say. With no time to think, I jumped into the nearest shallow trench. I felt a corpse under me which emitted a strong smell of decomposition. The stench was intolerable, but I had to endure it until the shells stopped exploding and the fragments were no longer whizzing through the air.

Senior Sergeant Tsiunel

Under Senior Sergeant Tsiunel, my scouts were going behind German lines to conduct a reconnaissance of the enemy's engineering constructions. I was supposed to accompany them as far as the frontline, making sure that they crossed the German trenches successfully. Accompanying us was our company nurse, the beautiful Anna Brovkina. We had to cross the frontline at night and we were waiting for darkness to fall. We were one kilometre away from the frontline, in a small, empty village which had been almost destroyed by artillery shells and aerial bombing. Suddenly the village was bombarded by an artillery raid. Immediately we all rushed in different directions. I jumped into a shallow trench which had been dug out some time earlier. But Anna was there! She was already lying there. I could do nothing but lie on top of her and press myself tightly down on her to keep below ground level. The bombardment, consisting of about ten shells, eventually ended and none of us was killed or wounded. Many years later, when I was telling my wife about this episode, she asked whether there had been something more to it! Under such desperate circumstances when everything was touch and go, I certainly would not have thought of what my future wife might have made of it.

Tsiunel and the scouts successfully crossed the frontline, completed their mission and returned safe and sound. Tsiunel (whose mother was Russian but father was German) had an interesting career, as you shall learn.

FOR THE MOTHERLAND! FOR STALIN!

We had a separate motorised reconnaissance company in our brigade, but this company was not doing very well. It is one thing to carry out engineering reconnaissance on your own territory, but quite another to do it in the enemy's rear. Particularly challenging missions, especially those in the enemy's rear, were delegated to teams of five to ten scouts led by twenty-year-old platoon commanders who had recently completed crash courses at military school. Failure followed failure. Either scouts returned with casualties, or they didn't come back at all for reasons which would remain unknown, or they came back without any useful information at all. So the commanders decided not to send scouts into the enemy's rear, but to use my second-in-command, thirty-year-old Senior Sergeant Tsiunal, instead.

Tsiunel carried out superb reconnaissance work and afterwards these missions were assigned to him alone. He was always lucky. By the end of the war Tsiunel had been awarded two Orders of Glory (3rd and 2nd class), the Order of the Patriotic War (2nd class) and a medal for courage in successfully completing challenging missions in scouting and reconnaissance. After carrying out yet another successful mission in the enemy rear and obtaining valuable information, the commander of brigade HQ asked Tsiunel which award he should recommend him for: the Order of Glory, 1st class, or the Order of the Red Banner for military valour? At a veterans' meeting, Tsiunel told us: 'I thought that as I had already had two Orders of Glory, the Order of the Red Banner would be better, so I chose that. Only when the war was over did I realize my mistake, because the bearer of the Order of Glory of all three classes is equal to the award of Hero of the Soviet Union with all its ensuing perks and privileges. The Order of the Red Banner doesn't give you any perks!'

I must add that after he was discharged from the army Tsiunel worked in agriculture and was subsequently awarded the Order of the Red Banner of Labour for great merit.

17

SANDOMIERZ

HOW I HELPED TO REPEL A GERMAN ATTACK

Our foothold on the Vistula near the town of Annopol didn't prove promising, so our battalion was transferred forty kilometres south to Sandomierz to provide technical support for our troops who were attempting to enlarge their foothold there.

The commander of our battalion, Major Kalyniuk, who had just received his Order of the Red Banner for our breakthrough near Gorokhov, set me the following task:

Firstly, to go to Sandomierz with my scouts and, on the way, put them in positions where the actual terrain differed from the data shown on our topographic maps (which were twenty years old and somewhat out of date). The scouts would act as beacons to point the battalion in the correct direction.

Secondly, once in Sandomierz, to contact the commanders of units engaged in fighting in order to assess the situation and map

Boris in Sandomierz, Poland, October 1944

out the battlefields; to carry out engineering reconnaissance (locating and mapping out the positions of minefields, land mines and booby traps—from information supplied by military scouts we knew that a German sapper battalion had been located in Sandomierz); and to find suitable billets for the battalion's personnel.

Thirdly (on a more personal note), ... at this point, the major turned his head to make sure no one else was listening, then told me about an old monastery in Sandomierz where there might be some gold. 'So carry out a thorough search of their cellars,' he said. 'But no one must know a thing!'

I was stunned by the last order, but I said nothing. How could I, an officer and prospective member of the Communist Party, just grab gold for him? What about my officer's rank—and mere decency? After all, I came from an officer's family. In 1918 my father, a Moscow factory worker, a member of the proletariat, became a member of the Communist Party and one of the first red commanders (as officers of military units were called at that time) before fighting with the 1st Ukrainian front as a lieutenant colonel, with the Order of Lenin and the Order of the Red Banner pinned on his chest.

'Very well,' I thought, 'we'll see what happens...'

So I set off on my mission immediately, accompanied by Tsiunel and five scouts with automatic weapons. At nightfall we put our coats on the ground, wrapped ourselves up in them, then lay tightly pressed up against each other. We slept soundly for about three hours. Those who have never experienced war would be surprised by our deep sense of fraternity and comradeship. But this feeling is built up of such moments.

We were walking fast and our spirits were high. We had only recently escaped encirclement during the furious battle at Gorokhov, before building, under murderous enemy fire, a light assault bridge for our infantry to cross the Vistula as well as piers on both banks of the river so that our tanks could cross the river on pontoons to the foothold. Many of our soldiers and commanders had been awarded orders and medals.

When he had presented me with the Order of the Red Star, Major Kalyniuk had said that it was for courage shown in the battle at Gorokhov and for crossing the Vistula, for military professionalism, for using my initiative and taking correct actions in difficult battle situations, and for the skilful management of my men.

As I walked, I glanced occasionally at the new Order of the Red Star attached to the front of my shirt. This, my first award during the war, was especially dear to me. I saw it as a sign that the commanders of my battalion and brigade were thoroughly satisfied with my service. And what could be more pleasing to a military man than admiration of his professional conduct, and the awareness that in the course of victory over the enemy he has done his bit, however small?

Early in the morning we reached the bank of the Vistula. We crossed the river on the ferry. The enemy was regularly covering the crossing zone with artillery fire. Great columns of water shot up around us. Sinister fragments whizzed past. We were very anxious. The current was flowing at half a metre per second. If you were hit by shrapnel on land, your comrades could bandage your wound, but what would happen if you fell into the river? For those who have never been in such a situation it would be difficult to understand our state of mind.

We crossed the river safely. We had to walk about two kilometres along the bank to the town. About ten metres away from the bank was an embankment standing five metres high and four metres wide. Our soldiers were lying on the top of the embankment, twenty to thirty metres away from each other, shooting now and then. We were walking along the path when suddenly we were deafened as the soldiers opened fire from rifles, automatic- and machine-guns to repel a German assault.

We had to carry out our mission so we continued walking. Suddenly, a general in field uniform appeared out of nowhere. Three soldiers stood behind him with automatic guns at the ready. Many medals, including various Orders of the Red Banner, glittered on the general's chest. In an authoritative voice he asked who we were, then ordered us to climb up the embankment and take part in repelling the German assault.

My humble attempt to explain that I was on a mission was totally ignored by the general. So I looked at my scouts, then at the general's entourage. They were waiting for me to make a decision. I understood that in such a situation I had to comply with the general's order. I ordered my scouts to climb up the embankment and repel the German attack with fire.

So here were the Germans! Real, live Germans—not just pictures on the targets which we shot at during firing practice at Bukhara. Even now, so many years later, I can see the Hitlerites in their mouse-coloured uniforms going into attack in a widely spaced line, the sleeves of their jackets rolled up to the elbows, their machine guns propped against their stomachs, erupting deadly fire. The German attack was supported by artillery fire. On the top of the embankment where we lay there were no trenches or gun emplacements. Swarms of bullets whistled past and shell fragments screeched overhead.

The distance between us was rapidly becoming smaller: 300 metres... 200 metres... 150 metres... The tension grew. The Germans advanced in short dashes, shouting—and it felt that like were not really humans but scarecrows stuffed with straw and I just shot at them with my automatic gun in cold blooded indifference. While they continued to approach, I targeted a German running towards me, but before I could pull the trigger he took one short bound, then fell down. He couldn't be seen in the grass. I directed my gun sight to the place where he had fallen, but then the German suddenly rose up two metres to the left. While I changed my aim, he fell down again and promptly emerged in his previous position. And he did this several times.

As cadets at artillery school we had not been taught to crawl aside while running in bounds. At last I contrived to take aim at the place where I thought the Nazi could be lying and when he got up I caught him in a short burst of gunfire. I saw him fall with his arms in the air and he never rose again. He was the second Hitlerite whom I killed in close battle during the war.

The German attack was repelled. The German soldiers who were alive crawled back, one after the other. I took a rest, my cap on the ground. I was only nineteen and I found it very difficult to bear the huge physical and psychological tension of battle. Who knows what it was like for middle-aged soldiers of nearly fifty with three or four small children at home?

Once we were sure that the formidable general wasn't around, my scouts and I set off on our way along the embankment towards Sandomierz.

Still hot from battle, we told each other about our experiences. Other scouts had also killed one or two Hitlerites. In one place the embankment had been breached, letting through a small rivulet. The soldiers warned us that the breach was targeted by the enemy, but we couldn't wait until dark so we started fording our way across. Although the Germans shot at us from long range machine guns, they didn't hit anyone.

Much later I found out that the formidable general was Grigory Ivanovich Vekhin, (born 1901), commander of 350th Zhytomyr rifle division. For his role in the resolute crossing of the San and Vistula rivers, and for retaining control of the strategic Sandomierz foothold, he was awarded the honourable title of Hero of the Soviet Union (with our help, I would add!).

Sandomierz

Sandomierz is a small regional town situated on the high left bank of the Vistula. In 1241 Tatars led by Batu Khan (the grandson of Genghis Khan) occupied Sandomierz, then went into Poland, Hungary and Serbia, reaching the Adriatic. Weakened by battles with West European knights in full armour, the Tatars retreated to the steppes near the Volga. On the lower reaches of the Volga, they set up their state, the Golden Horde, with its capital, Sarai (the Tatar word *sarai* translates as 'palace').

The great commander or hetman, Bogdan Khmelnitsky, led his rebel Cossack army into this region, defeating the troops of the Polish nobility or *szlachta*. Khmelnitsky was a legendary personality. His family were members of the Lithuanian nobility who ruled Ukraine in the late sixteenth and early seventeenth century as part of the Polish-Lithuanian Commonwealth. Khmelnitsky had been a Catholic, but in Turkish captivity he became a Muslim and on his return to Ukraine he became Orthodox Christian.

The battle for Sandomierz was taking place in the western suburbs, but in the town centre shells were exploding and stray bullets were whizzing through the air. I contacted the commander of the 1180th rifle regiment of the 350th rifle division, Colonel Vasliy Skopenko (born 1912). Two Orders of the Red Banner, the Order of Alexander Nevsky and the Order of the Red Star adorned his chest. I could see that Skopenko was very tense. The Germans were putting up a desperate resistance—there were not enough troops on the frontline, ammunition was running low and his superiors were putting on the pressure in immoderate terms, to put it mildly. He had enough on his plate, so his answer to my report was 'do what you think best'.

Several days later Skopenko would be killed in action while leading his soldiers into an attack. For taking Sandomierz he was awarded the title Hero of the Soviet Union, the Order of the Red Star and the Order of Lenin. Skopenko was buried with full military honours in the town cemetery.

We carried out an engineering reconnaissance of the areas of Sandomierz which had been liberated. The German sapper battalion's base at the barracks had been booby-trapped with mines. These mines had fuses on their tops, bottoms and sides—each one contained certain death. It was impossible to disable such mines and they could only be detonated. So we confined ourselves to putting up notices: 'Beware mines!'

After dealing with the situation I sent a scout to report back to the battalion which was on its way, then we embarked on our third 'combat' mission. My scouts and I came to the old and majestic Catholic monastery. The scouts put a notice 'Beware mines!' outside the gates. This, we thought, should keep everyone away. Once inside, my scouts kept guard in the corridors while I wandered around the rooms, accompanied by a respectable but bewildered abbot in long black robes. Then we went down to the cellars.

Pointing to the heavy doors with huge locks and wax seals, and to a notice in Polish, 'Polish Church Property', the abbot warned me that I would be personally responsible if I, of my own will, unsealed the doors in the cellar. Even their sworn enemies, the German Nazis, during five long years of occupation, hadn't dared appropriate the monastery's property.

His arguments had an effect on me. If there were any problems with opening up the cellars I knew that Major Kalyniuk would deny any responsibility. There had been no witnesses to our conversation and I could very easily face a military tribunal for crimes against the Polish-Russian Slav friendship. And on the frontline during war the decision of the tribunal would be to shoot me for looting. We apologised to the abbot and left the monastery, putting a guard outside the gates near the notice 'Beware mines!'.

We started looking for a convenient billet for the battalion. The scouts were roaming around the houses, assessing them for suitability. They were a daredevil, reckless and enterprising bunch. One of them found a red skirt, and suggested making it into a flag and hanging it from the town hall tower which rose up high above the other buildings. For our agile, energetic scouts, this wasn't a difficult feat. High above Sandomierz, with only random bullets whizzing past, the red flag started flying from the tower, announcing the town's liberation from the Nazis.

At the same time the scouts found a German food depot with supplies of flour, sugar, butter and jam. One of them suggested baking pastries for the battalion, and the local Polish women and girls, the *pannies* and *pannochkies*,[1] were willing to make them. I gave them the thumbs up and the work began. The next day the 300-strong battalion marched into Sandomierz. Ten baking trays laden with pastries awaited them on tables. Not far away was the group of cooks, looking on proudly.

At the head of the battalion marched its commander, Major Kalyniuk. I ran up and told him that the mission had been completed. I said that the cellars of the monastery had been sealed and I couldn't get access to them, but I had put a guard near the entrance to the monastery, the flag had been raised on the town hall, and that pastries had been baked for the battalion.

He wasn't impressed. He swore at me angrily. I stepped back and the soldiers rushed towards the pastries. I didn't dare mention that we had taken part in repelling the German attack, killed several German soldiers and deserved some recognition or reward.

Sometime later I started being ostracised. I was demoted from being commander of the battalion staff platoon to commander of the manoeuvring platoon of the 2nd sapper company, although I didn't have any specialised training in engineering (before coming to this battalion I had been a platoon commander in a mortar regiment at the front). During the following eight months of active participation in battle I was never rewarded, although my soldiers received two or three orders or medals during the same period. Several days later the troops who had crossed the Vistula and liberated Sandomierz received a meritorious commendation by the order of Stalin and a firework display was organised in their honour.

On the Sandomierz foothold

On the Sandomierz foothold I witnessed for the first time in my life a German bombardment from mortars with six 158.5-mm calibre tubes. Each mortar bomb weighed thirty-four kilos. Although the bombs exploded a safe distance away it was a horrific experience. I could just imagine what those who directly experienced that bombardment were going through and their suffering. I noticed that when this mortar fired the bombs it made a sound very much like donkeys braying and you could hear it several kilometres away.

Nowadays I fall asleep with great difficulty and wake up several times during the night. Even the slightest noise disturbs me.

'Old age does not bring joy', or *starost ne radost*, as the old Russian proverb says. But when I was young I could sleep soundly as heavy artillery shells exploded around me.

While we were on the foothold our battalion hurriedly laid anti-tank and anti-personnel mines along the frontline of our defence. Very tense and bloody battles were taking place around us. The mining was done at night. In addition to night duties, as a management platoon commander I had to carry out dozens of missions given to me by the battalion commander during the day. For some periods I had only two or three hours of sleep. I became very exhausted during that time. So once, when we were in a small village after laying mines all night and the soldiers were sleeping on the grass, I decided to sneak off for a sleep without saying anything, even to my orderly. I climbed up to the first floor of a barn where several lightly wounded soldiers were sleeping on the hay. Just before I went into the barn I noticed a big air balloon rising into air—it was rising from a lorry 200 metres outside the village. This was the aerostat or air balloon, which was used for observation from the air and directing artillery fire. I took off my high boots and, despite the terrible stench of the soldiers' foot cloths which overpowered the scent of hay and meadow flowers, I fell fast asleep.

When I woke up there was no sign of the wounded soldiers, or my high boots. Only someone's ripped soldiers' boots remained. I put them on, then went out. There was nobody around. The lorry with the air balloon had gone. About two dozen craters from heavy artillery shells could be seen clearly, black against the green meadow.

In a peasant's hut which served as the battalion HQ, I found only a communications soldier who told me that the German artillery had started shooting at the air balloon and that all personnel had been evacuated from this dangerous place.

During the war I had to sleep on the bare earth many times when I couldn't find any straw or twigs to make a mattress. I used to lie on my coat and pull it over me, fold my cap down over my ears, put my hand against my cheek and go to sleep, closely pressing myself to my comrades on both sides. One great man said: 'The people who win wars are those who can sleep on the bare ground.' Russians and Tatars could, but the Germans couldn't.

I suffered from several attacks of malaria which I had caught in Central Asia. On those occasions I remembered that the poet Byron had died of malaria during the war in Greece.

I can remember another episode on the Sandomierz foothold. I went to the rifle division HQ with several scouts to meet the commander of its engineering unit and agree to a joint plan of action for our assault battalion and his men. I could see that they had no time to talk to me; the division commander, a colonel, grave, pale and tense, was giving orders to his subordinates. They were also tense.

The headquarters was on a hill and from there the terrain was clearly visible. I saw three heavy German tanks slowly crawling along a field and firing. I had never seen such tanks before. They turned out to be the new German models—King Tigers or Tiger IIs. Each had an 88-mm gun and two machine guns. Their front armour was 190 millimetres thick and they weighed 68 tonnes. The German tank gun was so powerful that it could penetrate the armour of our T-34 tanks from a distance of two kilometres.

Our guns nearby were firing continuously, but to no avail. The tanks were moving steadily forward as if they were charmed. Our infantry was retreating at a run. The ground was shaking heavily and the air was filled with the non-stop rattle and boom of exploding shells along with the roar of tank engines and creaking of caterpillar tracks. The densely falling shells ripped the ground into shreds. Even now I can see those armoured German monsters as their tank turrets turn to the left and fire, then to the right and fire. And between the firing each iron monster with its long trunk of a gun inhales the air and scents its next victim.

FOR THE MOTHERLAND! FOR STALIN!

German King Tiger tanks

Next to me the division commander's last reserve stepped into line—a company of scouts with automatic guns. The division commander ordered them to stop those who were running away and take them back to the trenches. The scouts ran forward to fulfil their mission. Eventually two of the three German tanks were hit by our artillery fire and the third turned back and disappeared. The tank crew who were trying to escape from their damaged vehicles were shot by automatic guns.

The King Tigers were new heavy tanks; they were manufactured in conditions of top secrecy and first deployed on the Sandomierz foothold. The tank's designer, Porsche, rode in one of them, as he wanted to see for himself how his invincible wonder-tanks would destroy their Russian counterparts. He died with his creation in battle. It is possible that this is what I witnessed.

When the battle was over I went up to a damaged tank which had stopped burning. The infantry soldiers nearby were so exhausted by this episode, as well as by previous fighting and long marches, that they had taken the first available opportunity for a rest and were already sleeping soundly in the shallow trenches—they didn't care about trophies and tanks.

I found a German Schmeisser submachine gun among what was left of the tank crew. I used it for some time afterwards until I ran out of cartridges and handed it over to the ammunition commander. Our cartridges of 7.62-mm calibre were not suitable for German automatic guns as their calibre was 7.92-mm.

There was an appalling incident in our brigade. A sapper unit under the command of Junior Sergeant Khardzhiev was caught in an artillery attack while laying mines along the frontline. The sappers had nowhere to hide. A nurse was with them and she was hit by a shell fragment. Her heel was torn off and she was crying for help. But everyone ran away and no one gave her any help. At HQ, Khardzhiev said that he saw the nurse die from a fatal wound. A message of condolence was sent to her relatives informing them of her death—'the death of the courageous in the battle for the socialist motherland'—but the nurse didn't die. She was found by nearby soldiers, who bandaged her wound and sent her to hospital. From the hospital she wrote a letter to the brigade commander to tell him what had happened. Khardzhiev was promptly demoted to the ranks.

This disgraceful episode was angrily discussed at meetings in companies and platoons as well as at party and Komsomol meetings. While carrying out research at the archive in Podolsk I read the minutes of those meetings and what was striking was the fact that everyone who took the floor mentioned the name of Stalin at least once, if not twice or more, in a way that was typical of those times. Such was the cult of personality.

FOR THE MOTHERLAND! FOR STALIN!

My acceptance into the Communist Party

On the Sandomierz bridgehead in August 1944, the battalion's party bureau accepted me as a candidate member of the Communist Party.[2] We were sitting on the ground in a gully while a battle raged around us. In the sky was the ceaseless roar of planes. Not far away we heard bombs exploding, shaking the tortured land. German planes were bombing the division's artillery firing positions. Our IL2 fighter planes were dashing through the air just above our heads. Meanwhile our PE2 bombers were flying slowly in the blue sky, covered from above by our quick YAK3 fighters.

Shells were whistling overhead as our heavy artillery launched them towards the enemy. Those with very sharp vision could even see them flying through the air. We could hear machine guns firing along the frontline. It was difficult for us to hear each other. My application was read out, including my statement: 'I want to go into battle as a communist.' Then the party organiser summarised my personal details and the battalion's deputy political commissar gave me a brief, positive character reference. The decision was unanimous: 'Worthy to accept.' Several days later I was handed a candidate member's Communist Party certificate. I became a communist and continued to be a communist for forty-five years.

The commander of the platoon, Lieutenant Andriy Rilskiy, was a good friend of mine and the nephew of a famous Ukrainian poet, Maxim Rilskiy. Shortly before I joined the Communist Party we both attended five-day training sessions for platoon commanders which were held between battles to develop proficiency. We lived in the same dugout and became friends. When you are young you make friends quickly.

While laying mines at night on no man's land in front of our trenches, a stray bullet from a German machine gun entered Rilskiy's heart and he died immediately. He was twenty years old: a courageous warrior, good friend and member of the Young Communist League. A handsome, young, tall, slim fellow, he was lying in his roughly made plank coffin as if he were alive. His hair had not lost its lustre and a kind half-smile remained on his bright lips which were now silent for ever.

Before the war he had lived and studied in Kiev. He could have lived and enjoyed life, but the pitiless destiny of the front disposed of him in its own fashion.

My platoon organised the funeral of our comrade-in-arms. We buried him on a clear bright August day on a small hill near a tall, lonely oak tree which could be seen for miles around. The sky was blue. The sun was shining. The grass on the hill was lush and green. There was a field of golden wheat around the hill. This exuberant blossoming of nature in all its variety contrasted sharply with the sombre sense of death in its midst.

Near the grave a company of assault sappers stood in line. Some had tears in their eyes. One by one, they left the line, gathered lumps of warm black earth in their hands and threw them into the freshly dug grave.

On the grave we placed a wooden four-cornered pyramid with a tin star on the top. On the pyramid was a white wooden plaque with Rilskiy's name and surname. 'We swear on your grave,' said the battalion commander, Petunin, 'that we will carry the red banner bathed in your warm blood through all our battles with the hateful enemy until we achieve complete victory over the fascist beast.' 'We swear,' the line of soldiers answered. The speaker went on: 'Years will pass but we will remember you. We will always remember you, as will mankind for whose freedom you gave your young life. You gave your life for the sake of people's happiness. Eternal memory and glory to you. Rest in peace.' 'We swear,' answered the line of soldiers. There were three gun salutes. We felt a sacred hatred for the enemy in our hearts. In a way, the powerful artillery cannonade of our army that was driving our enemy to the west provided a suitable gun salute in honour of Andriy Rilskiy.

In the 1970s I sent Colonel Pavel Ryumin's book about the 16th assault brigade (where Andriy Rilskiy served) to the Writers' Union of Ukraine in Kiev with a request to forward it to Andriy's relatives as I didn't know their address in Kiev.[3] But I didn't get any reply and the book was never sent back to me.

In October 1944 I came to the town of. Dębica on a mission. The Germans had set up a firing range nearby for improving the V-2 rockets which they had used for bombing London. Our weapon designers were scouring the site excitedly, gathering various fragments and metal components from the V-2s to make similar rockets in Kaliningrad near Moscow.

In Poland assault unit officers like me were paid a decent salary in Polish złotys, so I ended up with a lot of money as there was nothing to buy at the front. In an empty street in Dębica I saw an old Polish man selling meringues. As I have a sweet tooth, I fell greedily upon them: I bought five or six meringues, ate them, then bought more and carried on until I had finished the whole tray, leaving one very surprised Polish man!

18

IN THE REAR IN POLAND
MEETING COLONEL POKRYSHKIN

In October 1944 our brigade was moved from the frontline and transferred to the rear. There in the forest we built dugouts, then reinforcements arrived and we did combat training. Among my scouts was a man from Siberia (a *Sibiryak*) who was a professional hunter. Colonel Pokryshkin, three times Hero of the Soviet Union, whose aircraft division was located on an airfield not far from us, learned about this. Pokryshkin arranged with our commanders for our experienced hunter to be in charge of hunting. There were plenty of animals in the forest—deer, elk, roe deer and boar. Because I couldn't allow one of my soldiers to leave the unit unaccompanied I went with him.

While hunting the hunter was in charge and everyone obeyed him without question, including Pokryshkin and his fellow com-

manders who included Glinka, Rechkalov and Klubov, all twice
Heroes of the Soviet Union (there were forty-six Heroes of the
Soviet Union in the division). Shortly afterwards, Klubov was
killed in battle and later buried on the Hill of Glory in Lvov.
Every time I go to the Hill of Glory I visit his grave. Pokryshkin
was in charge of the 9th aircraft division and he carried the ban-
ner of the 1st Ukrainian front in the victory parade in Red
Square in Moscow on 24 June 1945.

During one hunt I was standing behind a tree with my automatic gun at the ready. Suddenly I heard an ominous crackling
in the undergrowth to the side of the beaters and it was coming
nearer. It was clear that a wild boar was charging towards me—
and it was not a small one. I decided to stand my ground
although I felt uneasy as I remembered from hunters' stories that
a burst of automatic gunfire could not always kill a large wild
boar. A large boar is powerful and fierce with fifteen-centimetre
long tusks, and he is immensely agile and resilient. So he can
endure twelve to fifteen bullets without faltering, and even when
mortally wounded he will try to reach the hunter and tear him to
pieces with his huge tusks.

But I was lucky this time. I don't know why, but the boar
stopped fifteen metres short of me, stood still for a moment,
then galloped back. He must have taken me as a formidable
enemy and decided not to run any risks.

Grenades and Panzerfaust

I have already written that in my opinion every fifth person who
was killed during the war died as a result of their own carelessness and stupidity. Here is an example of my own stupidity. I
was walking alone through a field past some deserted trenches.
On my way I found a German grenade with a forty-centimetre
long handle. I spotted a large crater made by a bomb and decided

to throw the grenade into it. I assumed that the grenade would explode at the bottom of the crater and I would be safe.

The crater was about twenty metres away from me. I pulled out the safety pin, then lobbed the grenade into the crater. But it didn't go into the crater—it landed on a raised lip on the edge. I was dumbstruck. At once I threw myself flat on the ground, covering myself with my hands and my automatic gun. A thundering explosion followed and grenade fragments whizzed past me. But thank goodness nothing happened. I returned, safe and sound.

That wasn't the only example of my stupidity. At the end of 1944 the Germans had invented a powerful anti-tank weapon, the Panzerfaust 100.[1] Its warhead could penetrate a tank's twenty-centimetre metal armour or the fifty-centimetre thick brick wall of a house from a distance of eighty to a hundred metres. When we found these trophy Panzerfausts we quickly learned how to use them in battle. A Panzerfaust consists of a hollow one-metre long pipe with a cone-shaped shell at one end.

A German soldier with a Panzerfaust

You put the pipe on your shoulder and press the trigger and the five-kilogramme shell is launched from one end, while a four-metre long flame comes out of the other end, together with lots of smoke which covers everyone. But there is no recoil.

So in the presence of my soldiers, I decided, for no good reason, to fire a Panzerfaust which we had found on the roadside. I pulled the trigger, but instead of hearing a blast I only heard hissing. The shell flew out of the pipe and landed two metres away. We all fell down flat on the ground expecting it to detonate, and I had already said farewell to life—but the explosion never happened.

Once there was a session of the military tribunal in our battalion. A soldier had stolen an automatic gun with cartridges from a sleeping fellow soldier and given it to a Polish man in a nearby village in exchange for *samogon* (homebrew vodka), lard and bread. The guilty soldier was soon found out, the stolen weapon was returned and he had to stand trial.

The military tribunal was held in a forest clearing in front of the whole battalion. The trial was short—it lasted just an hour. After listening first to the accused and two witnesses describe the circumstances, and then to the military prosecutor (there was no one acting for the defence in accordance with the law during wartime), the members of the tribunal went aside, discussed the matter then pronounced the sentence: ten years' imprisonment. This was commuted to service in a penal company, so that the soldier could atone for his guilt with his blood.

19

MINE-LAYING IN POLAND

NEW YEAR 1945—LAYING MINES

I saw in the New Year of 1945, in the village of Pustynia, not far from the town of Mielec. All the officers of the battalion gathered together in a hut, had a drink, became very merry and danced to the accompaniment of an accordion. Suddenly the soldier on duty rushed into the hut. 'There's shooting at the medical unit!' he yelled. We grabbed our pistols and ran to the house where the medical unit was based. It turned out that two of our officers had downed quite a few drinks before going to the house to see Nurse Varya. They had a quarrel which resulted in a duel. They started shooting at each other in the dark. Fortunately all ended well and the culprits found themselves locked in a peasant's cellar overnight.

In Moscow thirty years later, I heard people speaking Polish in a household store near Kievsky Railway Station. 'Where are you from?' I asked. 'From Mielec,' they replied. 'Do you know Pustynia?' 'We certainly do,' they answered and stared at me in amazement. They couldn't believe that they would be reminded of a small Polish village in the great city of Moscow.

We were laying mines near this village along the front of our defences as our position was dangerously open to German tanks. As usual we were laying mines at night in the dark because this area was clearly visible to the enemy during the day. The mission was urgent and it had to be completed at all costs.

We carried out our task in the following way. A long cord with knots showing where the mines were to be laid was stretched out from the middle point of our defence, then other cords with knots were pulled out to the sides like branches. This overcame the problem of being unable to see in the dark, allowing mines to be placed in a grid as if on a chessboard. Different tasks were distributed among the sappers—some brought mines one in each hand (a mine weighs five kilos), while others bored holes in the frozen ground with pointed iron bars, pickaxes and axes. The holes were twenty centimetres deep and forty centimetres in diameter. The sergeant in command of the unit placed each mine in a hole, screwed in the explosive, then buried it and disguised it.

The frozen ground was very difficult to dig as it was hard as stone. Once I had sorted out the logistics I joined in and dug holes until my hands were bleeding. The minefield was big, about 200 metres wide. There were no rest breaks. As dawn approached we were exhausted. But no one complained. As well as laying mines, we had to mark out the area of the minefield on a local map, with reference to landmarks such as houses, trees, roads, the edge of forests and so on. That was done in daytime, but secretly.

It was almost morning and we were still out on the frontline when there was a bizarre incident. A lieutenant from the infantry in the nearby frontline trench appeared, bringing one of my soldiers under escort with his hands tied behind his back. The lieutenant asked me to identify the soldier. I confirmed that he was one of my subordinates, and the lieutenant and the escort party left. It turned out that the soldier had been carrying mines and lost his bearings in the dark, so instead of returning to us he had ended up on the wrong side. He said that as he had made his way back he blundered into a Bruno spiral (a thin spiralling barbed wire one metre high and about twenty-five metres long— if you attempt to go through one you get trapped in its coils), so for five minutes he wondered what was going on. There weren't any such spirals on our side. Then it dawned on him that he had gone to the enemy side by mistake. He went back, though not to his sappers but to the riflemen in the infantry trench who started shooting at him, taking him for a German scout. Only when they heard his four-letter curses did they realise that he was one of us.

Once at night the battalion deputy commander, Captain Petukhov, came to our base. He had decided that we were taking far too long to mine the frontline so, in front of all the soldiers, he hurled curses at our 2nd company commander, Lieutenant Khvarukia, using a string of four-letter words. Khvarukia was from the Caucasus and very hot tempered: he couldn't put up with such humiliation in front of his subordinates and went to a house nearby. Several minutes later, his orderly ran up and told us that Khvarukia had shot himself. We all rushed into the house. Khvarukia was lying on the bed wounded and shouting: 'Give me my pistol! I will kill myself. Life to the motherland, honour to nobody!' The bed and floor were covered with blood. The pistol lay on the floor. Khvarukia was hastily bandaged, lifted onto the cart that we used to transport mines and quickly taken to the battalion's medical unit. His wound was not lethal even though the bullet went near his heart.

FOR THE MOTHERLAND! FOR STALIN!

When in 1991 I was looking for addresses of veterans from our brigade in the military archive at Podolsk, I learned that Khvarukia had been posted to the far eastern island of Sakhalin before retiring from the army with the rank of lieutenant colonel and settling down in Odessa. I found his address in a local directory and went to visit him. But I was too late. His wife said Khvarukia had died four months previously. And that was it. I had lived in the same city as my company commander without knowing it.

While working in the archive I analysed our battalion's data to find out why people left the battalion. The reasons included: being killed; taken to hospital wounded or ill; sent to another unit; arrested by the secret service SMERSH; convicted by war tribunal; leaving for military school; or deserting.

Of interest are the causes of death. People were killed by artillery and mortar fire during bombardment, by snipers, by detonating mines or through carelessness with weapons; they were poisoned by methylated spirits captured from the Germans, killed in vehicle accidents, by exploding petrol tanks during electrical welding; or they were drowned during river crossings or struck by lightning; or they committed suicide.

POZ: the mobile mine-laying detachment

In early January 1945 our battalion was urgently sent to another part of the front. The front's high command had learned that the Germans had transferred scores of troops to that area and were preparing for an offensive which would start with a tank attack. I was to act as a POZ commander. POZ stands for *Podvizhnoy Otryad Zagrazhdeniya*, which was a mobile mine-laying detachment. The detachment's task was to mine an area in the path of German tanks, scattering anti-tank mines at one-metre intervals. To signal the start of our mission two white rockets were to be launched behind the forest where the rifle division's HQ was located. Our platoon had sixty mines. On each side of my platoon there was another platoon from our company with the same mission. It was extremely dangerous because we would be laying the mines in full view of moving enemy tanks which could fire at us with guns and machine guns. If a shell exploded nearby it could detonate the mines as the fuses had already been screwed in. Fortunately, this did not happen.

I remember that place very well. It was the site of an earlier tank battle. Three of our T-34 tanks and two German Panzers were standing there, motionless. The three graves of our tank crew weren't far away, comprising three small mounds of earth, each with a wooden pole bearing a plywood five-pointed star and a board with a surname, first name and patronymic. There was a senior lieutenant, born 1924; a lieutenant, born 1923; and a junior lieutenant, born 1922.

Their names were written in indelible pencil. I took off my cap and stood for a long time, thinking sadly that time would pass, that nobody would look after those lonely graves in a field in a foreign country. Rain would wash off the inscriptions, the poles would rot away, the heaped earth would sink and become level with the ground... There are so many of them, soldiers' graves with poles and stars, and sometimes without them, scattered on the way from Moscow to Stalingrad, from Berlin to Prague.

We spent ten long days and nights waiting for our signal. Every two hours the sentry was changed. We became tired of doing nothing.

The secret agent

One event brought some variety to our boring life. Senior Lieutenant Gushin, a SMERSH special agent, joined my platoon. The reason he came was that some days previously a young conscript from our battalion's new reinforcements from western Ukraine had tried to defect to the Germans. He had attempted to run up to the enemy's trench but was killed by a burst of machine gun fire.

So Gushin had come to carry out precautionary work with the soldiers and remind them of the inevitable fate of any traitors. Gushin's behaviour was always mysterious. He looked on everyone with suspicion—his profession had made an impact on him. But he worked with skill. No matter how hard we tried to find out who among us was his informer we did not succeed. Our only lead was the fact that some soldiers were occasionally summoned to clean floors or chop wood at the battalion's HQ, where Gushin could meet them unobserved.

His map holder where he kept his informers' data and reports was the apple of his eye; he guarded it even more closely than his pistol. Once he spent the night with the other officers around the bonfire. He must have been very tired; relaxing in the warmth of the fire, he nodded off and the map holder fell out from his hands. Some of my companions decided to play a joke. They put his map holder behind him. When he woke up and did not see it he grew increasingly worried and started to look around frantically. Then he found the map holder and calmed down. While it was happening we sat in silence, trying hard to resist laughing. But we knew that it would be very foolish to sour relations with such a dangerous man.

Now, looking back dozens of years later with all my experience of life, I realise that he was actually a decent man because during my ten months of service in the battalion no one was arrested for 'high treason and attempts to defect, or for praising German technology or better life in capitalist countries'—the reasons that many sly and underhand secret service agents gave for arrests in order to win orders and promotions for themselves.

At that time and later when I worked as a judge in a military tribunal I kept wondering why secret service agents had never tried to recruit me. I have always been active and sociable; I had (what was then) a rare quality—I fulfilled my duties honestly and conscientiously; I tried to follow the principles of Leo Tolstoy: always to speak the truth, keep my promises and to serve my motherland as much as I could. As any normal person with normal character I hated being a puppet and never succumbed to the herd instinct. As a result of my upbringing by my honest father and mother, my experience at school, pioneer camps, Komsomol and military school, and the influence of Pushkin, Lermontov, Chekhov and Nekrasov, I hated lies, meanness, cowardice and treason. The recruiters were mainly motivated by their love of the motherland and I loved the motherland more than my life. Most likely my qualities did not suit the secret agents—I was too straightforward.

Like many others, I knew about the wide network of secret informers within the military. There were one or two informers in each platoon of thirty to forty; among the five or six company officers one was inevitably a SMERSH secret agent.

I did not want to participate in that foul business and be a hypocrite, but neither did I want to be caught off guard. So just in case, I prepared a response if anyone attempted to recruit me. I knew just what to say on such an occasion: 'I love my motherland but I can't denounce my comrades and get rewarded for this because of my nature. Also I talk too much, I can let things slip out—especially when I am tipsy. But if I come across an enemy of the Soviet state, I will denounce him on my own initiative.'

20

A TANK RIDER OF THE
1ST UKRAINIAN FRONT

THE 1ST UKRAINIAN FRONT'S OFFENSIVE BEGINS

The signal to begin laying mines never came. Instead, early in the morning, we heard a powerful artillery cannonade from the Sandomierz foothold, far to the right of our position. Thousands of artillery weapons of various calibres were firing and we could hear the wild howling of Katyusha rockets. It all merged into one solid, deafening noise. Something incredible was going on there.

A contact arrived with an order that all officers should come to the battalion HQ immediately. There we were told that the 1st Ukrainian front's offensive had started. We must go on a fifty-kilometre forced march (seven kilometres per hour) to join the 22nd Nevel self-propelled artillery brigade of the 4th tank army.

After our infantry breached the enemy's fortified lines, the 4th tank army headed by Lieutenant General Lelushenko would

Boris, Poland, January 1945

attempt to break through the enemy's rear. Simultaneously, the 3rd guard tank army headed by Lieutenant General Ribalko would join the infantry's assault.

Our task as assault sappers riding on the tank armour was to provide technical support for the successful advance of our brigade. We did our bit to contribute to the brigade being awarded the title of 'the guard brigade' and later 'the Berlin brigade'. Sappers were necessary everywhere—in every reconnaissance and in every assault force.

The panic

On 12 January 1945 the 2nd assault sapper company, where I was a platoon commander and lieutenant, was transferred to the

A TANK RIDER OF THE 1ST UKRAINIAN FRONT

22nd Nevel self-propelled artillery brigade. The brigade had self-propelled 76-mm artillery guns, Valentine tanks and a division of 88-mm trophy German guns which we used as anti-tank weapons.

Our company, which comprised three platoons with a total of eighty people, was to provide technical support for the brigade's advance during the offensive. It took our company a day to walk to our destination and we set up camp at the foot of a hill where there were some old German trenches. The company commander Lieutenant Ryumin and his orderly went into the forest to establish links with the brigade which was based there. I was left in charge of the company. Along the unsurfaced road was an endless line of slow moving vehicles and horse-drawn carts.

Suddenly we heard sounds of a fierce battle on the other side of the hill, with shots and explosions from shells, tank guns and artillery weapons. Afterwards we saw people running down the hill in panic, vehicles began accelerating and cart drivers whipped their horses on, their faces distorted with fear. When we asked what had happened no one replied. There was just sheer panic!

A car braked near us. An officer jumped out. In front of our eyes, he smashed the flag pole of a banner against a post as it wouldn't fit in the car, then got back in and drove off.

What could we do? The shooting behind the hill continued. I could see the tension in my soldiers' faces; they were looking at me silently for a decision. My brain worked quickly. Those who were running away were non-combatants. We were a combat unit. We could not retreat. We had three anti-tank rifles and anti-tank grenades, hand-held machine guns and automatic guns. If we ran away from battle, we would face the tribunal and then the firing squad. The laws of war are harsh. That is why there could only be one decision. I gave the command: 'Prepare for battle!' But we didn't have to fight. The firing behind the hill had subsided.

When he returned, the platoon commander told us that a retreating German tank unit had run out of fuel and hidden in the forest. They were thrown barrels of fuel from planes. After refuelling they left the forest and drove onto the road where they started smashing into our unit's transport vehicles (the cars and carts), which blocked their line of retreat. One of our artillery units which happened to be on the road started fighting the tanks. But some of the tanks managed to break through and head west. When we entered the forest we saw three members of a German tank crew who had been captured by our self-propelled vehicle crew. To my surprise, although they were surrounded by a crowd of our soldiers, the German tank crew behaved in an insolent and arrogant way. But it was not 1941 anymore—it was now 1945.

The self-propelled artillery brigade

At first we were grouped into assault parties of two to three men riding on the self-propelled guns, the SU-76s. The SU-76 was based on our light T-70 tank chassis. It had wheels at the front and caterpillar tracks to the rear. It weighed ten tonnes, had a four-man crew and its weapons were 1943 models. Its firing range was 8,600 metres, with a speed of ten shots a minute, holding sixty shells as ammunition. The vehicle's front, top and sides were armoured, while the rear was covered with tarpaulin.

This self-propelled artillery brigade was one of the most distinguished during the war, and afterwards it would be listed on page 485 of the *Military Encyclopaedia of the Great Patriotic War 1941–45*, published in Moscow in 1985. It was headed by Colonel V Prikhodko who was killed when the brigade was bombed by German aircraft. The house where he was living at the time was destroyed by one of the bombs. His body was transported from Poland to Lvov and buried in the military cemetery on the Hill of

A TANK RIDER OF THE 1ST UKRAINIAN FRONT

Troops riding on an SU-76

Glory. After his death the brigade was headed by Lieutenant Colonel N. Kornushkin who was awarded the title of Hero of the Soviet Union for success in subsequent battles. The brigade was part of the 4th tank army after it was re-formed in June 1943.[1] As part of the 1st Ukrainian front, the 4th tank army took part in the liberation of Ukrainian and Polish territory on the right bank of the Vistula, the storming of Berlin and the liberation of Prague. Its members would include a total of 119 Heroes of the Soviet Union as well as twice awarded Heroes of the Soviet Union, Generals Lelushenko and Fomichev.

As troops on the self-propelled guns and tanks, our company joined the self-propelled artillery brigade in combat with a long raid deep into the enemy rear. The brigade was in the front detachment of the tank army and my platoon was on the offensive several times as part of the front patrol, with the objective of ensuring the successful advance of our tanks and self-propelled vehicles. My platoon of assault sappers comprised twenty-two people, including seven sergeants. We had one hand-held machine gun and one anti-tank rifle. The patrol comprised three tanks (accompanied by my platoon) which advanced two to three kilometres ahead of the brigade's main forces.

The front detachment of the 1st Ukrainian front consisted of a tank and self-propelled artillery brigade, an anti-tank division, an anti-aircraft division and our sapper company. Our combat tactic was as follows: after our infantry broke through three fortified enemy lines the tank army would swiftly advance deep into the enemy's rear, leaving the infantry eighty to a hundred kilometres behind. The front detachment and main units of the tank army would bypass areas showing strong resistance. As it stormed ahead, the tank army, comprising hundreds of tanks, self-propelled vehicles, armoured vehicles and artillery weapons, would kill any who resisted, throw enemy defences into disarray, intimidate the enemy and cause panic by breaking communications, halting supplies and disrupting the organisation of enemy troops. During the advance it was the 22nd self-propelled artillery brigade that liberated the towns of Milicz (22 January 1945), Rawitsch (now Rawicz) (23 January), Freystadt (now Kożuchów) (13 February) as well as scores of other towns and villages. By order of Stalin, gratitude was expressed to the troops who liberated these towns and twenty salvos of fireworks were fired from 224 weapons in Moscow in their honour.

Our sapper company's main task was to defend the tanks from German Faustpatrone. It was difficult for the tank crew to spot disguised Faustpatrone launchers through the narrow slots of the tank compartment, but it was possible for riflemen on the outside of the tank. That is why during the last stage of the war our tank crews always operated with additional troops riding on the tanks.

The British Valentine tanks, which had been delivered to our brigade as part of the USA's Lend-Lease policy, had very weak armour which was only sixty-six millimetres thick.[2] The Valentines were not very fast and as they had narrow caterpillar tracks they couldn't negotiate uneven territory. They were also highly inflammable because their engines were petrol-driven (Soviet tanks ran on diesel) and they were armed with just one 40-mm gun. The tanks weighed sixteen tonnes and had a four-man crew. Our own superb medium-sized tank, the T-34, was in a class of its own. It weighed thirty-two tonnes, had a five-man crew, an 85-mm gun, two 7.62-mm machine guns and wide caterpillar tracks which enabled it to move over open country. Its front armour was 110 millimetres thick, while its bottom armour was ninety millimetres and its speed was fifty-five kilometres per hour. It was a steel giant, emitting thundering gunfire and showers of lead from its two machine guns, blasting past all obstacles in its way.

The front patrol

After painting the general picture, let's return to my platoon. Three T-34 tanks are rattling loudly along in the front patrol. On each tank there are four or five assault sappers looking carefully at the road ahead for disguised anti-tank mines. Each mine contains five kilos of explosive (200 grammes of explosive can splinter a piece of rail). We, the sappers, are in a constant state of anxiety because at any moment an enemy anti-tank gun might open fire, and if we are hit even the most courageous among us will be blasted into pitiful fragments of flesh hanging from the bushes. Each man holds an automatic gun with a round of seventy-two cartridges; on his belt he has two F1 grenades, a spare round of cartridges and a sapper knife in a sheath. On his back he wears a backpack containing an anti-tank grenade, four or five explosives and a length of fuse. He keeps the detonators in his chest pocket. A platoon commander also has a TT pistol in its holster on his belt, binoculars around his neck, a watch on his left wrist and a compass on his right.

In front of us lies a wood—what is in there? As soon as we hear the first shots from enemy anti-tank guns and the rattling of machine guns we spring off the tanks and run forward, hiding behind our tanks and firing as we go.

One of our tanks stops to take aim at a target. The enemy is using every weapon available to fire at the tanks and therefore at us. The tank crew is in a better position behind their armour. Yet no one wants to swop places with them.

There are jokey suggestions: 'Hey trooper! Get into the tank!' But none of us takes up the offer. To us a tank is like an iron coffin. We feel much more comfortable outside, on Mother Earth. You can press yourself against her and cover yourself. The tanks are two and a half metres high, and the German artillerymen know their business well, unlike their counterparts in films, who are depicted as caricatures. In films our soldier kills five to six Germans in one burst of automatic fire, and there are no wounded. In real life there are three to four wounded for each person killed.

During the war, on average ten of our soldiers were killed for every German soldier killed. Marshal Zhukov appreciated many of the qualities of the German soldiers and officers. He wrote: 'A German soldier is literate, disciplined and brave in battle. The Germans resisted bravely and efficiently until the last days of the war, even though it was evident that the war was completely lost six months before it actually ended.'

On more than one occasion we witnessed an entire tank crew being killed by a shell breaking through the tank armour. When this happened the tank caught fire and a plume of black smoke rose a kilometre upwards. Sometimes the shell or Faustpatrone detonated the tank's supply of forty to fifty shells and there would be a horrific explosion. In one case, the tank broke into parts and its turret was hurled twenty to thirty metres to the side, and once a turret and its gun was embedded in the ploughed earth. In such cases nothing was left of the crew. There was no one to bury. Only a crumpled medal for courage could be found.

A TANK RIDER OF THE 1ST UKRAINIAN FRONT

So the tank crew wasn't to be envied: somehow it's easier to die outside, on the earth, rather than in the iron coffin.

What does a man feel as he rides on the outside of a tank that rushes into attack amid squalls of gunfire? Nothing good. Each attack is a potential encounter with not just one, but with hundreds of deaths. Your nerves are strained to the limit, your brain works in overdrive. All your concentration and attention are directed onto your surroundings. You must be resolute in your actions. And you must never, ever show your subordinates that you are afraid, or at a loss.

In the rules of war you have special powers during battle. If an order is not carried out you have the right to shoot the transgressor without prior investigation or trial. Somehow we never thought about heroism or awards. We simply clenched our teeth and went into battle with the aim of following our orders and annihilating the hated enemy. The instinct for self-preservation also kicked in: if you don't kill your enemy, he will kill you. It was said long ago that the true warrior is not the one who is unafraid, but the one who can suppress his fear.

Numerous skirmishes with the enemy left us exhausted. We had to have superhuman stamina that was verging on the incredible. Soldiers were deathly tired after so many long days of tension with hardly any sleep or rest and no hot meals, constantly out in the biting frosty air on the cold armour of a moving tank where they could fall asleep at any time. There were cases of soldiers who fell asleep falling off moving tanks.

I am coming back to my story. We passed the wood without complications. There was a small town ahead. Once again everyone was in a state of tension. Our automatic guns and the hand-held machine gun on the tank turret were primed. I was sitting on the front tank. Someone on the middle tank noticed something, so three of our soldiers rushed into a house where they found two unarmed elderly German soldiers with red crosses on their sleeves, possibly members of an ambulance patrol. One of the Germans was put on my tank—he looked worried and met our eyes questioningly, as if expecting to read his fate.

On noticing that one of our soldiers was looking at his watch, the German took it off his wrist and gave it to him. Another soldier touched the German's sweater which he wore under his coat. The German took off his sweater and gave it to him. Our soldier took it willingly as we didn't have sweaters. Trying to make ourselves understood, the tank platoon commander and I asked the German about the situation around us and we gathered that there were no large enemy units nearby. We couldn't find out more as our German was quite poor.

After speaking on the radio to the brigade commander, the tank platoon commander ordered the tank commanders to advance along the roads on either side of the town to carry out a reconnaissance. The Germans were taken off the tanks and kept under guard in the central square.

When our tank came back to the square we saw those two Germans with their red cross bands lying in the flowerbed, shot dead. Who had shot them and why? I would never know. But where would we keep prisoners like them when we were in the deep rear of the German line ourselves, always on the move? It would be dangerous to send them back to our own forces, under guard, because there could be more retreating German units behind us.

By the end of the war, as far as we Russians were concerned, we valued each and every soldier. We had almost no reinforcements: it even happened that when a POW camp was liberated the brigade conscripted all those who could hold a weapon. Some were killed in battle and lay in the snow in their dark civilian clothes because there was no opportunity to give them a military uniform. Some were killed before their names could be added to the lists of military personnel, and they would remain unknown because POWs didn't have any identification documents.

A TANK RIDER OF THE 1ST UKRAINIAN FRONT

Once, as we moved from one place to another on the front, we saw the bodies of sixty or seventy Germans lying in a pile. Our forces hadn't bothered to lead them to a POW compound but had simply shot them. People might say that I shouldn't write about such things. But it did happen.

In yet another case, a German POW, who could have been a colonel judging by his imposing physique and the epaulettes on his shoulders, was forced, by a tank crew, to run in front of their tank for fun. The tank commander was sitting on the front of the tank and threatening the runner with his pistol. The German finally wore himself out and fell down under the tank's caterpillar tracks. There was a 'CRACK' as his skull was crushed. All those on the tank regarded this episode as perfectly normal, and they would not have understood any objections. Only in films is war waged in white gloves and the horrors not shown.

I remember one case especially well. One early February morning as dawn broke, a tank formation with troops on the tank armour stopped on an earth track in a field. The mist was spreading. You couldn't see further than fifty metres. At the head of the formation, the commanders, holding torches, were working out the route on the map. Suddenly a guard from another unit came up with three German POWs, his automatic gun at the ready. The group stopped near our tank. With shouts and gestures the guard ordered the Germans to remove their high boots. It was obvious to any spectators that afterwards they would be shot.

The Germans were taking off their boots when one of them, who wasn't wearing high boots, suddenly pushed the guard over and began to run away. The guard rose to his feet, shot the other two before they could escape and started shooting at the running man. Our automatic gunners who were sitting on the tanks also started firing at him. As the bullets hit the frozen earth they sent up sparks and the German ran as if in a halo of fire. Soon he disappeared into the mist.

By then, it had become normal to shoot Germans who were surrendering during battle. In battle you become brutalised. You're running into attack with your automatic gun, your finger on the trigger, and you see a German in front of you, with his hands up, his automatic gun at his feet. He shouts: 'Drei Kinder!' ('Three children!'). You shoot him in a burst of automatic fire and carry on running, without even considering whether he can shoot you from behind if he is still alive.

> In harsh times we must become harsh
> And kill without mercy
> Those who would enslave our children
> And desecrate our soul

> When hawks swoop down, you cannot be a dove
> A dove will die in vain
> No one should call us murderers
> For killing murderers in battle

I remember another case; during our offensive a young woman, who was the 10th brigade's medical instructor, went into a shed to have a pee. Suddenly she ran out, shouting: 'There's a German in there!' Soldiers nearby rushed into the shed and brought out a Kalmyk man in German uniform.[3] During the German retreat he was left behind by his unit and when he saw Russian tanks enter the village he decided to hide in the shed. The woman ordered him to walk out of the village and followed him, holding a trophy woman's Browning rifle. Then she shot the Kalmyk in the back of the head and he fell silently to the ground. The order to board the vehicles was given and everyone hurried away. No one was surprised.

We also knew about the time when the commander of a neighbouring tank company lined up the POWs. They were Vlasovists. He shot every second person until his pistol ran out of cartridges (there are seven cartridges in a pistol). Nobody dared object. How could you object if you knew that the

Germans had taken his next-of-kin hostage and shot them? In the occupied region of Kiev the Germans would shoot 100 hostages for each German killed by the partisans.

I remember Kornushkin, our brigade commander, during our offensive (by then we had been advancing for two and a half months and covered 700 kilometres, with battles almost non-stop) when he gathered officers from the brigade and other units and read out the order of the front commander, Marshal Konev, which forbade the shooting of prisoners because if the Germans found out about this it would harden their resistance. Kornushkin's comment was: 'Well, if you decide to shoot him, why shoot him on the road? Take him to the side and shoot him there.' You will never see such a scene in a film, or read about it in a book. This is among the reasons why veterans, when remembering the war, can't hold back their tears. The cruelty during the war is impossible to describe—it can only be experienced.

In mid-January 1945, during the Sandomierz-Silesian offensive, the 22nd Nevel self-propelled artillery brigade, with assault sappers on the tank armour, liberated a small village near the Polish town of Kielce. After the battle we spent the night in houses, which was very unusual during an offensive. That night it was −5–6°C.

Early in the morning my unit commander, Sergeant Andreyev, came into the house and said: 'Comrade lieutenant, follow me. I want to show you something interesting.' We walked about fifty metres up the road and in the ditch he showed me a German corpse lying in the water under thin ice. On seeing my bewilderment, he said: 'Look! There's a watch on his wrist and it's still working.' I looked carefully. And indeed, there, in the water under the ice, the watch's second hand was still moving around the face. What technology! Having admired this wonder (it was a Swiss watch), we left. For us it was out of the question to take it as a trophy. During war, when death is everywhere, people believe in omens. We felt that taking that watch from the dead man would be looting and this would bring bad luck.

One of the tank brigades in the 4th tank army, the 62nd guard tank brigade, was awarded the title of Kieletskaya in honour of its participation in the liberation of Kielce. It had already been given the title of Molotovskaya because it was formed in March 1943 from volunteers from the town of Molotov.

Since 1780 the town had been called Perm, but in 1940 it was re-named Molotov, the party nickname for V.M. Scriabin, who had been a member of the Communist Party since 1906. In 1957, aged sixty-seven, Molotov was expelled from the party for his anti-communist behaviour and the town and tank brigade were subsequently renamed Perm and Permska.

For those interested in the history of the war, I can say that in the battle for the liberation of such a small town as Kielce, which had no natural obstacles or defensive fortifications, a surprisingly powerful Soviet force was deployed, consisting of four rifle divisions (comprising three rifle regiments and one artillery regiment as well as six separate units and battalions: anti-tank, anti-aircraft, sapper, reconnaissance, communications and a medical unit); two artillery divisions (a total of five artillery and mortar brigades); three aircraft bomber divisions (six air regiments in total); two tank brigades and two tank regiments; one artillery brigade and nine artillery, semi-propelled artillery, anti-tank and anti-aircraft regiments; one communications regiment and three communications battalions; one special regiment of trained dogs; and four separate sapper and flamethrower battalions. In total, there were six brigades, thirty regiments and thirty-four battalions.

In honour of Kielce's liberation, twenty-eight military units were given the title of Kieletskaya and thirty-two units were awarded orders. All the personnel and troops who took part were given official thanks, and in Moscow twenty salvos from 224 guns were fired in their honour by order of the Supreme Commander, Stalin.

A TANK RIDER OF THE 1ST UKRAINIAN FRONT

On 23 January 1945 our front detachment rushed into battle in the German town of Rawitsch (now Rawicz in Poland), deep in the enemy rear. A battle in a town is the most dangerous scenario for tanks. In towns a tank and any assault troops riding on its armour are highly vulnerable. It is practically impossible to manoeuvre, and the enemy can fire Faustpatrone or throw anti-tank grenades from any window, roof, balcony or basement.

Having been caught off guard in the early morning, the Germans rushed out of the houses in panic, some just wearing underwear, and ran along the streets, firing randomly. They were so bewildered by the sudden attack that they couldn't put up any organised resistance. Most of them were killed by firing from tank and machine guns and assault sappers' automatic guns. Only a few could escape. Some hid in basements, attics, wardrobes and sheds, only to be caught by our troops who were ransacking houses in search of trophies.

Once in the mid-1980s I came home one evening and my daughter Masha told me that some Polish tourists had called for me. They came from Rawicz and were staying in the Krasnaya Hotel. They had invited me to come and see them the next day. Accompanied by a fellow veteran from the 68th tank brigade, I took a bottle of vodka to the hotel and met the Poles. Several years earlier, I had sent my congratulations to the people of Rawicz on the anniversary of their town's liberation by our brigade, but I hadn't received a reply. And now the Poles had found me!

But I was disappointed. They were members of a tourist party, about twenty or thirty years old—all born after the war. What should I talk about? I told them about the liberation of Rawicz and the route which our tank company had taken through the town to the western railway station. After a bottle of vodka the conversation became very lively! A Polish man who had been about ten years old during the liberation kept asking me whether I had been on the first or second tank when our tanks were moving up his street, with assault sappers firing at running German soldiers from guns, machine guns and automatics.

I couldn't remember which tank I was sitting on. During the 1st Ukrainian front's offensive of January–March 1945 our brigade was in the front detachment of the 4th tank army. We were in the frontline and we liberated dozens of towns and villages. When I asked, 'Does it matter?', the Polish man explained that when the tanks were passing his house, an assault soldier on the second tank released a burst of automatic gunfire at the window where he was standing looking out at the street, but fortunately the bullets flew ten centimetres above his head and didn't hit anyone. I had to run quickly to the nearest shop to buy another bottle of vodka in order to restore Soviet-Polish friendship! (The Polish like free drinks even more than the Russians!) We said goodbye and promised to keep in touch, but none of us kept our promise. And so the accursed war would still stir up bad memories many years later. I didn't tell the Polish man that at the end of 1944 the Germans had invented the Faustpatrone, the anti-tank weapon that could be used by a single soldier. During battles in towns German soldiers fired Faustpatrone at tanks from roofs, attics, windows, basements, fences and any other cover. That is why before an offensive we were instructed to immediately fire our automatics wherever we saw the slightest movement—which is exactly what our assault trooper had done.

21

THE ADVANCE INTO GERMANY

HOW WE WERE FEARED!

As we approached, German civilians evacuated their villages and fled to the west. For a 100-kilometre stretch the villages were empty. Chickens and geese roamed around the yards. Hungry and thirsty pigs were squealing in pigsties. Dogs howled.

I came to a good solid village house with a corrugated iron roof. On the table, covered with a clean tablecloth, there was a meal of bread, homemade biscuits, sausages, vegetables and pickles. Knives, forks and spoons were laid out, with a bowl of salt. The Germans had been waging wars with their neighbours for their entire 1,000-year history, so they knew all too well what a soldier needed during war. To stop such a soldier kicking up a row and smashing up the house the owners had prepared everything for his meal. At first the political commissars issued a strict warning to soldiers not to eat the food, which could be poisoned, but then the first 'Ivan' tried the food and it was all right, so everyone eventually tucked in. In fact, the only cases of poisoning were those caused by drinking methylated spirits, which could be found in a factory, a workshop or at a railway station. The result was blindness then death, and it was impossible to save the victims. But there were only a few such cases, and just at the beginning.

After 100 kilometres we started to come across people who hadn't managed to run away. People from the village gathered in several neighbouring houses, waiting in horror for the appearance of the awful avenging conquerors. When you come into such a house dozens of eyes stare at you, frozen in fear. Some villagers start trembling.

The propaganda produced by Goebbels had depicted the soldiers of the Red Army as fearful savages with fangs sticking out of their mouths, narrow eyes and horns on their dishevelled heads.

Red Army soldiers in winter uniform

We certainly looked unsightly: we wore felt boots, padded trousers and short sheepskin coats; on our heads were dirty *ushanka* (Russian caps with earflaps); warm mittens dangled from strings; on our belts we had a grenade and a Finnish knife, and we held automatic guns. We had alert, unfriendly expressions on our raw red faces. Our faces were red from constant exposure to the cold frosty air, and our eyes were red and sore from sleep deprivation. I remember an episode in Rawitsch, where we had been stationed for three days waiting for our brigade's infantry and rear units. During our ten-day offensive our kitchen wagons had been left hopelessly behind, so we had to eat anything we could find in German houses, including Christmas presents which soldiers took as trophies. There were rusks, biscuits, sausages and chocolates which we gobbled up very quickly.

We needed hot food badly. Our stomachs were burning from our cold, dry diet. On the morning of the second day my aide, Sergeant Major Korolyov, left the house where we were staying and spotted a small flock of chickens in the yard opposite. Korolyov suggested going into the house and asking the owners to cook us chicken soup. We went into the house which was evidently the residence of a wealthy person. Out of curiosity, we walked around the rooms. Everything was intact: large wardrobes and cupboards, expensive crockery, big mirrors and a hall with a fireplace. On the walls were drawings and oil paintings of ancestors in full dress uniforms, with orders and medals, hunting rifles and daggers, and heads of wild boar and stags with huge branching antlers.

We were met by two German women—one was about thirty or forty years old, the other older. They were bewildered and trembling with fear. They couldn't understand our request, no matter how hard we tried, using gestures and pointing at the chickens running around the yard and the cooking pot. They just trembled even more in panic and horror. In the end we had hot tea with bread and butter. When we were about to leave the younger woman made a gesture inviting me to follow her to a separate room. I followed her out of interest into a bedroom and she started to undress near the bed. When I realised what she was driving at I protested strenuously. She was bewildered, then she started tugging off her big golden wedding ring convulsively. At any other time I would have taken up her offer, but at that moment, wishing to be consistent, I objected and we left. The next day the older German woman saw me in the street and, gesturing energetically, invited me into the house. She led me into the same bedroom where, on the floor covered with yellow sand, I made out the contours of a human body under a white sheet. I raised the edge of the sheet and saw the naked younger woman. Our peaceful visit the day before had affected her so much that her heart had failed and she had died.

Damn the war and those who started it!

Our offensive had started again. We were the first to make our way across Germany. On the highway ahead there was a long convoy of refugees. They travelled on long carts with high sides drawn by two horses. Each cart was loaded with hay, with old people, women and children sitting on the top surrounded by suitcases and knotted bundles of household goods and other belongings. A foal or colt would run alongside the cart while a cow, roped to the back, walked behind.

As we came nearer the refugee convoy, consisting of fifteen to twenty carts, stopped to let us by, moving onto the verge with trees along the side. The left wheels of the carts were still on the road. As usual I was standing on the front tank, behind the turret, and my men were sitting on the armour next to me. Suddenly our tank, approaching a cart, moved sharply to the right and crashed into its left wheels. The cart was upturned and toppled over into the trees. The cracking of broken wood, the wild, desperate shouts and screams of people falling off, horses neighing, cows mooing, everything was blended in a bloodcurdling howl along the whole convoy.

Sometime later, when we stopped to rest, I asked Sergei, the senior mechanic who was driving the tank, why he did it. He answered: 'For Kharkov.' 'Why for Kharkov?' I asked. 'Because during the second occupation of Kharkov, the SS men[1] arranged round-ups in the market square, took hostages and with rifle butts and Alsatian dogs they herded people into lorries—old people, women, children—and locked the doors. When the lorries were moving they released gas—carbon monoxide—and the people were poisoned and their bodies were dumped into a deep ravine in the suburbs where POWs covered them with earth. My mother was killed in that way. Have you got any more questions?' I didn't have any more questions.

In Rawitsch something happened to me which I remember very clearly. After crossing the entire town during constant fighting under the command of Lieutenant Kuzmin, our tank company gained control of the railway station, cutting off a route for German retreat. During the ferocious battle the tanks of the brigade and my sappers killed about 300 and took 250 prisoners. We also captured valuable equipment: two trains loaded with ammunition, 400 vehicles, five guns and five warehouses storing fuel and ammunition. For their superior skills and heroism Kuzmin and his mechanic and tank driver, Katchalin, were awarded the title of Hero of the Soviet Union.

At night I wasn't sleeping, as usual, and every hour or two I checked the guards at their posts. Seeing a light in one of the station windows, I decided to check who was there. I came up to the gate by the corner of the station building and was about to step onto the platform when I bumped into a German as tall as me who had suddenly emerged from the corner of the building.

In a patriotic war film I would have caught him by the throat and strangled him. But this wasn't a film: it was real life. In real life it happened so suddenly that I stepped back. The German did the same, then he turned and started running. I quickly took my pistol from its holster and shot an entire round of seven bullets at him. He fell. Hearing the shots, my soldiers ran up. The German was dead. Once I had recovered from the excitement I went to the part of the building where I had seen the light. The light turned out to be a candle in the post room where two of my soldiers were rummaging through parcels for trophies.

Some people might regard my behaviour as unheroic and if they were in my place they might have embarked on a hand-to-hand fight. Perhaps... But you can only judge my behaviour if you have found yourself in a similar situation.

Before the next tank attack with assault sappers the commander of the brigade, Hero of the Soviet Union Colonel Kornyushkin, read the list of those recommended for awards and orders for courage in front of a dozen soldiers and commanders, to the accompaniment of sounds from a nearby battle.

I was recommended for the Order of the Red Banner and the Order of the Red Star. My soul glowed with patriotic pride. We immediately went into battle and fought heroically, and the proof of it lay in the many towns and villages which we liberated from the Germans, as the five orders glittered gold on the red banner of our Nevel (later renamed Berlin) self-propelled artillery brigade.

Later I found out that my name wasn't put on the list of recommendations for awards thanks to the negligence of a clerk at HQ, so I never received the award which I deserved and my award papers, which were signed by all the competent high commanders, now lie forever in folders on dusty shelves in the archive of the Russian Ministry of Defence in Podolsk.

At a reunion of veterans from the 4th guard tank army in Moscow on 9 May 1984, I met Nicholai Kornyushkin, our former brigade commander and lieutenant colonel (now retired), and told him that his recommendation for my award back in

February 1945 was never met because of the negligence or malicious intent of bureaucrats and clerks. He sympathised, saying that during the war there were many good and heroic deeds, but also much injustice.

He told me that he too hadn't received what he deserved: during the war he was in charge of the famous self-propelled brigade and, after the war, of the 180th motor rifle division where the commander is supposed to have the rank of general. But he was only made a lieutenant colonel, even though he had commanded both of these military units for a long time and with much success. At the same time, he said, Stalin's cook was a lieutenant general and the head huntsman at Stalin's estate in Zavidovo in the Moscow region was a major general.

We stayed in Rawitsch for three days. Our offensive was temporarily halted. We were 100 kilometres ahead of our infantry, and we were running out of fuel and ammunition (shells, cartridges and grenades), so it was risky to advance further.

When the infantry reached Rawitsch, accompanied by our brigade's rear units, we handed over the wounded and took ammunition and fuel for tanks and vehicles. A month later, the 22nd self-propelled artillery brigade joined the 2nd echelon of the front detachment of the 4th tank army and our platoon of assault troops was transferred to the 93rd tank brigade which would advance in the 1st echelon of the front detachment of the tank army.

I must say that during the war, awards, which played a very important part in our life of combat, were the responsibility of commissars and political wheeler dealers, the clerks at HQ, who, as a rule, didn't take part in battles themselves but hid in the rear, turning up to their offices only once battle was over. But they were the first to reward themselves. In an analysis of the number of awards given they received the highest number while the lowest went to those who directly fought the enemy on the front.

Reconnaissance

In late January 1945 the 4th tank army swiftly crossed the Oder and established a bridgehead on the left bank. The Germans made a great effort to win back the bridgehead, as it would be very important for our future offensive, but all their attacks were successfully repelled by our forces.

We received a message from high command that according to air reconnaissance a large motorised German tank formation was advancing towards us along the right bank of the Oder with the aim of cutting off our troops fighting on the bridgehead from their bases and supplies. It goes without saying that it is impossible to fight without shells and cartridges.

At night the brigade commander summoned me and our tank platoon commander (who was in charge of three T-34 tanks) to explain our mission to us. We were to follow the road along the river towards the German formation and engage it in battle, so gaining time for our brigade to construct strong defences, including trenches for motorised riflemen and firing positions for artillery. We didn't have time to think. My assault sappers jumped onto the tanks and we moved ahead in pitch darkness, our caterpillar tracks rattling along the cobbled road. We understood that we were being sacrificed. But war is war. Small sacrifices bring big gains. This is the cruel law of war.

The racket from our tank engines could be heard for tens of kilometres in the still of the night. All of us were tense. We didn't notice the cold as we sat on the tanks' frozen armour in the frosty wind. Once the Germans heard us they would certainly get ready for battle by mining the road and preparing their anti-tank guns (a German 88-mm anti-tank gun could break through the armour of a T-34 tank).

If a tank hit a mine the assault sappers, if not ripped apart in the explosion, would suffer severe shell shock because of the powerful effect of the blast. There was no medical staff with us, so no one could have given qualified medical help to the badly wounded. We understood our situation perfectly well, holding our automatic guns tightly as we looked into the darkness, anxious and trying to see what lay ahead. We would fight our hateful enemy until we had shed the last drop of our blood... But all ended well. After about fifteen kilometres we received the radio command to halt from our brigade commander, so we stopped and prepared for battle, but nothing happened, and then at daybreak we returned to our brigade. For some reason the German formation never approached us.

Once, when we were moving from one part of the front to another, our tank brigade stopped for lunch in the forest. Groups of soldiers were cooking lunch on fires near the tanks. An unknown soldier suddenly appeared, playing a harmonica. Telling jokes, he moved from one group to another. No one suspected a thing. Then he vanished. Half an hour later, nine bombers flew over on a raid. The bombs were falling on us, but we hadn't dug any trenches and had to take shelter under our tanks. In spite of this people were killed and wounded. Several days later, we learned from our counter-intelligence SMERSH officer that the soldier was a German spy. He was caught and shot without trial after revealing the location of the radio which he had used to summon the bombers.

The offensive in Silesia

> Our enemy called us 'red devils';
> Our friends called us the 'guards of the front';[2]
> But we simply called ourselves
> A sapper company.

The Sandomierz-Silesian operation (part of the Vistula-Oder offensive) was carried out from 12 January to 3 February 1945 from the Sandomierz foothold. The German front was breached—

the opening was seventy-five kilometres wide. The 1st and 4th Ukrainian fronts, and the 1st Belarus front took part in the operation.

The 1st Ukrainian front, under the command of Marshal Konev, comprised eleven armies including two tank armies and one aircraft army. Areas in south-west Poland were liberated and military operations moved onto German territory. Our troops crossed the Oder and established a base on its west bank. For their excellent performance during this operation 246 units were awarded honourable names after the towns which they had liberated and 350 units were awarded orders. For the twenty-three days and nights of the offensive our troops advanced 500 kilometres, covering an average of twenty-five kilometres per day while engaging in battles during which huge numbers of Nazi troops were destroyed.

The Lower Silesian operation followed, from 8 to 24 February 1945. Starting from the Oder foothold, the troops on the 250-kilometre-wide front advanced 100 kilometres to the River Neisse and surrounded the fortified towns of Breslau (now known as Wrocław) and Głogów.

After a short break the Upper Silesian operation took place from 15 to 31 March 1945. The opening artillery bombardment lasted for ninety minutes. Tens of thousands of shells, mines and bombs were dropped on the enemy positions. Five Nazi positions were surrounded and destroyed; 280 tanks and assault guns and 600 field guns were destroyed or captured; 40,000 Germans were killed and 16,000 were taken prisoner.

As well as our 4th guards tank army, three armies, one rifle corps and one aircraft army took part in the Upper Silesian operation. In total, there were thirty-one rifle divisions, 988 tanks and self-propelled guns, and 1,737 planes from the 2nd aircraft army. In all three operations we were in the front section of the 4th guard tank army. For a week at the beginning of

March the tank brigade and the entire 4th army were withdrawn from battle to carry out repairs on equipment, and to receive reinforcements of personnel and ammunition.

During that week the 4th tank army received a new T-34 tank, the gift of Maria Orlova. She had asked Supreme Commander Stalin to give the tank to the 6th guard mechanised corps, which was under the command of her son, Vasiliy Orlov (born 1916). Her request was granted.

With Junior Lieutenant Kashnikov as commander, this tank took part in the battle of Berlin and in the liberation of Prague, destroyed ten enemy tanks, one self-propelled gun, several armoured vehicles and cars, and killed about 300 German soldiers. Our political commissars told us about the family history of the Orlovs. The head of the family, Fedor, was commander of the people's militia division near Moscow. Their eldest son, Vladimir, fought the enemy near Leningrad and was killed defending the city. They had two other sons: Vasiliy was the commander of the mechanised corps, while Yevgeniy was in charge of an anti-tank rifle company. Their daughter Maria was fighting in the famous female regiment of night bombers, under the command of Hero of the Soviet Union Marina Raskova. The new tank was named *Motherland*. After the war it was put on a pedestal in Berlin near the entrance of the building in Karlshorst where the act of complete and unconditional surrender of Nazi Germany was signed on 9 May 1945.[3]

But great sacrifices were made to achieve this victory. On 18 March, twenty-nine-year-old Vasiliy Orlov was seriously wounded and later died while repelling an enemy tank counter-attack near the town of Neisse (now Nysa, Poland). He was awarded the posthumous title of Hero of the Soviet Union and was buried in Novodevichy cemetery in Moscow.[4] My platoon also suffered many casualties. During an attack on a German village which had been fortified by German troops, a section commander, Sergeant Kyril Andreev, was mortally wounded and fell off the tank armour. I ordered a soldier to jump off the tank to help him while we continued to advance. After the battle the soldier caught up with us and told us that a bullet had entered Andreev's head and that he was already dead. The soldier had buried him, keeping his documents for our records.

While our brigade was being transferred to another part of the front we set up camp in a German village for the night where I met a group of soldiers who were passing by. They told me that they were from the 111th rifle division which I had fought with at Rzhev in July 1942, and had then left after being wounded. I also found out that my 532nd rifle regiment was billeted in a village three kilometres away and I could see the lights in the distance. Although it was dark and I was tired and didn't know the terrain I went straight to that village, cross-country through the snow. I was so eager to meet my comrades and find out what had happened to them. When I found the regiment I discovered that none of my comrades from 1942 were still there except for the head of supplies, but he was away. But I didn't regret going to the village. It was a great pleasure for me to visit my first regiment. In the morning I returned to my brigade and slept on the moving tank. My soldiers had to hold me on to stop me falling off as the tank jolted and jerked. After the war I managed to find only two veterans from the 532nd regiment.

During our stop for lunch we learned that the post had come and we could send parcels. This was the first time throughout the war that I had been able to send a parcel. My father, mother and brother were in Dubno. I didn't know what to send to them. I had nothing apart from my rucksack in which I kept my wash kit, some spare underwear, grenades and cartridges. But I still sent a parcel with a trophy camera, a short sheepskin coat and some darning thread which my soldiers had obtained from a village shop. The parcel reached my family: the camera was later stolen from my father by a worker repairing the house; the short sheepskin coat lay around unworn for fifty years; and the thread was used for darning socks and stockings. I used the camera to take photos of me and my comrades-in-arms. My father developed the film. Those were the only photos I took during the war. I still keep them in my photo album.

The deputy commander of the battalion in charge of supplies and ammunition, Captain Movergan, was tragically killed. He died in an absurd way, as so often happens in war. At this stage of the war we didn't dig trenches during offensives, knowing that we would soon be advancing beyond them. The frontline of our position wasn't indicated on the road. Movergan was in a lorry with his driver and they couldn't make out where we were, so they ended up crossing the frontline. Our soldiers shouted, yelled and fired shots behind the lorry which was heading off to the German side, but to no avail. As it approached the German frontline the lorry came under fire. Movergan and the driver got out and started running, but they were killed and the lorry went up in flames. It all took place in front of our eyes, but we couldn't do anything as it happened so quickly.

In March 1945 the 3rd company of our battalion suffered a great misfortune. The company commander, Captain Zilberberg, the platoon commander, Lieutenant Paukov, and the company sergeant major, Karpenko, together with the military engineer of the 68th guard tank brigade, Major Korneev, died while attempting to take apart a one-metre long German anti-tank mine. They were all sitting in the trench when the mine exploded. We were told about it by an eyewitness, the company commander's orderly, who had sensibly left them to it and so remained alive. All the rules and regulations had been broken. There was no need to take the mine apart. They had tried to do it purely out of professional curiosity. The sapper's job is considered the most dangerous of all: according to the regulations, a sapper must work alone, away from his comrades, and when in danger he cannot rely on them but must find the way out of the situation himself. The deaths of Movergan, his driver, Zilberberg and his comrades made all of us very sad. However, there was no time for sadness during the war. We had to keep fighting.

The closer to final victory we came the stronger was our determination to survive and witness it with our own eyes and live in a time of peace. Never before had the possibility of dying or being maimed seemed so cruel and unfair as during those final months and weeks of battles. In the army people thought it was easier to die in 1941 or 1942, but I don't agree. To die in a swamp near Rzhev in 1942 without knowing whether victory would come or whether your sacrifice was in vain was much more unfair.

Our company commander, Lieutenant Ryumin, who became a lieutenant colonel after the war and also a writer (he was a member of the Union of Writers of the Soviet Union), wrote a poem which conveys the atmosphere of that time. He dedicated this poem to me:

Assault Force
to Boris Bogachev

For days we clung to the rough metal of our tanks
Bound for Berlin not for glory
But for the survival of Russia herself.
Our command
To shake up the SS rear.
Our rucksacks were packed with TNT.
The battlefield was ridged and cratered
No rescue was in sight.
With a jolt I was thrown to the ground,
My revolver still in my hand.
Missiles screamed overhead.
Snipers took aim at us.
Tanks hit land mines
And exploded into flames.

THE ADVANCE INTO GERMANY

You can't say it wasn't terrible
To see their Tiger tanks advance...
The shells whistling down on our gun turrets
And ripping them apart
Still resound in my mind.

We were given an order to comb the forest for Germans. In a line ten to fifteen metres apart from each other, in full readiness for battle, prepared to open fire, our fingers on the triggers of our automatic guns, we walked two kilometres through the forest. It's a very unpleasant sensation as you constantly feel that you are the enemy's target. But all ended well.

I recall another episode in the same offensive. The tank battalion headed by Hero of the Soviet Union, Major Ivan Medved, was quickly moving towards the enemy's rear (Medved would be killed in battle a few days later). A unit of assault sappers from our 2nd company headed by Sergeant Kukhtik rode on the tanks at the front to ensure the safe advance of the tank battalion. They saw a narrow river ahead, which was a serious obstacle for the tanks. We could see German soldiers running over the bridge, then smoke appeared. This meant that the bridge had been mined, the fuse had been lit and the whole thing was due to explode any minute. Under cover of fire from our tank guns, Kukhtik, the target of heavy enemy fire, ran up to the bridge, cut the fuse and crawled back to safety. But he didn't manage to do it properly and the fuse soon started burning again. Kukhtik, risking his life, rushed back to the bridge and cut the burning Bickford fuse yet again. The bridge, prepared by the Germans for demolition, was saved. The tank battalion successfully reached the opposite bank and swiftly moved into battle. Then the whole tank brigade of the front detachment of the 4th tank army crossed the bridge.

According to the practice of the time, the reward for such a heroic deed would be the title of Hero of the Soviet Union.

FOR THE MOTHERLAND! FOR STALIN!

Sergeant Kukhtik was nominated for this award by the commander of the tank brigade, Colonel Maryakhin. However, as quite often happened, someone in the higher echelons at HQ, who perhaps throughout war hadn't heard as much as the whizz of a bullet, considered this honour excessive and Kukhtik was awarded the Order of the Red Banner instead.

The years fly by quickly. Our children are grandparents and our great grandchildren have grown up. But we will never forget our youth spent in combat during the war, and I feel like repeating the words of a poet who was at the front.

> Now we are few and we grow old
> But every hour we must vow
> That what we saw in those war years
> Must never happen in this world again.

22

SOLDIER SIDAMETOV

Once my granddaughter Elena was ill. She was ten years old. 'Grandpa, tell me about the war,' she said. 'I'm very interested in it.' She didn't have to ask me twice! An old soldier will always find time to talk about the war, whatever else he might be doing. But what should I tell her? I decided it was not suitable to tell her how we were killed and how we killed others. And then I remembered a story about a soldier in my platoon called Sidametov who was an ethnic Uzbek. Sidametov's Russian was very poor. He only knew about thirty Russian words—apart from four-letter ones.

One night Sidametov was standing guard. Usually at the front the lieutenant didn't sleep but checked the guard every hour, so I came up to Sidametov in the dark. He shouted: 'Freeze! Where to goes there?'[1] I answered, then approached him. There was a long night ahead and there was no need to hurry, so I decided to teach Sidametov a bit of Russian. 'Sidametov,' I told him, 'you should say: "Freeze! WHO goes there?" Repeat.' 'Freeze! Where to goes there?' he said. Then I decided to change the method. I told him to say 'freeze'. He said: 'Freeze.' Then I told him to say 'who'. He said: 'Who'. I said 'goes'. He said: 'Goes'. 'And now repeat "Freeze! Who goes there?"' He repeated: 'Freeze! Where to goes there?' So nothing came of my lesson.

The soldiers in my platoon made fun of Sidametov because he always carried a small hand sewing machine in his rucksack. This was a trophy which he had found somewhere and no persuasion could make him part with it. He didn't pay any attention to the jokes. As it was, we were all acquiring small trophies—watches, fountain pens, rings, knives, pistols, compasses, lighters, cameras and so on. My comrade, the commander of 2nd platoon, Junior Lieutenant Redkin, who was killed during a tank attack when we were taking a small German town, used to take watches as trophies from dead prisoners of war or civilians (both men and women) and kept them in a stocking. Once after a battle he was tipsy and showed them to us. He climbed on a table and pulled a woman's stocking out from his rucksack. It was half full of watches and stretched down to the floor.

The generals would take bigger trophies. The scouts found gold for them and expensive jewellery, mirrors, tableware, sewing machines, chandeliers, hunting guns and carpets—anything that could be transported by car. Once a month after each offensive the commander of our brigade, Colonel Boris Kordukov, dispatched one or two lorries laden with such spoils to Moscow, with armed guards carrying certificates to prove that this was an official transport of goods.

The more senior generals sent trophies home by train, in carriages or on flatbed trucks. These included not only everything mentioned previously, but also small boats, yachts, cars and prefabricated wooden hunting lodges. Some commanders were so shameless that they started openly cohabiting with their girl-friends from the front, who became known as 'front-line wives'. The award which those women received, the medal for 'merit in combat', was renamed 'merit in bed' by the soldiers (in Russian 'combat' is *boyevie*, and 'in bed', or sex, is *polovie*). Other commanders asked their wives to come and take care of them and choose trophies. This kind of thing became increasingly common in the second half of the war when the Nazis were driven back to the west.

The commander of our brigade not only had his wife with him (the soldiers called her 'mum', while he was called 'dad'), but his son too, who was promoted from sergeant to captain. A far more senior commander and Hero of the Soviet Union, Colonel General Galitsky, also had his wife and son with him. Galitsky not only sent trophies by lorry from the front to his home and to his patrons in Moscow, but he also sent sappers from the front to build dachas for himself and other marshals in the quiet forests around the resort of Archangelsky on the bank of the Moscow river.

It is worth mentioning another little known aspect of the war concerning the sons of superior marshals and generals. Ostensibly they were at the front the whole time, holding positions of command—platoon, company or battalion commanders, and so on. However, they only appeared on their brigades' lists of personnel; in reality they were back at the army or front HQ with their fathers. They would turn up at the HQ of their unit once or twice a month and put their signature on the payroll to get their salary. None of them ever took part in offensives nor were they wounded in action, but when the war was over they all received four or five combatant orders and immediate entry to the military academies in Moscow.

This unhealthy trend causes society to decay, and after the Great Patriotic War it intensified. Statistics show that none of the sons of military commanders and senior officials, or those of the heads of regions and districts, took part in the ten-year war in Afghanistan or in the war in Chechnya.[2] The elite had not only succeeded in freeing their sons from war, but from conscription too.

This was how the courageous and legendary Red Army of workers and peasants gradually started to degenerate and change into the army of a totalitarian evil empire and the world gendarme of an absurd and unviable social system. However, we didn't understand this back then.

But I have digressed; I will return to Sidametov. By now we were assault troopers riding on the tanks of our brigade and taking part in battles that ranged for hundreds of kilometres along the German rear, and I had become an experienced fighter. After being wounded twice I knew that during battle it is very important to have a loyal orderly who can carry you to safety under fire if you're seriously wounded, bandage you rather than let you bleed, and not leave your side to save his own skin. So I chose Sidametov as my orderly. He was a head taller than me and physically stronger because he had been doing hard peasant work before conscription. At that time he was forty years old. In a bold attack our front tank detachment had captured Rawitsch. We were told that we would have to wait three days for the infantry and rear to catch up. During this time we had to send our wounded to the rear and obtain fresh supplies of ammunition, armaments, food and equipment. During continuous battles and while we were on the move some of us would lose a cap, mittens, a coat or a belt—and it was winter.

So I was walking up a street with my orderly, Sidametov. I came up to a T-34 tank. The tank crew were nearby, their faces dirty and their overalls and short coats covered in oil. They were standing around or sitting on chairs brought out from neighbouring houses, drinking trophy wine. Wine bottles, full and empty, stood on a barrel of diesel. The tank driver, a sergeant major, was absolutely out of his head. He came up, grabbed me and started shaking me while putting his pistol to my head and asking: 'Do you know who I am?' 'A sergeant major,' I answered. 'No,' he said, 'I am a major.' He did this several times. I was afraid even to try knocking his pistol out of his hand because his finger was on the trigger and, with the slightest movement, my head could have been blown apart. All my hopes rested on Sidametov who was standing next to me. But he never made a move to help me. At last the sergeant major was called over by his fellow drinkers and he let go of me, swearing violently. I started upbraiding Sidametov for being so unhelpful and unable to defend his commander. But now, as I write these lines, I think that maybe Sidametov did the right thing after all. If he had snatched the sergeant major's hand, the shot could have been fired.

We had walked about twenty metres when, in the silence, we heard a pistol shot. It was the drunken sergeant major who had shot his comrade, the tank battalion cook, in the chest. After this the sergeant major instantly sobered up and ran into a house, fearful at what had happened. Soon the battalion commander, a captain, arrived to investigate. Through the window of the house I saw the captain beating the sergeant major with a thick stick as he crawled under a bed. The sergeant major kept crawling under the bed while the captain kept pulling him out by his legs to continue beating him. That was the end of the affair. It wasn't reported to the tribunal or the prosecutor's office. The sergeant major continued to fight courageously in the war and the cook, a huge chap, returned to his unit fifteen days later, and both of them, having a drink after a battle, just laughed at what had happened.

After that episode I appointed a new orderly, Yefremov from Vologda region: I was confident of his loyalty and felt sure that he would be prepared to do anything to save his commander, even if it involved laying down his own life. Although he was of peasant stock Yefremov was physically weak and clumsy. Once, after battle, we were sent to a German village for a short week's rest. No one was there, as all the people from the area had fled to the west away from the advancing Russian troops. I asked Yefremov to catch a chicken, as there were plenty running around, and cook some soup. Our kitchen wagons were hopelessly lagging behind and we never saw them during the offensive, so our stomachs ached from our constant diet of dry food.

Yefremov put aside his automatic gun, then, still wearing his grey coat, helmet, rucksack (with his grenades and small sapper spade strapped on the side) and a Finnish knife on his belt (all the sappers had Finnish knives), he tried to catch a chicken. But it easily escaped. So I took off my belt, my short sheepskin coat and my padded jacket, put down my weapons, then, wearing my tunic, came up to the chicken, grabbed it and voilà—there it was, flapping in my hands. I left the rest to Yefremov.

Now to continue Sidametov's story. Instead of having a thirty-strong platoon of sappers with automatic guns, I had just eighteen men, a handheld machine gun, a Degtyaryov handheld machine gun and a Simonov anti-tank gun. At that time my platoon was in one of the brigade's battalions that deployed English Valentine tanks. As I have already mentioned, our tank crew didn't like this tank. It was very tall with narrow caterpillars and its armour was thinner than that on our T-34 tanks and it used petrol, not diesel. If a shell hit a Valentine tank, it instantly turned into a fireball, and there was no chance of escape.

During an attack Sidametov was sitting alone on the tank armour behind the gun turret, armed with a Shpagin automatic gun. The tank came up to a passage between two clamps of sugar beet.[3] The upper hatch of the tank was open and the tank commander looked out, a pistol in his hand. In a Valentine tank he was the gunner. The other crew members couldn't fire the tank gun. At that moment a German emerged from the clamp with a Faustpatrone on his shoulder and aimed it at the tank. The tank stopped and the commander fired his pistol at the German, but missed. The German hid behind the clamp. The commander was about to get inside to fire the tank gun but the German stood up behind the clamp, so the commander shot at him with the pistol and missed again. Then the commander shouted to Sidametov: 'Shoot the German while I go down to the gun!' But Sidametov, who was still sitting behind the turret, didn't shoot. Eventually the commander managed to fire the tank gun and kill the German. After the battle the commander dragged Sidametov over to me, holding him by the collar (Sidametov was two heads taller than him). The commander was furious and told me what had happened in a spate of four-letter words. If the German's Faustpatrone had hit the tank it would have pierced the front armour and detonated the explosives inside. The resulting explosion would have ripped the tank to pieces and nothing would have been left of the crew. A Faustpatrone pierced armour as thick as twenty centimetres.

The last time I saw Sidametov was during an offensive when my platoon was lying on a frozen field about 300 metres from a line of German soldiers. We were shooting at each other with rifles and pistols. Suddenly Sidametov ran up to me, shouting in Uzbek, and showed me his hand from which a bloody finger was hanging, attached only by the skin. I took out my knife to cut through the skin, but Sidametov wouldn't let me, so I had to bandage his finger to his hand while lying on the ground away from the bullets. After this Sidametov crawled to the rear and I never saw him again. We all envied him at that time—he had remained alive, but what would happen to us?

Another reason why I remember him is because he could never believe that man (himself included) had evolved from apes. He would object and get very angry, with his bloodshot eyes open wide, his face reddening, pulling horrible faces. He also couldn't comprehend that we live in a universe with no end or edge, which is expanding all the time, or that the earth is flying through space at a speed of thirty kilometres per second.

In 1991 I went to Podolsk for the fiftieth anniversary reunion of the Podolsk cadets who had held the Germans back from Moscow before the Siberian reinforcements arrived. We were received very well and stayed in a tourist hotel free of charge for three days with food and alcohol provided. Among the events, four buses were laid on to take us to the battlefields near Maloyaroslavets, then to Moscow to lay flowers on the Tomb of the Unknown Soldier by the eternal flame.

One evening a slightly tipsy veteran organised an amateur concert in the hotel's assembly hall, with dances, songs and poems. I took part and entertained them with my memories of Sidametov. The veterans felt young again, cast away their sticks and danced so vigorously that the young people looked at them with surprise saying: 'You're so full of energy—we can't imagine what you must have been like fifty years ago when you were winning Berlin!'

There were other guests at the hotel as well as the veterans, including two young Uzbeks. They came up and asked me to repeat my stories about Sidametov the following evening when they would be meeting ten of their fellow Uzbeks who lived in Podolsk. So I had to repeat my reminiscences. The Uzbeks were very pleased that their compatriot had taken part in the defeat of the German enemy which had conquered most of Europe and part of Africa. They asked me for Sidametov's address, but I didn't have it.

In the Ministry of Defence's archive at Podolsk I found out that Sidametov, as we called him, was actually called Satmetov. He was born in 1905, so he had been twice my age during the war and by that time he already had five children, four of whom were daughters. Only then did I realise why he had been carrying a sewing machine in his rucksack. In 1991 he would have been eighty-five, so I didn't try and look for him because it would be too late.

23

THE END IS NEAR

150 KILOMETRES LEFT BEFORE BERLIN

We were several days away from Berlin. We started thinking more frequently about what would happen and what life would be like after the war. But Death lay in wait at every step, his scythe in his bony hand. The offensive continued and the Germans resisted with the desperation of the doomed.

After a battle many of us, myself included, would drink alcohol to distract us from negative thoughts. We had a plentiful supply. Nearly every German cellar was fully stocked with alcohol, from champagne to cognac, robbed from the rest of Europe. We would take control of a distillery in one town and top up our supplies, then see the chimney of another distillery on the horizon and become very upset if the direction of the march moved away from it. On the armour of our tanks there was almost always a boar's flayed carcass from which we cut pieces of fat for snacks, a bag of sugar which soldiers would burn somehow to make caramel, and a full cask of spirits from the last distillery. Incidentally, we didn't even have to open the cask. During a tank attack the top of the cask was hit by a bullet so we bent it a little to fill our mugs and mess tins with spirits. Before an attack, or if we were expecting an enemy attack, we tried not to drink, or drank very little. Discipline among the tank troops was strict in this respect. But after a battle, once guards had been posted, we drank a lot. Regarding my subordinates, I was guided by Maxim Gorky's famous saying: 'I don't like drunkards, but I don't trust teetotallers.'

I remember one such drinking session particularly well. After a battle in which we captured a small German town we learned that the commander of the 3rd platoon in our company, Junior Lieutenant Redkin, had been killed. He was from Siberia (a *Sibiryak*, associated with stamina) and had the unusual name of Nikander. Redkin was born in 1925 and was a good friend of mine. Many a time we slept together on the bare earth, pressed tightly against each other for warmth, one grey coat on the ground, the other one covering us. We ate from the same mess tin and drank from the same mug. His death—and I had seen quite a few during the three years of the war—particularly upset me, even more so because it was senseless. While capturing the town he had jumped off the tank, drunk, run up to a shop in the town square, broken the window, thrown a shop dummy on the floor then hit it on the head with the butt of his automatic rifle. The breechblock had gone back, pushed the spring and discharged a round of gunfire into Nikander's head. Meanwhile the tanks had moved on and nobody knew where he had been buried or who had buried him. A condolence letter was sent to his home: 'He died in battle for the socialist homeland, the death of the brave.'

I was already quite drunk (we had been drinking spirits) when I learned about this. I had been in a house drinking with the sergeants and soldiers from my platoon. Those who have never been in war won't understand. How can you drink with your subordinates during war? But this was living proof of the principle which my experience had shown to be true: 'In battle I am your commander—after battle I am your comrade.' By following this principle I was sure that if I was heavily wounded my soldiers would carry me out of the line of fire and get me to the medics, even at risk to their own lives.

When I heard about Redkin's death I got even more drunk and started mourning my friend. In the hope of alleviating my anguish with physical pain I took my Luger pistol, a German trophy, out of its holster. I clutched it in my fist and hit my forehead with it once, and then again. My soldiers took it away from me. Then I snatched my TT pistol from its holster and began hitting my forehead with it. My soldiers took that pistol away too. Then I reached into my breast pocket and pulled out a small Mauser pistol which I had taken from a captured German officer and used it to hit my forehead. They took away that pistol too. By the morning I had sobered up and was completely fit for battle. Those who have been in such situations themselves will understand; those who haven't cannot pass judgement. I remember this episode well, perhaps because I had been hitting myself on the forehead. My memories of numerous other battles have faded away in the course of time after drinking and sound sleep.

During battle, when you are surrounded by death, everyone is extremely tense. My section commander, Junior Sergeant Kirichenko (born 1925), distinguished himself by his calmness. I asked him: 'Why aren't you afraid?' Surprised, he answered: 'Why should I be afraid? I would be afraid in a cemetery at night, but during the day it's not frightening.' About this Gilyarovsky (a famous writer) said:

Let the devil frighten the timid,
but he won't frighten us—

while we are alive,
there is no death for us,
when death comes
we won't be here to bother.

All potential risk should be minimalised in war. But only those who were never young are never reckless. When I was young I liked to walk on the razor's edge, so to speak. And I can confirm this with an example. We were in the front detachment during the offensive and found ourselves far ahead of the tank army's main forces. It happened that our reinforcements couldn't reach us as the road was blocked by the retreating German tank formation of 200 tanks and self-propelled artillery. We were running out of fuel and ammunition. The wounded couldn't be evacuated. We were forced to eat whatever we could find in our pockets and rucksacks. We received the radioed order from command to halt the offensive. We hid in a gully about 200 metres from a small village where a local German military unit was based. White snow lay everywhere. We were warned not to poke our heads out of the gully as there was a sniper. But it is intolerable to sit still in the cold for hours doing nothing. I decided to take a look at the village. I put a white handkerchief over my cap so that it wouldn't be spotted and quietly looked over the edge of the gully. I heard a single shot from the village. The icy surface of the snow near my ear crackled. The bullet left a small mark in the snow just two centimetres away from my left temple. It was my fate to be saved again.

On 10 March 1945 I was admitted to the Communist Party. This took place during a break between two battles several days before I was wounded. The head of the political department of the 93rd tank brigade, Lieutenant Colonel Inin, gave me my party membership card, no. 3890707. This red card with its portrait of Lenin which I kept in my left pocket near my heart didn't give me any privileges except one—to be the first to go into attack. This card was our greatest prize. As a member of the

Communist Party I couldn't be taken prisoner by the Germans under any circumstances because at best I would face the firing squad, at worst cruel torture. I knew that you don't live twice on this earth and that we can't repeat our lives. I understood that the war would soon be over. I remembered my mother's plea in every one of her letters: 'Take care of yourself.' But I couldn't hide behind my comrades. I had to think about how to complete my mission rather than save my own skin, as I was in charge of my platoon of twenty to thirty soldiers to whom I was supposed to set an example.

Incidentally, before the offensive I had seven sergeants in my platoon—one was my deputy, four were section commanders, another was the submachine gun commander and the seventh was the anti-tank gun commander. I remember one of them well: Junior Sergeant Kazakov (born 1912), the submachine gun commander. On winter nights it's not easy to fall asleep on the frozen ground. So the soldiers would light a fire using anything to hand, then a group of eight to ten would listen to Kazakov's stories. He was a former schoolteacher and an inspiring story-teller. He would recount, almost in its entirety, Alexandre Dumas' *The Three Musketeers*, with the soldiers hanging on his every word. Some of them were illiterate: most of them had three or four years of education—only a few had seven years. All those with eight or nine years of education had been sent off to officers' schools, or to train as junior lieutenants. Kazakov used to tell his stories without a break for hours on end. Then he would break off and start singing his favourite song, and the soldiers would join him, in low voices.

Quite often we argued over what was the most dreadful thing that could happen to you in the war. There were different opinions:

– to be taken prisoner;
– hand-to-hand combat;

FOR THE MOTHERLAND! FOR STALIN!

- when a German tank is a metre away from you;
- to go into attack against submachine gun fire;
- to come under sudden artillery fire or air bombardment in an open field;
- to cross a river under heavy fire from guns, submachine guns, artillery, mortars and aircraft—while not being able to swim;
- to disable an anti-personnel mine at night fifty metres away from the enemy's trenches;
- when your commander loses his nerve during battle;
- when you have to bury a comrade-in-arms who has been a close friend for a long time;
- to see the children's faces when a letter of condolence arrives.

At our reunions after the war my fellow veterans, after a drink or two, would reminisce. One veteran said:

When I was sitting in a trench I would be so comfortable in that frozen trench that I seemed to be able to sit there all my life. I would be sitting and praying for the damned Nazi to get past and go somewhere else, praying not to hear the order 'Prepare for battle!' However, the Nazi rarely got past and the order was given in time. I used to get out of the trench and run forwards. I saw a friend fall down, then another one. And I kept running with my rifle at the ready. I won't lie—at that moment I had no fear. I felt a kind of excitement: if I managed to make it that would be great; if not, nothing doing, it wasn't meant to be. You can only die once. As for heroes, we had a man from Vyatka. Before an attack he used to cross himself and be the first to jump out of the trench. He used to run shouting not 'Oorah!', but swearing obscenely at the Nazis. He was a good man, a hero. He was killed by a mine.

Another veteran told us:

We used to sit in the trench, lice all over us. It's impossible to imagine what it's like until you experience it yourself... When I watch a film about the war on telly, it doesn't look like real war at all. Bang-bang and the Germans are running away and we're shouting, 'Oorah!' I ask myself: 'Who makes these films? I daresay they won't remember how we were running away from Lvov, how young chaps were crying and calling for their mummies before the attack.' I say this because I did this myself.

A third veteran, a former member of a tank crew, remembers:

After a battle I came up to a tank and knocked on its burnt turret—nobody answered. I opened the lid—a man was sitting there, we had gone into battle with him... Then the wind blew—and a pile of ash was all that was left of him. Lots of our chaps were blown away like this.

It is interesting to note that at the front I kept dreaming about life during peacetime: about my mother and father, my brother, my school, my street, my chess club. But for a long time after the war I kept dreaming about fighting: a tank attack with assault troops on the tank armour; the enemies moving towards me and my automatic gun won't fire; enemy aircraft bombs are being dropped on me... I used to wake up in a cold sweat. Thank goodness I am alive. But in my dreams I never saw my comrades who had been killed in battle as dead. In my dreams they were always alive.

According to the data kept in the military archive at Podolsk, the USSR had 1,320 divisions during the war, of which 500 were rifle divisions while the rest were cavalry, airborne, artillery, tank, anti-aircraft and mechanised divisions. The commander of each division was changed at least once and up to nine times during the war.

As for their nationalities, the commanders of the divisions were 75 per cent Russian, 8 per cent Ukrainian and 2 per cent Belorussian. The remaining 15 per cent included all the other nationalities of the USSR—Tatars, Jews, Georgians, Armenians, Bashkirs, Ossetians and so on. There were no Germans: Stalin did not trust them and those who were not behind barbed wire served in the far rear.

FOR THE MOTHERLAND! FOR STALIN!

Once I had thought about it, it was obvious why, after the victory parade in Moscow in June 1945, at the reception of the supreme military commanders and the leadership of the country, Stalin had raised a toast to the great Russian people; why, during the most difficult period of the war, he had remembered Russian patriotism and established guards units and orders named after Alexander Suvorov, Mikhail Kutuzov, Alexander Nevsky, Pavel Nakhimov and Fyodor Ushakov.[1]

The countdown of days before victory had started, the countdown before the end of the bloodiest war in the history of humanity. What stamina, what willpower must one possess to go into battle and risk one's life in the last days of the war—but we would go to any length for the sake of victory, for the sake of the homeland, for the sake of peace on our planet.

The third wound

On the night of 15 March, after a long and exhausting march (we were being transferred from one part of the front to another), we stopped in a small village near the River Neisse and waited for daybreak. We were given the command to fight the 20th German infantry SS Estonian division. The Germans opened fire on our position with 88-mm and 105-mm medium calibre shells. You have a horrible feeling during such night-time bombardments. In daytime you can see the location of the explosions and you can act accordingly. At night all the explosions seem to be near you.

After warning the tank crew we jumped off the tank and took cover underneath. The explosions continued for half an hour. A German artillery director was evidently nearby, radioing where to fire. We were on the alert because in this situation the tank crew could easily forget about us and move off, crushing us under the tank. Such things happened.

It was pitch black. The darkness was interrupted by flashes of explosions from German shells which made the ensuing darkness seem even denser. Dawn started breaking. The tank engine began to rumble. Somewhere a wounded man was crying, 'Nurses, nurses, help me!', then the cries stopped. Our tanks received the radioed command 'Forward to attack!', then, as the engines roared we rolled out from underneath and climbed onto the armour (we looked horrible, with crumpled, unwashed faces, hands blackened with dirt and eyes red with lack of sleep). Riding on the front tank, we approached the crossroads about 300 metres away. A storm of artillery fire was hurled at us. That place must have been very well targeted by the Germans. With a cry, Soldier Tkach fell down from the moving tank onto the highway. He had been hit in the head by a shell fragment (I later learned from documents in the Podolsk archive that he died from his wound in hospital).

It was dangerous to stay on the armour of the one and a half metre high tank. I ordered my soldiers to jump off, which they immediately did and hid in a ditch by the road. Then I jumped— I had to jump after them as they had surrounded me on the tank and I had to wait until they were out of my way. In mid-air I felt a strong blow on my right buttock. A shell fragment hit me, ripping through my greatcoat, my padded trousers and my underwear. Somehow I didn't feel the pain at first; it would come later. A split-second thought flashed through my mind that if I landed and wasn't able to stand on my feet it would mean that the fragment had broken my hip, which would count as a serious wound. But I managed to land and make it to the ditch where I quickly took cover from the fragments singing around me. Because of its awkward position I couldn't bandage the wound myself so my orderly, Sergeant Yefremov, took control. He bandaged me clumsily, taking a long time. I was bleeding heavily and my strength was ebbing away.

Once the shooting was over I handed over the command of the platoon to my deputy, First Sergeant Korolev, and, leaning on Yefremov's shoulder, I slowly walked to the rear along a heavily ploughed field. It was dangerous to go along the road in case there was more shooting. After walking for two kilometres I reached the medical aid point of the 113th rifle regiment where I was bandaged again and they filled in a form to confirm that I had been wounded on the battlefield. Yefremov said goodbye and returned to the front. I was taken on a lorry with the rest of the wounded to the rear.

In comparison to a bullet wound a fragment wound, even a light one, very often develops severe complications. This happened to me. Along with the fragment there were shreds of clothing in my body, causing severe inflammation.

About a week after I was wounded, when I was being treated in the brigade hospital, we were told the good news. In recognition of its courage, discipline and successful action against the Germans, the 4th tank army was to be known as the 4th guard tank army and would receive the guard banner. This was by the order signed on 17 March 1945 by Stalin, the People's Commissar for the Defence of the USSR and Marshal of the Soviet Union. It was pleasant to realise that I had played a role in this great event. Later, when the war was over, I found out which offensive I had taken part in while I was studying the history of the Second World War at the Military Law Academy. The Upper Silesian offensive operation of the left wing of the 1st Ukrainian front was carried out from 15 to 31 March 1945. The German side consisted of twenty divisions, sixty battalions, 1,420 guns and mortars, 750 planes and 100 tanks and assault weapons. We confronted them with our troops: thirty-one rifle divisions, 5,640 guns and mortars, 988 tanks and self-propelled guns and 1,737 planes. After breaking through 245 positions on enemy lines our troops surrounded and annihilated five German divisions, killed more than 40,000 and captured 14,000 officers and men. For its active role in the battles on the River Neisse foothold our brigade was awarded the Order of Kutuzov.

For taking part in this offensive Captain Vladimir Markov (born 1923), who had shown courage in battle, was awarded the title of Hero of the Soviet Union. In a letter to a friend Markov describes the operation as follows:

> And then there was the Ratibor operation. It was there that I drank the full cup of bitterness. If you come across some of our comrades, ask them about the Valley of Death (that was what we called it). After two days of battles, the battalions of the brigades were destroyed and the remnants of all these large 'enterprises' of Belov were handed over to me. With these remnants I organised twelve attacks a day, losing four to six 'boxes' each time, and many people. And the radio receiver was shrieking: 'Lelushenko and the marshal are not happy with your actions!' Then I wished to be dead because no nerves can stand this.

I will explain some of the jargon in this letter: the Ratibor operation was the encirclement of German troops near the town of Ratibor (now Racibórz in Poland) and the River Neisse; the remnants of the large 'enterprises' of Belov were the remnants of a tank corps under the command of Lieutenant General P. Belov; boxes are tanks; the radio receiver was shrieking means that radioed commands (each tank had a radio) were given in the form of four-letter words.

Lelushenko was a general and the commander of the 4th tank army. Vladimir Markov was awarded five orders and in 1955 he was a lieutenant colonel and deputy commander of the mechanised regiment in Tbilisi. He died of an anaesthesia overdose in a hospital operating theatre during an operation for appendicitis. His heart gave way, overstrained by the war. He was only thirty-two years old. May his memory live forever and may he rest in peace.

By end of the war the majority of officers in our army had been wounded once, twice, less often three times, although I came across some who had been wounded five times. In the German army an officer would remain in rear after recovering from an injury and an officer from the reserve would be sent to the front to serve in his place. We didn't have such a policy, neither did we take leave after being wounded unless it was necessary for our state of health.

The life of an officer during the war went as follows: graduation from military school as a junior lieutenant; formation of military unit in the rear; sent to front; wound; hospital; personnel department; back to the front; and the same cycle would repeat itself several times. By the mid-point of the war both sides had become brutalised. Those who surrendered during an attack weren't taken prisoner—there was no time for this—and the wounded were killed so they wouldn't be a burden.

The officers, who were mostly members of the Communist Party like me, understood that if they were taken prisoner they would be tortured and killed (although in reality it wasn't always so). Everyone knew the tragic story of Junior Sergeant Smirnov which was used as propaganda. As a member of a tank assault unit he was taking part in an offensive on the enemy rear when he was wounded and fell off the tank. His comrades didn't notice what had happened in the heat of battle. The tank continued moving. Bleeding, Smirnov was taken prisoner. The Germans couldn't get any information out of him, so they crucified him with daggers on the wall of their HQ bunker. Later he was given the title of Hero of the Soviet Union. We were also told that in 1941 near Kiev drunken Germans entertained themselves by putting prisoners in a line and competing to see whose bullet could hit the most heads. Being experienced in war, we officers knew that in the heat of battle you could use up all your cartridges and be taken prisoner without an effective weapon. We also knew that those taken prisoner, whatever the circumstances, were automatically regarded as traitors by our side, with all the consequences.

After the war I found out that the 126,000 officer POWs were stripped of their military titles and awards and sent to gulags; very few came back. That is why we were psychologically prepared to shoot ourselves and not be taken prisoner. It is impossible to understand this in peacetime when everything is normal. In the pouch on my belt, together with my black plastic 'death medallion' identity disc, was a scroll of paper with my parents' names and a spare cartridge for my TT pistol. If you're facing capture you put the cartridge in the pistol, then put the pistol to your temple and press the trigger and... your problems are over.

In the Berlin operation the 63rd tank brigade, which was next to our unit, distinguished itself under the command of Colonel Fomichev. They seized a concentration camp guarded by SS officers in a Potsdam suburb. Among the prisoners was the former prime minister of France, Edouard Herriot, who sent Fomichev telegrams of thanks for his liberation until his death in 1957.[2]

At 3 am on 9 May this brigade was the first to enter the capital city of Czechoslovakia to help the insurgent Czechs stop the Germans destroying 'golden' Prague. In gratitude for the heroism of the Soviet fighters, the first tank that entered Prague (tank no. 23, under the command of Lieutenant Goncharenko, who was killed in the ensuing battle) was later put on a high granite pedestal in the city centre in a square which the Soviets named after Soviet tank crews. Fomichev wrote a book, *Moy Put Nachalsya v Uralom* (*My Way Began in the Urals*), about his youth and participation in the war, and gave me an autographed edition which I have kept with gratitude. After the war I met him again in Siberia when I served in the town of Chita from 1961 to 1967 and he was the first deputy commander of the Zabaikalsky military zone, behind Lake Baikal.

It was the last day of the war, 9 May 1945. For me it looked as if it would be yet another day in the brigade's mobile hospital. Discharge was coming out of my wound and it was still not healing although more than a month had passed since I was injured. I wasn't sent to the rear. During the last months of the war virtually no reinforcements were sent to our military units, but we still had to fight on. So in the 4th guard tank army, as in the other armies, the lightly wounded were not sent to the rear. Instead they were treated at their unit's mobile hospitals, or at the army's frontline hospital. As soon as they recovered soldiers and officers were sent back to their military units.

Our mobile hospital, consisting of four covered lorries and a captured bus, was in a wood about fifteen kilometres north of Prague, together with the other sub-units. At that time the sappers from our assault battalion and Colonel General D. Lelyushenko's tank army were fighting a battle with Germans on the outskirts of Prague. Early in the morning we were woken by loud shouts. It was the hospital duty officer: 'Victory! Peace! We've won!' He was shouting this over and over again. We were half asleep and for a fleeting moment we didn't understand and were somewhat bewildered. Then, in our underwear, we all jumped out of the lorries and started shouting joyfully and repeatedly: 'Hurray! We've won! The war is ended!'

Random firing started—rifles, automatics, pistols, machine guns with tracer bullets. Anyone who had a weapon was discharging it. Groups of military men were everywhere, firing in the air. Some of them were firing signal pistols and flares exploded in bright colours across the early May sky—yellow, red, white and blue. Soldiers and officers were congratulating each other joyfully, hugging and kissing each other, slapping each other on the back, dancing, singing, crying.

Several days later, with the permission of the brigade commander Colonel B. Kordyukov, I went to Dubno, where my family were living, for further treatment.

24

VICTORY!

THE WAR IS OVER

We learned about the victory at 3.30 am on 9 May. At that time the combatant units of our brigade were approaching Prague, and their rear services were fifteen kilometres behind them. Among these was our brigade's mobile hospital in a covered lorry where the lightly wounded were being treated, including me.

At night we were woken by sudden gunfire from machine guns, automatics, rifles, pistols and cannons at the nearby anti-aircraft battery. Thinking that we were under German attack, we jumped out of the lorry with automatics and pistols, ready for battle. But it turned out to be an extempore fireworks display to celebrate the victory and the end of the war. Our radio operators got the news and passed it on. So on top of the fireworks shots rang out from our automatics and pistols—and this time we didn't spare the cartridges! The alcohol wasn't spared either; the rejoicing was universal.

The four-year war comprised 1,418 days and nights full of mortal danger and superhuman endeavour, leaving the soldiers immensely war weary. They say that soldiers once asked Marshal Zhukov's driver to ask him when this damned war would be over. The driver carefully chose his moment and was about to ask, but Zhukov spoke first: 'Damn this bloody war! Ivan, can you tell me when it will be over?'

But everything comes to an end. This war was over—the cruellest in the history of mankind. Our people had to suffer to the utmost degree. The sacrifice was enormous. Among soldiers born between 1922 and 1924 (those who were fighting when our army started its offensive), of every 100 who fought at the front only three survived and at least one of them was maimed.

What is important is not how long someone stayed at the front, but what he did there. I happen to know a man who used to say, not without pride, that he fought during the war from beginning to end. That is totally correct—with one proviso that during his entire time at the front he was performing in a song and dance ensemble. I was not at the front as long as him, but I fought like a man with a weapon in my hand amid whizzing bullets and the whine of shrapnel, face to face with Germans.

The newspaper *Krasnaya Zvezda* (*Red Star*), published by the Soviet Ministry of Defence, reported on 25 August 1945 that the camp of engineer sapper troops was looking festive. On a green lawn in the suburbs of the Austrian town of Tulln, thirty kilometres from Vienna, the participants in numerous battles lined up—sappers, miners and pontoon bridge builders. Hero of the Soviet Union, Colonel General Galitsky, was riding his horse up to the line. The ceremony to award orders to the battalion and brigade began. There was a solemn silence as the general read the decree of the Presidium of the Supreme Soviet of the USSR that awarded our battalion the 4th order, the order of Bogdan Khmelnitsky.

During the war, under the command of Major Kalyniuk, our battalion covered about 9,000 kilometres on campaign, dug 4,755 metres of trenches, built twenty-two bridges and detonated and placed 448,790 mines. Three representatives from our battalion took part in the victory parade in Moscow on 24 June 1945. After the war dozens of poets who fought at the front considered it their duty to write about the great victory on 9 May 1945. My favourite is the poem *On the Day the War Ended* by Ivan Ryadchenko, my fellow townsman from Odessa who fought at the front as head of the rifle battalion HQ.

> The land still lay in silent darkness
> And in the mist
> The grass shed tears of dew
> But the great ninth of May
> Had already dawned
> The army telephone rang, ever so faintly
> Everyone woke up
> The operator jumped to his feet, then hurled the receiver down
> And that was all!
> No one called the signallers.
> No one barked out orders.
> The camp exploded with joy.
> A lieutenant started dancing.
> Jubilant shots rang out.
> His voice hoarse from cheering
> The chief catering officer fired his Walther revolver
> For the first time in four years.
> Over the dark waters of the fast-flowing Tisza
> Came the joyful rattle and roar of our guns.
> The bald-headed cook, used to the heat of his stove,
> Unbuttoned his collar, not knowing why.
> Our yak fighters no longer rumbled

FOR THE MOTHERLAND! FOR STALIN!

Above dawn's distant glow.
And someone was singing.
And someone was crying.
And someone was lying, dead in the damp earth.
And suddenly there was silence,
And in this all-pervasive silence
A nightingale began to sing, as yet unaware
That the war was over.

Those who have never been to the front often idealise it, thinking that everyone who was there was a hero and a hard worker. Soviet propaganda helped to create this impression through the mass media, using books, radio, TV, speeches and so on. Accordingly there were no people who changed sides, no deserters, no cowards and no scaremongers, and everything was good and correct. This gave a very one-sided view of the war. Then why did state security workers and officers, military prosecutors and the chairs of military tribunals receive awards after the war? I'll give an example: in the 1970s I happened to attend a readers' conference in Odessa on a book by Lieutenant General Shafarenko who had been commander of a rifle division during the war. The general wrote his book *Voyennye Memuary* (*War Memoirs*) about his division's participation in the war and the men who served in it.

Among the many questions, I remember this one: 'Comrade general, why did you mention only one woman in your book? There were plenty of them in the division, weren't there? Doctors, nurses, radio engineers, draughtswomen, cooks and so on.' The general answered: 'Dear friends, in my manuscript I wrote about the twenty-two women who served in the division, but the deputy head of the war memoirs department of the publishing house in Moscow crossed out twenty-one of the women, saying, "Do you want young people thinking that our war was won by women?"' No comment.

Another example comes to mind. When I was searching the archive of the Ministry of Defence at Podolsk for veterans serving in my regiment, I browsed through a volume listing awards for the soldiers and commanders of the 81st rifle division which our battalion helped to cross the Vistula in August 1944. In the list I found an award for a soldier who drove a horse and cart. It was written that this man had been sent to another commander with a message and had been attacked by two Germans on his way through the forest. However, he showed courage and handled the situation with honour, capturing both Germans and delivering them together with his message to the other military unit. So in the recommendation it was pointed out that he deserved recognition of his courage and he was subsequently awarded the medal.

I went on browsing through the volume and came across another description of the same heroic feat, word for word, this time for a cook also awarded a medal for courage. And later the same feat appeared again and again. There were about a dozen recommendations, absolutely identical in content, but for different people. I realised that if it had been said or written in a recommendation that the man who drove a horse and cart had carried out his duties honestly and conscientiously, then the HQ officials who had never smelt powder nor heard a bullet whizzing past would not have given him an award—there is nothing heroic in driving a horse and cart, so to speak. But this man did deserve his award for the fact that during his four years of not eating enough, not sleeping enough, being out in the cold, in the rain and the slush, he made it possible for his sub-unit to carry out its combatant mission.

When a famous actor and comedian, Yuriy Nikulin, was asked how he had fought at the front, he usually replied with the following joke: a discharged soldier came home and told all his relatives how he had fought. When he had finished, his little son asked: 'So what did all the other soldiers do at the front, Dad?'

FOR THE MOTHERLAND! FOR STALIN!

The war was over. The fireworks ended and there was peace. We couldn't believe it was possible just to sit on a tank and not be hit by bullets, that you could walk along streets, not trenches, not bent over but walking tall, that you could look up at the cloudless sky without feeling danger, that there was no need for blackout blinds, that you could take a photo in the centre of Berlin near the Reichstag, and that a Russian accordion would be playing a famous Russian song in the main square of the capital city of Germany.

I think that Major General Fyodorov, twice Hero of the Soviet Union and commander of the partisan force which fought in Ukraine, gave a very precise description of war. 'War is cruel... We called it great because our courage and anger were great. We called it patriotic because there is nothing more sacred than the struggle for freedom of your homeland. We called it the people's war because all Soviet people took part in the struggle.'

After the war German tourists to the USSR saw the poverty we lived in and said 'We were lucky to be defeated and you were unlucky to win.' It was a shame and it hurt to hear these words. The victory for which we paid so dearly didn't give us prosperity.

25

VICTORY IN MOSCOW—NINA'S STORY

MOSCOW 9 MAY 1945

The people of Moscow had also experienced the terrible impact of the war. From its beginning they had lived under a state of siege and blackouts were introduced. When night came the city sank into darkness with no lights to be seen. Rationing of food and household goods was introduced. Some 800,000 Muscovites joined the armed forces, 800 of whom were awarded the title of Hero of the Soviet Union. During the war the enemy carried out 134 air raids on Moscow using 9,000 planes, but only 243 managed to make their way through our defences. A total of 1,392 planes were shot down during the air raids. About 1,800 bombs and 120,000 incendiaries fell on the city, which resulted in the destruction of hundreds of buildings, 45,000 fires and more than 2,000 deaths, including those of 100 people in the Kremlin.

FOR THE MOTHERLAND! FOR STALIN!

On 9 May 1945 my future wife Nina and her elder sister Natalia, who were living in Moscow, learned about the victory on the radio and went to Red Square. Nina says:

> I was in the tenth form at school. Both at school and at home we had been preparing for this long-awaited day. The radio informed us daily about the advance of our victorious troops closer and closer to the beast's den—Berlin, the capital of Nazi Germany. We knew we would win for certain, but when it finally happened on 9 May, it came as a shock! There would be no more war, there would be peace! We had been waiting for that day throughout the four long years of the most murderous and destructive war in the history of the mankind. And now that day had come!
>
> On that first day of peace tens of thousands of people, both young and old, from Moscow and its surrounding areas gathered in the main square. People were standing close to each other. Everyone was jubilant. They were shouting: 'Victory! Victory! Hurray! Hurray! Hurray!' Strangers hugged, kissed and slapped each other on the shoulders. Tears ran down their joyful ecstatic faces. People in military uniforms, especially those with orders and medals, got the worst of it... Girls hung like grapes on a handsome young lieutenant with artillery emblems on his epaulettes and a medal for courage on his chest. It is impossible to count how many times he was hugged and kissed! Next to him a middle-aged captain from the air force had bought all the ice cream from an ice cream van and was handing it out to everyone. An invalid with two yellow ribbons on his jacket to show that he had been seriously wounded was shouting and waving his crutches over his head. Someone else was given the bumps. Many people were tipsy. Military and civilian bands were playing popular songs from the war in different parts of the square. Some members of the crowd were singing, others were dancing, while others were crying. The mood on that great day is conveyed well in this song:
>
>> This Victory Day smells of gunpowder,
>> This is our holiday with grey hairs on our temples,
>> This is our joy with tears in our eyes.

VICTORY IN MOSCOW—NINA'S STORY

I remember in particular the festive fireworks in commemoration of the Victory—thirty salvos from 1,000 guns accompanied by colourful rockets and illuminated by beams from anti-aircraft searchlights.

26

AFTER THE WAR

FROM DUBNO TO LVOV, VIA NOVOSIBIRSK

The war was over. Our joy was indescribable! The victorious salvos of automatic guns and pistols resounded in our ears. Then came the first nights of calm sleep and the joyous feeling that the war had ended and we were still alive. Whoever has experienced such intensity of feeling will understand. Whoever hasn't, let him thank God that he has been spared the ordeal of war.

We were also proud of the fact that all the soldiers in our brigade were awarded medals for our victory over Germany, for taking Berlin and for the liberation of Prague. Some officers, including me, were awarded Czechoslovakian medals for courage and Polish medals for our operations on the Neisse, Vistula and Baltic.

My diagnosis was confirmed: the shrapnel lodged deep in my body had pulled in fabric and cotton padding from my clothes

Boris in Dubno, western Ukraine, 1945

and this had caused infection. In the conditions of the brigade's makeshift field hospital further treatment had turned out to be useless. My wound wasn't healing. I sent a request to finish my treatment in Dubno, where my father was military commissar and head of garrison. Permission was given and I went to Dubno after saying fond farewells to my brothers-in-arms. There wasn't a military hospital in Dubno, so I stayed with my father and finished my treatment in the town hospital.

In July my father was appointed the head of a faculty in Novosibirsk, in charge of a professional development course for the managing officers of military committees. By then my wound had healed, so to stop me hanging around with nothing to do my father sent me to deliver his papers to the Siberian military region's

HQ in Novosibirsk. Just as I arrived in Novosibirsk and registered with local military commandant, the Soviet Union declared war on Japan. It was 8 August 1945. The commandant delayed my return to Dubno, giving no explanation. I was worried. Nobody knew then, of course, that the war would be so short. After all, Japan had been successfully fighting the United States and Britain for four years. I decided that I had been held back in order to be sent off to fight in a new war—and I was sick and tired with the last war. But a week later the war with Japan was over, so I came home to Dubno and my father went to Novosibirsk.

When I returned I was sent to the artillery reserve of Lvov military region where I served as an officer for about two months. The reserve was stationed in the village of Dubliany near Lvov; an agricultural academy is currently based in the building which used to be its headquarters. From there I was posted to the 147th rifle division which was stationed in Berdichev. Our barracks were on the outskirts of the town, at Lysaya Gora. The division formed part of the 102nd rifle corps of the 13th army.

From Berdichev to Zhytomyr

The commander of the 13th army was Colonel General N. P. Pukhov, Hero of the Soviet Union. Pukhov subsequently became commander of Odessa military region. He belonged to a cohort of military commanders who had succeeded in carrying out impossible missions. During the war Stalin used the following method of choosing personnel: whoever failed to carry out a mission was sacked, ceding their position to another. Pukhov always succeeded and this is confirmed by the fact that in the six-month period from June to December 1941 the 13th army had four commanders: Lieutenant General Filatov, Lieutenant General Remizov, Lieutenant General Gerasimenko and Major General Gorodensky—and from January 1942 to May 1945 just Pukhov.

FOR THE MOTHERLAND! FOR STALIN!

I was appointed commander of the 1st artillery platoon: it was the ninth platoon that I had commanded since military school. The studies began. The days dragged on, one just like another. The three-storey barracks at Lysaya Gora were ranged around a quadrangle which was used for military and artillery drill.

I remember one episode clearly. A girl was walking across the square. The barrels of six 76-mm anti-tank guns were pointing at her. I gave the command: 'Target Tanya!' Six gun commanders loudly repeated my command and six gun barrels steadily followed the girl. And so it continued until Tanya disappeared behind the barracks.

I learned from my friends that the division had been marching back from Czechoslovakia to Berdichev. Trophies, including cattle and lathes, were brought back from Germany by rail, in carriages and on flatbed trucks. Meanwhile the regiments marched home with their banners flying in the air, singing along to the triumphant sound of bands, their soldiers and officers glittering with medals.

Behind them lay the countless graves of our brothers-in-arms. The victorious soldiers had covered more than 1,000 kilometres on foot before they reached Berdichev. Every town or large village had greeted them and seen them off with flowers and displays of heartfelt joy. The bands played, songs were sung and passionate speeches were made.

During the war Berdichev was liberated by the 44th guards tank brigade. Berdichev had been jokingly known as 'the Jerusalem in Volhynia'[1] or 'the capital of Jewish Cossacks', as before the war 70 per cent of the population were Jewish.[2] I was walking up streets where a century earlier the great French writer Honoré de Balzac led his Polish bride and last love, Eveline Hańska, to their wedding at St Barbara's Church.

Also of interest is the fact that in the summer of 1920 an American aircraft squadron was stationed in Berdichev. The squadron supported the Poles during the Polish-Soviet War of 1920 and bombed formations of Budyonny's cavalry army.[3]

I served in Berdichev until November 1945. I lived in a private flat on the outskirts with two other lieutenants from the same division. Our landlord constantly insisted that we should marry his daughters, who were about our age—but nothing came of it; we stood our ground!

There was an incident that could have ended in tragedy but for the grace of God, as they say. One night I was taking a girl home from a dance. She lived in a suburb of Berdichev, on an island in middle of a lake. The path led through thick reeds. We stood near her house, talking; our conversation must have been heard from the house. Someone stomped down the creaky staircase. 'Run!' said the girl. 'It's our lodger! He's a sergeant major and he's got a gun.' Without a second thought I ran back along the path, then quickly made two side steps into the reeds. And then, one after another, three shots whistled past my ear. I had escaped by the skin of my teeth. I waited until the sergeant major and the girl went into the house, then walked home to the opposite side of the town, thanking God for my narrow escape.

An artillery brigade was formed in our division, consisting of a field gun regiment together with a new howitzer regiment and a mortar regiment. As a result, our brigade was transferred to the village of Guyva, seven kilometres from Zhytomyr along the Berdichev highway. Cold weather had set in and at the barracks everything had either been broken or stolen. The windows had no glass, doors were missing, the ceilings and floors were pitted with holes, the walls were dirty, scuffed and burned, and there was no water or electricity. Little by little we started improving our living conditions by hanging our greatcoats and oilskin ponchos over the doors and windows. Rank-and-file soldiers and sergeants who had taken part in the war and had medals on their chest to prove it lived in those barracks all through winter, while the officers lived in private lodgings in the village two kilometres away.

FOR THE MOTHERLAND! FOR STALIN!

Boris at Guyva, Zhytomyr, December 1945

Once I was walking home at dusk. The women were digging potatoes in the field. I saw a girl running from the village towards them, shouting something. Suddenly everyone stopped working and ran to the village. When I reached my lodgings my landlady told me that a teenage shepherd had found an artillery shell in the forest and set fire to it. His more astute companions had moved away and the shell had exploded. Two boys were killed and several were injured. Shortly afterwards, I was called to the home of one of the dead boys, along with Lieutenant Alexei Velousov, who was in the same regiment. The villagers needed our help because there were almost no men left to do what was required. I looked at the remains of the boy, torn to pieces by the explosion, and felt sick. There was just bloody meat and white bones. We had to use this to construct a human figure which could be presented to the boy's relatives for burial. I performed the man's role of holding the door shut to stop the women who were crazy with grief from bursting into the room. I had to use all my force. Meanwhile Alexei formed the remains into the shape of a body. Once we had done all we could, we left. We didn't attend either the funeral or the wake. That episode made a very strong impression on me. The war was over, but it continued to devour its victims.

I have never met a battlefield veteran who could bear the sight of blood and wounds. Some people are surprised by this but I understand how my comrades feel. They saw too much blood and witnessed too many deaths during the war and can no longer stomach such experiences.

When I had some free time I went to Zhytomyr and admired the architecture of its old buildings and cathedrals. The city was founded in the ninth century. From 1320 it was under the rule of the Polish Lithuanian state and from 1569 it was ruled by Poland; it was only ceded to Russia in 1793 during the division of Poland.

At the end of 1945 an order was sent to our regiment. Rank-and-file soldiers and sergeants who had been wounded two or more times were to be dismissed from the army without any delay. It was believed that even after a wound had healed it still had a malign influence on the body. Nothing was said about officers, but the order made me think... I had three wounds.

Guyva was a godforsaken place. It was an extremely remote, provincial military base surrounded by forest. An officer's life in such a dead end place is vividly described by Aleksandr Kuprin in his story *Duel*. All your life is spent either in barracks or on parade. Such a life kills any yearning for knowledge and future aspirations. Everyday garrison life with its ignorance, petty squabbles, gossip, drunkenness and gambling destroyed many talented people who couldn't find enough inner strength to resist its temptations and depressing tedium. Although I could only sense this vaguely at the time, I was yearning for a better career with challenges and the opportunity to move upwards. I was not content to go with the flow and end up being sucked into the quagmire of a humdrum, trifling existence. They say that the optimist invents a plane and the pessimist a parachute. I consider myself an optimist.

On 5 November I heard that the officers in the regiment would be given presents, that is to say trophies brought back from Germany, to mark the anniversary of the October Revolution. There was a queue by the storehouse. Every officer was to be given a piece of leather for high boots. While I was waiting in the queue I saw a pile of small calibre German rifles in the corner of the storehouse. They looked exactly like full-size rifles. According to the Treaty of Versailles, the Germans were only allowed to have a limited number of full-size rifles so they made small calibre rifles for training which looked like and weighed the same as the full-size ones. I asked the head of the storehouse to give me a small calibre rifle instead of leather. He was surprised by my impractical request, but he gave me the rifle, telling me to get a certificate for it from the regiment's HQ, which I did.

27

MY ILLEGAL TRIP TO AUSTRIA

MY AWARDS ARE VETOED

By now I had received a reply from the deputy head of the brigade's HQ concerning my awards of the Order of the Red Banner and the Order of the Red Star. It turned out that the military council of the 1st Ukrainian front had vetoed my awards. The reason was not stated. I was profoundly shocked and upset. I couldn't understand why the front's military council should have had any say in the matter. The front had not just thousands, but tens of thousands of lieutenants like me. I decided to return to my former assault brigade, the 70th guard propelled artillery Nevel Berlin brigade, which had recommended me for the orders and sort out the issue myself.

Somehow I found out that the brigade was stationed near Zhytomyr, in the town of Novograd-Volinsky. I decided to go

The Order of the Red Star

there to track down my military service record so I could have the proof to back up my claim to my awards. With the regiment commander's permission, I came to the brigade's HQ in Novograd-Volinsky and spent a night in the heavy atmosphere of the barracks (as a rule, the soldiers were fed peas and rye bread!).

Most of the brigade's personnel were new, but some remembered me and sympathised with my plight. I was given a detailed record of my military service. During the war there had not been much opportunity to write about heroic deeds at great length, so the notes in my record were brief: 'He skilfully commands the unit in battle, he shows courage and he is faithful to the socialist motherland and the party of Lenin and Stalin.' The contents had been written by reasonably literate clerks at HQ and the commanders had just signed their names.

MY ILLEGAL TRIP TO AUSTRIA

From my comrades-in-arms' letters I learned that my battalion and brigade were stationed in the Austrian towns of Tulln and Klosterneuburg on the Danube. To get there I would have to go through Poland and Czechoslovakia. By now the Soviet border had been restored and it was guarded; the guards were part of the Ministry for State Security (the MGB, the precursor of the KGB). You could only cross the border if you had a special pass which was issued by the government in Moscow.

I realised that there was no way I would get permission, so I decided to resort to low cunning, or rather to be more exact, I would take a gamble. I knew that the Polish town of Przemyśl had been ceded to the USSR in September 1939, but several months ago it had been returned to Poland. It had been in the newspapers, but few people paid attention during the stormy, worrying aftermath of the war. I decided to tell my regiment commander that my brigade was in Przemyśl and ask him to let me go there.

I didn't plan in advance exactly how I would cross the border. I hoped that I could sort that out once I was there. If I was detained at the border I would show my permission for leave and just plead ignorance of any rules about crossing the border.

I reach Kraków

Everything went to plan. I handed in my request for ten days' leave to go to my former unit stationed in Przemyśl and find out about my awards. The request seemed plausible enough and permission was granted. Having sorted out my leave, I went to Lvov and took the train to a station on the Polish border. I hung around the station, assessing the situation. In the evening I climbed into a freight carriage of a train bound for Poland and closed the door. I hid in the front right hand corner of the carriage and waited. The border guards came up and opened the door, shining their torch into the carriage, but the light didn't reach me. They shut the door and left. Soon the train started and I gave a sigh of relief. It was difficult to stand and there was nothing to sit on. I lay down on the floor. I was wearing my officer's coat and I had my TT pistol with two magazines of cartridges. There was much unrest at that time, with roaming bands of deserters, nationalists and thieves, so officers always carried a personal weapon.

Suddenly, when the train was moving I sensed there was someone in the corner opposite me. I took out my pistol, loaded a cartridge (it made a definite sound) and asked 'Who's there? I'm going to shoot!' The answer came: 'Sergeant Major Mabler.' We started talking. He turned out to be a Polish Jew and sergeant major in our army who was also illegally crossing the border to see his relatives in Kraków.

The train was travelling slowly with frequent stops. I did my best to stop falling asleep. Falling asleep was dangerous. You would never know whether the other person was all that they seemed to be. My life experiences prompted me to be on the alert. I was lying on my bag but I held the pistol on my chest, pointing towards the figure in the opposite corner, my finger on the trigger. Nevertheless I began to nod off towards the morning.

We got off the train in Kraków. The sergeant major invited me to his place for a wash, shave and a meal. I agreed: a long journey lay ahead across alien territory and I had to look respectable.

Early in the morning we walked around old Kraków. We passed the university where Copernicus had studied and worked. The university has a copy of his book *De Revolutionibus Orbium Coelestium* (*On the Revolutions of the Celestial Spheres*), published in 1543, in which he proved for the first time that the earth is round and that it rotates around its axis and around the sun. The Catholic Church only lifted its ban on his theory 300 years later.[1] It is interesting that Copernicus' statement that the earth was round was confirmed at first hand by our second cosmonaut Gherman Titov on 6 August 1961. When orbiting earth aboard *Vostok 2* at an altitude of 244 kilometres, Titov saw the horizon not as a straight line such as we see on land, but as a curve, so proving that the earth is round. He joyfully told the Centre of Flight Management about his observation. I remembered that Kraków had been the capital city of the Polish kingdom before Warsaw, and in 1813 Russian troops had passed through, driving the remnants of the defeated Napoleonic army back to the west.

When the concierge opened the door for us early in the morning, to my surprise the sergeant major gave her some money. We didn't tip the concierge at home. Later on in the USSR we too would start paying tips. I took a bath at his place, my pistol always by my side. Caution was my watchword. When we had wine with our meal I watched to make sure that they poured from the same decanter into my glass. But everything was fine. I went to the railway station, had a sleep then continued my journey.

Outside Kraków I passed the German concentration camp of Auschwitz where, during the war, 250,000 people were imprisoned and more than a million citizens of the USSR and other countries were killed.[2] Then I changed trains in the cities of Bernau, Bratislava and Vienna.

Reunion at Tulln

My battalion was stationed in Tulln on the River Danube, forty kilometres away from Vienna. I was overjoyed to meet my brothers-in-arms from my platoon, company and battalion. To survive such a war, to cover hundreds of kilometres in the frontline advancing towards the enemy, not hiding behind other people's backs, and to remain alive after scores of bloody battles... Some didn't make it through the war to enjoy that happy day of victory; some were seriously wounded, others were missing.

I was particularly shocked by the fact that in the same battle where I had been wounded, my platoon aide, Sergeant Major Korolev, had been killed. During the three months that we had fought together we had become great friends and he had been like a brother to me.

My soldiers were wearing their orders and medals on their chests—indeed, some wore two medals... So what had happened to my awards?

In autumn 1944 Private Shegartsov had joined my platoon at Sandomierz. He had been a clerk in the brigade's award department, but he had committed a misdemeanour and had been sent to my platoon as a punishment. Two months later he had taken up his former position at HQ. Now I met him again. 'What's the matter?' I asked. 'Why was I refused the rewards I deserved?' Shegartsov looked through the papers and showed me the recommendations for my awards. The recommendation for the Order of the Red Banner was signed by the commander of the self-propelled artillery brigade and Hero of the Soviet Union, Lieutenant Colonel Kornushkin, and the commander of the 4th tank guard army, Colonel General Lelushenko. But at the top, in red pencil, someone had written 'refused on account of him being awarded a second time for the same operation'.

Shegartsov explained that the sappers were nominated for awards by their tank commanders, but to avoid duplicating awards for the same deeds (this could sometimes happen with sappers and tank crew) the tank crew sent their recommendations to the military council of the front before they reached the sappers' command. So there, at the military council of the front, someone had written the words on my recommendation which no one dared to question.

But my recommendation for the Order of the Red Star was still valid! And it was signed by the same commanders. So why didn't it get onto the list? Shegartsov tried to think of an answer and supposed that it was because when I was wounded and left the brigade, a recommendation for an award for someone in the rear had been sent off instead of mine.

(Later during my military service I got to know one of those people who worked in the rear. He was the head chemist on the cavalry course. Although he had never been wounded he wore five combatant orders on his chest. The point was that as head chemist he had access to alcohol and to the girls who worked with him, both of which were much sought after by the cavalry commanders.)

The commander of my battalion couldn't come up with an explanation either. Soon it was New Year's Eve. I saw in the New Year of 1946 with the officers of my battalion at a restaurant by invitation of the mayor of Tulln and the local branch of the Communist Party of Austria.

Then someone advised me to contact the head of the engineering troops of the 1st Ukrainian front, Colonel General Galitsky. His HQ was in the suburban resort of Baden on the other side of Vienna. So I made my way to Baden.

Colonel Galitsky's letter

It wasn't easy for a humble lieutenant without any connections to arrange a meeting with such a high official, but I succeeded. Galitsky received me well, listened attentively, wrote something on a piece of paper, put it in an envelope which he sealed, and told me to give it to the brigade commander. Overjoyed, I rushed back through Vienna to my former brigade. At that time the brigade commander still had the right to give his subordinates national awards.

But the brigade commander wasn't there. I couldn't wait for him as my leave was coming to an end and I had to return across the border and the border guards would become suspicious if I was late. So I decided to hand Galitsky's letter to the acting brigade commander, Lieutenant Colonel Lunin, head of brigade HQ. He had joined our brigade after the war and I had never met him before. As he read the letter Lunin suddenly got very angry and started cursing and swearing at me, shouting that orders should be awarded in battle, not begged from high-ranking people. I was bewildered, indignant and highly agitated, but I managed to pull myself together. I couldn't insult him back because he could have had me arrested for ten days and this would be disastrous as I was abroad illegally and running out of time to return to my regiment.

I left Lunin, having failed to achieve my goal for which I had overcome so many difficulties. I was full of indignation because I had won all my awards in deadly battle, carrying out attacks from my exposed position on the armour of the tanks where I had spilt my blood. Never mind; as a poet said: 'The best reward for us is the eternal love of our motherland...'[3]

So what did Galitsky write in his letter? It remained a mystery. I tried to resolve this twenty years later, but failed. I read Galitsky's memoirs: he wrote, 'the sappers were paving the way for the infantry'. In his book he gave himself the lower rank of lieutenant general, but when I saw him in early 1946 he was a colonel general. I started to make inquiries among my fellow veterans to find out why.

It turned out that in 1938 Galitsky, then deputy head of the Military Engineering Academy in Moscow, wrote a denunciation of the head of the academy. The latter was arrested and died in the basements of the Lubyanka. In 1956 the former head's wife started campaigning for his rehabilitation. His case was subsequently investigated and the investigator asked Galitsky to write an assessment of his former boss. Galitsky wrote a positive assessment. The investigator showed this and the earlier denunciation to the wife.

Appalled by Galitsky's duplicity, the woman sent a complaint to the Central Committee of the Communist Party of the Soviet Union. The complaint reached the Minister of Defence, Marshal Zhukov. He ordered that Colonel General Galitsky be downgraded to the ranks. But when Brezhnev was in office Galitsky managed to prove that his denunciation was written after the head of the academy was arrested. For that reason they decided to meet Galitsky halfway by restoring him to the inferior rank of lieutenant general. During a trip to Moscow to meet fellow soldiers from the 111th rifle division I found Galitsky's address at the information desk. I went to his flat but I was too late. His daughter told me that he had died four months earlier. He died before his ninety-first birthday. I had been so eager to learn what exactly Galitsky had written in the letter to the brigade commander and discover why Lunin had so cruelly abused me.

Smoktunovsky's medal

For some time I was very upset about being deprived of the awards which I had won on the battlefield. After the war the battlefront veterans wore their orders and medals on their soldiers' shirts and coats every day. Of interest in this respect is a famous actor, Innokenty Smoktunovsky. In autumn 1943 as a rank-and-file automatic machine gunner and member of a landing party he was parachuted to the west of Kiev. Unfortunately he landed right where the Germans were stationed and was taken prisoner. Smoktunovsky managed to escape while being driven to a concentration camp and joined a partisan detachment. He fought bravely and was awarded the soldier's medal for courage. Smoktunovsky did not realise, however, that he had been awarded this medal. When the war was over he went to the Arctic Circle, to the remote town of Norilsk, where he became an actor in a local theatre. He considered that in Norilsk he would have a better chance of concealing that he had been taken prisoner and so avoid being sent to Stalin's gulags. With this in mind he even changed his surname from Smoktunovich to Smoktunovsky.

The point is that as a result of the Red Army's shattering defeat in the second half of 1941 most of the army was taken prisoner. Sometimes an entire regiment or division was captured without resistance. In revenge for this defeat, Stalin ordered that all POWs who returned to the Soviet Union after the war be sent to gulags in remote parts of the country for ten years. Very few managed to avoid this fate.

In due course Smoktunovsky, who had demonstrated his talent as actor in various theatres, became a celebrity and was awarded many orders, medals, titles and prizes. He worked at the theatre in Leningrad (now St Petersburg) for a long time, appeared in many films, went on tour in the US and became a favourite of the authorities and a great actor recognised during his lifetime.

So at the height of his fame he was summoned to the district military committee and awarded the medal for courage for fighting for the partisan detachment. His joy was indescribable. He was so happy that he visited all the city authorities, the theatre and his friends and relatives, wearing his medal. For a long time the medal was the only one of his numerous awards that he wore on his coat, and he would take pleasure in telling people why it had been awarded to him and that on his death the silver medal and award certificate would remain in his family for eternity.

Undeserved awards

After our victory at the end of the Great Patriotic War the front veterans were highly respected and wore their much deserved orders and medals on their chests with great pride and honour on both holidays and normal days. But the awards procedure became distorted and corrupt, and the value of combat and anniversary awards was diminished. Much of this was the result of the irresponsible actions of various heads of state—the ill-educated and ill-bred Khrushchev,[4] Brezhnev and others, who would lavishly award themselves both Soviet and foreign orders. Thus during peacetime Khrushchev was awarded the military honour of Hero of the Soviet Union and, three times, the title of Hero of Socialist Labour; he was awarded seven Orders of Lenin and many other orders. He was outdone by Brezhnev who, during peacetime, became a Hero of Socialist Labour and four times Hero of the Soviet Union, and was awarded eight Orders of Lenin and many other orders, both foreign and Soviet (he had thirteen titles of 'Hero' of various socialist countries). But the Soviet Minister of Defence, Marshal Ustinov surpassed them all, possessing along with his numerous other awards eleven Orders of Lenin.

During his leadership Brezhnev amassed more orders and medals than Moscow princes, tsars or Russian emperors possessed together. Other political figures acted in a similar way, including one of the first five Marshals of the Soviet Union,[5] Budyonny, who did not distinguish himself during the Patriotic War but was nonetheless awarded the title of Hero of the Soviet Union three times during peacetime.

Then awards started pouring down like rain. At the peak, awards were given to enterprises and institutions, plants, factories, cooperatives, divisions, military courses, armies, regions, fleets, citizens and towns. Even worse, awards for combat were awarded to murderers and terrorists. For the murder in 1940 of Lenin's first deputy, Leon Trotsky, the Spanish communist Ramón Mercader was given the title Hero of the Soviet Union, while the NKVD officers who planned the assassination, Eitingon and Sudoplatov, were awarded Orders of Lenin. The Order of the Red Banner was awarded to KGB agent Bogdan

Stashinsky for the assassination of the leader of the Organisation of Ukrainian Nationalists, Stepan Bandera, in 1959. That is why the Soviet people stopped wearing awards except for one day in the year, Victory Day on 9 May. Time is the best healer, as they say in the East. In time my pain from this flagrant injustice subsided.

All's well that ends well

But let's return to Vienna. Although I was very short of time I couldn't miss the opportunity of walking down the main streets of one of the most beautiful cities in the world. I looked at its luxurious palaces, magnificent churches, beautiful parks and bridges over the 'Blue Danube'. I even visited the grave of Strauss, composer and genius, who composed an incredible 500 waltzes!

The crusader knights had passed through Vienna on their way to fight against the Muslim Turks, including those on the 1148 crusade led by the German Holy Roman Emperor Friedrich Barbarossa. Hitler named the blitzkrieg against the USSR after him. Vienna is also the coffee capital of Europe. I certainly stopped for a cup of coffee.

On the way back I openly crossed the border, safely passing border control.

Many years later I worked in the Supreme Court of the USSR, dealing with hundreds of criminal cases involving the rehabilitation of people who had been unjustly sentenced.[6] Only once I had become familiar with the devious methods used by the NKVD, which had been falsifying such cases, did I understand how great a risk I had run during my illegal trip across the state border via Poland, Czechoslovakia and Austria. If my wildcat venture had been revealed I could have been sent to a gulag for ten or more years and ended up working in the mines of Magadan or Kolyma, or tree-felling in eastern Siberia.

28

THE ELECTIONS TO THE SUPREME SOVIET

I AM POSTED TO A VILLAGE IN WESTERN UKRAINE

When I returned to my regiment I learned the news. It turned out that the division's rifle regiments (without artillery) were being posted to Rovno region in western Ukraine to 'facilitate' the elections to the Supreme Soviet of the USSR, which were due to be held in February 1946.[1] About thirty officers from the artillery brigade were sent to the rifle regiments to strengthen the Communist Party's influence in the units. We were all members of the Communist Party (Bolsheviks), or *Vsesoyuznaya Kommunisticheskaya Partiya (bol'shevikov)* VKP(b) to give it its full name.[2] Wicked tongues claimed that this was an abbreviation of 'the second serfdom of the Bolsheviks' (*vtoroye krepostnoye pravo bol'shevikov*).[3]

FOR THE MOTHERLAND! FOR STALIN!

Boris as the deputy political officer of a company of the 15th rifle regiment, Rovno region, 1946

I was sent to the 15th rifle regiment as the deputy political officer of a reinforced company, which comprised eighty riflemen and three machine guns. We went by train to our destination, the Alexander district of Rovno region, travelling in freight carriages which were equipped with heaters. We came to a large village with a church. The village was near the River Gorin (Horyn), about thirty kilometres north of the city of Rovno.

We were staying in the villagers' houses. I was with a Baptist family—most people in the village were Baptists. The Baptists couldn't tolerate weapons in their homes, so to avoid conflict our soldiers left their automatic guns in the *ceni* or porch, while officers kept their pistols in their pockets rather than in holsters. When the villagers met us they were suspicious and unfriendly.

Once, out of curiosity I attended a Baptist service in one of the houses. There were twenty people sitting on benches and reading prayers. They sang psalms in unison, with blissful expressions on their faces. The service lasted two hours.

Our village was divided into sections. Our role was to prepare each section for the elections and urge people to turn out to vote. My section included a small hamlet of ten houses, which was a kilometre away from the village on the other side of the River Gorin.

One evening I rode over to the hamlet on horseback and stayed quite long. It was getting dark. When I returned to the village I saw handwritten Bandera leaflets on the walls of the houses; they had evidently just been stuck up, as the glue wasn't dry. Without dismounting, my automatic gun in my hand, I pulled the leaflets off the walls and wedged them between my sheepskin coat and soldier's shirt—there was nowhere else to put them. It took a long time to wash my shirt later on due to the amount of glue stuck to it.

It was alarming to be alone in the dark. I was always under pressure and on the alert, expecting a shot to ring out any second. I was riding up to the river. A bridge was ahead and there were steep slopes to my right and left. On the bridge I glimpsed a shadow. Ambush! Immediately I stopped my horse and got ready to shoot. I waited five minutes. All was calm. Slowly I rode across the bridge. It must have been an otter. There are plenty of otters in that region.

During the war the headquarters of the Ukrainian Insurrectionary Army, the military wing of the Organisation of Ukrainian Nationalists (*Banderovtsi*), was in a marshy and forested place ten kilometres north of the village. About fifteen kilometres west was the village of Veliky Zhitin, home of the first President of Ukraine, Leonid Kravchuk. Back then Kravchuk would have been twelve years old—exactly the same age as the boys from our village who took bags of food to the *Banderovtsi*.

On our arrival, the *Banderovtsi* main forces headed north to Polesie, an area of impassable marshy forests and swamps. Only small groups of four or five men from the Ukrainian Insurrectionary Army remained. They were hiding in well-equipped underground shelters.

It was the day of the election. No one from my hamlet went to the village to cast their vote. Accompanied by a unit of soldiers, I went to the hamlet. At every house the peasants told me: 'We won't go to the polls by ourselves. Give us a soldier with a rifle for company.' This was to make it look as if they were being taken to vote under duress, so we had to do it their way.

I went into a house where a married couple lived. The wife was at home but she didn't know where her husband was. I thought he must be hiding. I left a soldier with an automatic in the yard while I climbed up to the first floor of the barn, where I found the man hiding in the hay and gave him a telling off, using four-letter words. We were about to climb down when he suddenly rushed into the corner where his tools were, grabbed an axe and swung it at me, but I was quicker. I snatched my pistol and fired it above his head into the air. At that moment the soldier was running up, his automatic at the ready. The man was calming down. I told the soldier to lead him and his wife to the poll, then I went to the next house.

In another house I found a veteran from the front, an invalid with one leg and a medal for courage pinned to his chest. He said: 'I'm not going to vote.' I brought him a ballot box. He said: 'I'm not going to vote.' And no matter how hard I tried to persuade him, my efforts were in vain. He said: 'Put in your own vote—I won't vote.' Having spent half an hour achieving nothing, this is what I ended up having to do.

To avoid possible unrest the poll was guarded intensively. A machine gun was positioned in the attic of the house opposite. There were armed two-man patrols everywhere. The polling booths were open for all to see.

I was a member of the election committee. On some of the ballot papers people had added their own candidates or crossed names out; some papers were torn, while others were covered with anti-Soviet messages, but the majority voted for the party. During the day a T-34 tank arrived in the village. After midnight it took the ballot boxes, the minutes of the election committee and the election results to the centre of the region.

The Ukrainian nationalist prisoner

Once, during clashes, we captured a wounded *Banderovtsi* fighter and I had to take him on a thirty-kilometre journey by sleigh from the platoon's base to the centre of the region, accompanied by a guard.[4]

After the heat of battle we had cooled down and started talking. My prisoner turned out to be a history teacher in a village school and he spoke Russian. I asked him how he thought he could resist the invincible Red Army which had defeated the strongest army in the world, that of the Nazi German invaders. I said that Soviet rule brought freedom and a prosperous future to the people of western Ukraine. He answered:

> 'We don't need your "freedom". What is this "freedom" that you are talking about? With the arrival of Soviet rule in western Ukraine in 1939–40, tens of thousands of members of the intelligentsia—teachers, doctors, engineers, writers, actors, artists—were arrested and sent to Kolyma, to Magadan and the far north. Five years have passed and none of them have come back. Those who remained behind were driven into collective farms, their horses and cows were taken away and they were made serfs of the collective farm system. As for our "prosperous future", we will build it without your help. If people fight for their freedom they can't be defeated.'

> 'What is your political platform?' I asked. 'What do you want to achieve, through making such appalling sacrifices?' 'We want,' he said, 'an independent Ukrainian state with its own army and a true democracy with different political parties. We want to get rid of the collective farm, that

system of slavery where labourers can't use the fruits of their labour. We want to restore private property and private means of production. We want to have our own currency. We want the symbols of the Ukrainian state—its ancient trident, and its yellow and blue flag which symbolises our blue sky and ripe corn. We object to your red flag that is the colour of blood.'

I tried a different approach. 'How can you be so cruel to people who were sent to you from eastern Ukraine? You've killed doctors, postmen, teachers. Only recently a woman was cruelly killed in your region, a teacher who had come from eastern Ukraine.'

He answered: 'We told the teacher: "You can teach our children, but we will raise them as patriots of Ukraine ourselves. If you start denouncing us to the NKVD we will hang you from this tree." And we did, as we were convinced that she had betrayed us. Through her pupils she found out the names of relatives and accomplices of the *Banderovtsi* who were living in the village. They were arrested, their property confiscated, and then they were sent with their babies to the remote regions of Siberia and the far east from where, as a rule, people don't come back. Just remember how ruthlessly Lenin's entourage and even Lenin's deputy, Trotsky, were annihilated, along with Trotsky's wives and children.'[5]

I must say that even back then the teacher's opposition and his arguments made a deep impression on me.

The Ukrainian war veterans' congress 1995

Now, when more than sixty years have passed and a fifth generation has reached adulthood, it's high time to put aside mutual offence and reproaches and work together to construct a better life for our people in an independent Ukraine.

Moving forwards, I will tell you how these nationalists, the *Banderovtsi*, reminded me of their existence many years later. In the summer of 1995, fifty years later, a congress of delegates from the All-Ukrainian Union of War Veterans was held in Kiev.

About 200 delegates came from all regions of Ukraine. I was the only representative from my regiment's war veterans' group in Odessa. I was head of the group of veterans from the 4th guard tank army in Odessa, which consisted of 100 members. When the congress was in progress I handed a message to the presidium which suggested that we should discuss the reconciliation of *Banderovtsi* nationalists with communists, with reference to the fact that both had been struggling for a free Ukraine and that more than half a century had elapsed since the war. Mutual hostility had already passed down to children and grandchildren. What for? And how long would this continue? Nowadays Ukraine is independent—which is exactly what both sides had been fighting for—and now all their efforts should be put not into stirring up hostility between sides, but improving the standard of life for all Ukrainian people who had endured so much suffering in the past.

My message was read aloud by the chair of the presidium at the end of the session. My lord! All hell broke loose! There were shouts of 'show us where he is!' I stood up and walked into the aisle between the rows of seats. I was surrounded by a furious crowd of people, their faces beast-like and contorted with rage, swinging their fists at me and shouting: 'Disgrace! Traitor! Bastard! Scoundrel! He should be shot!'

I tried to explain that as a member of a rifle division I had fought against the *Banderovtsi* and that there was no gold, silver or jewellery in their underground shelters, but only weapons, food, water and warm clothes. When surrounded by our soldiers and fearing being taken prisoner and tortured in the basements of the KGB and NKVD, they blew themselves up with grenades while shouting 'Long live independent Ukraine!' They were not bandits but were fighting for an independent Ukraine on the basis that according to the constitution of the USSR, each republic in the union had the right of secession. But nobody seemed to be listening to me. It was through sheer luck that I managed to get out alive, safe and sound. Fortune was smiling on me again.

At this point I must say that I watched this brouhaha break out around me quite calmly. I understood that these people had never fought against the *Banderovtsi*. Warriors who meet each other in deadly battle respect their opponents. A vivid example is the case of the commander of the 63rd rifle corps, forty-year-old Lieutenant General Leonid Petrovsky, the son of Lenin's close associate, Gregori Petrovsky. Leonid Petrovsky skilfully commanded the corps in August 1941. During battle he was surrounded but fought courageously and did a lot of damage to the Nazi enemy before being killed and picked up by the Germans. Impressed by his heroism and courage, the Germans buried him with full military honours in his uniform with his orders.

The next day the head of the presidium was presenting jubilee medals from the Czech Republic to those who had participated in the liberation of Czechoslovakia in May 1945, to commemorate fifty years of liberation from the German invaders. My surname was also read out. I came up to the table to receive my medal. The chair asked me: 'Are you Bogachev from Odessa?' 'Yes I am.' 'Have you got a medal for the liberation of Prague?' 'Yes I have.' 'One is enough for you. You may go.' So head bowed I returned to my seat. Because of those nationalist *Banderovtsi* I was stripped of a state award from a friendly country.

In our cruel world where people kill each other for peanuts, where the concept of life itself has lost its value to its utmost, it is within our power to prevent this animosity.

29

THE MILITARY LAW ACADEMY

I DECIDE TO CHANGE CAREER

Five months passed. We were still in the village, tense and unable
go anywhere, surrounded by endless forests. Contrary to our
expectations, we were not sent back to our permanent base after
the election, but left in the village for an indefinite period.
Morale was low. Everywhere else life was peaceful and nights
were calm. Here, there was no rest for the exhausted soul—only
constant tension and service, with no diversions. We were not
given any orders or awards for our hard service because they
didn't want anyone in the country to know about it.

During an officers' meeting at the end of spring the battalion
commander asked who would like to take summer uniforms to
two radio operators who were on a course near Lvov. Several
people raised their hands, but I was the first so I was chosen.

FOR THE MOTHERLAND! FOR STALIN!

On the train I started talking to my neighbour in the compartment, a captain, who told me that he had seen the conditions
of admission to the Military Law Academy in Moscow in the
Krasnaya Zvezda newspaper. I didn't even know the academy
existed.[1] The captain couldn't remember the details, but I became
interested. I remembered that the writers Gogol and Korolenko
also dreamed in their youth of becoming lawyers who would
work for the triumph of truth. I also remembered another occasion at Guyva garrison when I was walking back from the artillery firing range after shooting practice with my colleague
Lieutenant Belousov. During the fifteen-kilometre walk
Belousov said that it was vital to get a higher education. I asked
why. 'To be able to read between the lines,' he said. This thought
went deeply into my mind. We were living through difficult
times—people said one thing, thought another and did something else. That was why it was difficult to find your way in life.

My military career didn't go well. I wasn't promoted during
the war, as some were. I started and finished as a lieutenant, a
platoon commander (the lowest officer rank) with one order and
three injuries. I had almost no prospects of promotion after the
war. The army was being reduced considerably. A captain who
was formerly a battery commander joined our battery as a platoon commander. By that time I had lost my romantic illusions
about military service as an artillery officer. I was sick and tired
of the dirt and the horrors of war, of service in forests, small
villages and remote garrison towns. On the other hand, I could
become a military lawyer. The career of an army lawyer is interesting and prestigious. I had long been thinking about the legal
profession and the sense of justice and the yearning to seek out
the truth, to judge people justly, honestly and decently. I had a
strong sense of right and wrong. And so I developed a fervent
desire to enter the academy. There are so many circumstances
that influence the role of fate in our lives.

THE MILITARY LAW ACADEMY

At 6 am I arrived in Lvov and immediately started searching for the nearest military unit so I could look through *Krasnaya Zvezda* in the library. A military hospital was nearby and the principal's wife was its librarian. I went to the principal's apartment and explained my errand to the sleepy woman. Realising that she couldn't get rid of me, she opened the library in her dressing gown, her hair dishevelled, and I went and read the conditions of admission to the academy. I fulfilled all the conditions: those eligible to take the entrance examination had to be officers who had served for two years, who were members of the Communist Party, fit for military service, with a secondary education, and positive political and service records. I had all these.

Actually, to tell the truth, I had only eight years of secondary education, but when I had checked out of hospital in 1943 the personnel department had filled in my CV using the details which I had given them. I had told them that my secondary education lasted ten years, so this is what appeared on my form. My first CV as an officer had been written in military school and was lost when the 111th rifle division was surrounded and annihilated near Kharkov in 1943. My second CV had been drawn up by the personnel department of the Kalinin Front and was lost when I left the mortar regiment after my serious injuries in February 1943. After my recovery in July 1943 the personnel department of the Central Asian military region drew up my third CV.

I decided to stay overnight in a hotel. As I checked in at reception I noticed that a major with a pistol in his holster was looking at me intently. My intuition told me not to start talking to him. At night, through the open window, I heard the continuous rattle of automatic gunfire, single shots and grenade explosions in different parts of the city.

When we went to bed my roommate and I put our pistols not under our pillows, but under the mattresses by our feet. Our reasoning was that if someone rushed into the room the first thing he would do would be to look under the pillows for weapons, like in the films. During the night we heard pistol shots in the corridor. We jumped off our beds and pointed our pistols at the door, preparing to shoot to save our lives. We knew there were many *Banderovtsi* in the city.

In the morning we learned that the major who had looked at me in such a strange way in the foyer had been firing his pistol in his room. Its door was peppered with bullet holes. The major turned out to have a mental illness.

After returning from Lvov a month passed before I was sent to my artillery regiment. After joining them I asked the commander of the regiment for permission to send my documents to the academy. 'Only lawyers are admitted there,' he said. 'Not people like you. Show me the newspaper.' Another obstacle! Where could I get hold of a two-month old newspaper that had probably been used to make cigarette papers?

At that moment I remembered that Pushkin was useless at maths, Beethoven couldn't learn his times tables, the poet Robert Burns couldn't learn how to write for a long time, the fifteen-year-old Einstein was castigated at his Gymnasium for his poor academic performance, Chekhov repeated a year in his third form after poor results in Russian, and Gorky was admitted to the church choir and Shalyapin wasn't. Nevertheless Shalyapin persevered and became one of the most famous opera singers in the world.

So I decided that I must fight at whatever cost! I found some spare time and went to the officers' club library in Zhytomyr where I found the newspaper I needed and secretly took it from the pile. The librarian was surprised. 'You must have read the newspaper quickly!'

I showed the newspaper to the commander of my regiment, who gave me permission to prepare my documents for the academy.

The secretary of the local party quickly wrote me a good reference. I went to the commander of my division who claimed to have read only two books in his life—the brief history of the Communist Party and an artillery manual which he knew by heart. I asked him to write me a reference on my military service. 'My dear boy,' he said, 'you need your reference, so write it yourself. I don't have time. You write it, then I will sign it.'

What was I supposed to do? How could I write my own reference? Nowadays it is quite common, but back then... I didn't have any alternative. I wrote four or five lines and was unable to write more. I brought the sheet of paper to the commander of my division. Where I had written 'disciplined' he added 'not' in front and did the same to all my sentences. I was extremely angry. Firstly it wasn't true; secondly it would have been impossible to turn up at the academy in Moscow with such a reference in order to take the entrance examination—it would have been out of the question. 'Come back in an hour,' he told me. For an hour I walked to and fro in front of HQ in a state of great anxiety. What was on his mind? An hour later he gave me my reference, a whole page of typed text where I was described in such positive terms that I could barely recognise myself. He said: 'That is the way you should write a reference for the academy.'

Now the hard work began. My documents had been sent to Moscow and I was waiting to be called to the academy to take the entrance examination. After work, while everyone was going home to rest, I was off on a second shift studying textbooks. The four-year war had knocked many things out of my memory—I felt as though ten years had passed since the beginning of the war. During the day I stole some hours for my studies and climbed up to the attic where no one could disturb me. In the evening I studied at the barracks, in Lenin's room under the dim light of the electric lamp on the ceiling.[2]

FOR THE MOTHERLAND! FOR STALIN!

My trip to the Military Law Academy—and Skopin

After receiving the invitation to take the examination I arrived in Moscow. I went to the academy which was on Smolensky Avenue near the future site of the Ministry of Foreign Affairs. I found out that there were 1,000 applicants for 120 places. One thousand candidates had already been rejected by the admission panel on the grounds of insufficient paperwork.

I went to the admission panel and—what a fiasco! I was not allowed to take the examination because my certificate that showed I had completed ten years of secondary education was not valid. I needed my secondary education exam certificate, or a copy. What could I do? Everything had started so well only to end in ruins! Extremely frustrated, my hopes shattered, I was going downstairs to return to Zhytomyr when...

Suddenly an unexpected meeting. A miracle happened! It really is a small world—mountains may never meet, but people will. Actually our life is full of accidental coincidences of which, like bricks, our fortune is constructed. The girl who was walking upstairs towards me was, I realised, the girl who had danced with me at a dance in a park in Petropavlovsk, north Kazakhstan, in the summer of 1943 during my month's leave after hospital.

Such luck! She was working as a secretary for the admission panel. Learning about my predicament, she said that the panel would accept a certificate that showed that I had completed ten years of school with the head teacher's signature and the school stamp. I am forever grateful to Fate for sending this girl to me who, in many respects, defined the shape of my future life. I expressed my gratitude to her and we parted.

But how could I get hold of such a certificate if I finished secondary school after only eight years? Later, on my way to Moscow's Kievsky Railway Station, an idea came into my head: what if I went to my school in Skopin where I had studied for two months of my ninth year. Skopin had been occupied by the

Germans in a sudden raid. I saw my school 'No. 2' after it had been looted—everywhere in the corridors and classrooms were scattered papers, textbooks and library books. All the offices in Skopin, including the town hall—all the places where there could have been information about my time at school—had also been looted. Maybe it would be worth trying my luck and returning to the school in Skopin to get the certificate I needed. Although it was a chance in a million I had to take it. With my plans laid, I went to Moscow's Kazansky Railway Station and took the train to Skopin in Ryazan region, 300 kilometres from Moscow.

I walked up to the school but couldn't pluck up the courage to enter. I was overcome with nerves. I waited until the school head teacher, an elderly woman, was leaving to go home. I was young, just twenty-one years old. I was wearing my lieutenant's uniform with three wound stripes, an order and three medals on my chest. I told the head teacher that she held the key to the destiny of a person who had been prepared to sacrifice his life and had fought for his motherland, and that she had to provide him with a new opportunity in life by giving him the certificate. I told her many things of this nature and pleaded with her while we walked to her house at the other end of the town. And I succeeded!

The next morning she gave me the certificate and stamp for finishing ten years of school. She gave it to me for nothing—she had done it out of the goodness of her heart. I will always remember her and be eternally grateful.

I arrived at the academy with the certificate and was allowed to take the examination. I met some of the applicants. What strong candidates they were! One said that before the war he had graduated from teaching college and worked as a schoolteacher. Another said that he had served in the Defence Ministry in Moscow throughout the war and had been preparing to enter the academy all through those years. (Neither was admitted.) The third applicant was a Hero of the Soviet Union. The fourth was the adjutant of a famous Moscow military commander. And so on. Listening to them, my prospects looked bleak. I was very nervous when I sat the examination, but to cut a long story short I passed both parts with good and excellent marks.

Hurray! I enter the academy!

I believe in destiny, but I don't believe those who say destiny can't be altered. The main thing is to listen to your inner voice and try to make your dream come true.

I had one more alarming moment. I was going through the most important stage—the document panel. The panel was chaired by the head of the academy, Major General of Law Sukhov. The head of first aid Colonel Zalkind said that I had a shell fragment in my body. 'How big?' asked the major general. I nervously showed them my index finger. 'Oooh!' gasped the entire panel. Only then did it occur to me that I was doing it the wrong way. In reality the fragment was the size of my fingernail, so I quickly told them and the head of first aid confirmed it from my papers. Applicants weren't told the panel's decision at this point.

The next morning I rushed to the academy to learn the panel's decision. The lists of successful applicants were pinned to the announcement board in the hall. I was nervously looking for my surname and... I found it! I am lost for words to describe my happiness and joy. I looked at my name on the list over and over again to make sure that I hadn't made a mistake. And when I finally convinced myself that I had been admitted to the academy I went for a walk around Moscow.

I was filled with tremendous joy. My soul was singing. Through my own efforts, without anyone else's help, I had made my life turn around for the better. There are moments when you feel you have power over the world. That was such a moment. It didn't matter where I went. I wasn't actually walking—I felt as if my soul was floating through the air. The sense of life's fullness went to my head like a young wine. Everything was ahead of me! Everything was within my grasp! As Leo Tolstoy wrote in *War and Peace* of his heroine Natasha Rostova when she cut a brilliant figure during her first ball: 'she was at the summit of her happiness when a person becomes kind and good, and doesn't believe in the possibility of unhappiness, or distress...' To celebrate my admission to the academy I drank a bottle of champagne in a cocktail bar in Gorky Street (now Tverskaya Street), having said to myself, 'the bigger the risk, the sweeter the champagne'.

My dream had come true! My difficult path had led to victory! I would study at the Military Law Academy in Moscow. In five years' time I would have a degree in military law. I would be able to study, fully paid by the state during a very difficult time for my country when there was rationing and everyone was living from hand to mouth. All Moscow belonged to me! Theatres, cinemas, museums, exhibitions, libraries, the circus, the zoo, the planetarium and many, many more attractions. And I would have a military career.

I was puffed up with pride and vanity—I would be a lawyer, a judge, a chair of a military tribunal. I would decide the fate of a person who broke the law, I would determine whether he should live or die. When the judge enters the courtroom the secretary commands: 'Be standing!' and everyone stands, including the president of the state. During the deliberation when the judge decides on the sentence no one is allowed to come into the room, even the president himself, and the sentence is pronounced on behalf of the state of the USSR. Everyone stands up at that point. And the judge obeys only the law and no one else. No wonder I felt dizzy!

Of the 750 officers serving in 1946 in the 147th rifle division, I was the only one who entered the academy.

FOR THE MOTHERLAND! FOR STALIN!

Where is my black gun?

(from a song *Gde Moy Chorniy Pistolet?* by Vladimir Vysotsky, 1938–80, actor, poet and singer)[3]

Length of life is measured not by the number of years you live, but the number of events you live through...

In early March 1945, during a tank attack near the German city of Cottbus, my machine gunner shot a German officer who refused to surrender and I was given his 9-mm Luger pistol. The Luger was a high quality weapon. This type of pistol had been used in the German army for seventy years, the longest period of continuous usage for pistols and rifles throughout the world.

After the war the Ministry of Defence issued several orders to hand in trophy weapons, pistols, rifles, cartridges and so on. But few obeyed. While I was in the army I kept the pistol in my suitcase or in my trouser pocket if necessary. When the war ended there was a spate of robberies, hooliganism, assaults and banditry, especially in the larger cities, and personal weapons were necessary for self-defence.

Many of our generals had this pistol in their possession after the war. Incidentally, it was a Luger which General (later Marshal) Batitsky used when he fired a whole round of eight cartridges into one of the greatest scoundrels in world history, Marshal of the Soviet Union Lavrenty Beria, in the basement of Moscow military district HQ in Zamoskvorechye in December 1953.[4]

Beria was the sixth Marshal of the Soviet Union who was shot by his own people. Before him five marshals had been shot in the dirty basement of the secret police HQ at the Lubyanka: Yegorov, Tukhachevsky, Kulik, Khudyakov and Blyukher (the latter was beaten to death). Their wives and grown-up children were sent to gulags, and their younger children were sent to orphanages and their surnames changed.

In late August 1946 I received my invitation from the Military Law Academy, left my garrison in Guyva where I was serving in the artillery regiment, and went to Moscow to take the entrance examination. I had my pistol in my suitcase. The applicants were staying at the academy, ten to a room. We slept on wooden pallets with mattresses and pillows stuffed with straw, and no sheets or pillowcases.

One evening a fellow applicant complained: 'I can't lie down on this. There's a damned nail sticking out.' We had nothing with which to hammer down the nail so I took the initiative, forgetting that it is never a good idea to stick your neck out. I unpacked my Luger and with several blows used it to drive the nail back into the board. Everyone seemed happy and I put the pistol back in my suitcase.

After passing my exams I went to my regiment to hand in my resignation then returned to the academy on 1 September to begin my studies. I stayed in a hall of residence in the academy building. I continued to keep my pistol in my suitcase.

From 20 September onwards the cadets at the academy started preparing for the annual parade on Red Square on 7 November to commemorate the great October Revolution.[5] Rehearsals lasted from morning until 2 pm every day, with the cadets marching along the bank of the Moscow river near Smolensky Square accompanied by a military band. The front section of our formation was called the 'box' and consisted of twenty columns in ten rows, making a total of 200 cadets.

As you passed the platform on the mausoleum where members of government of our great state were standing together with the greatest man of our time, Stalin, it was said that you would be overcome by awe. As a result you could stumble or walk out of step, or lag. To avoid such occurrences, we cadets would link our little fingers together.

In mid-October, after our classes, the duty officer's aide came to my room and told me to go to room 217 immediately. When I asked who wanted me and why he didn't tell me. The duty officer was the infamous Colonel General Vasiliy Ulrikh, who was later appointed the course director of the Military Law Academy in 1948. From 1926 until 1948 Ulrikh was the chairman of the Military Collegium of the Supreme Court of the USSR. Under his chairmanship hundreds of criminal and other cases were considered, and marshals, generals, admirals, ministers, senior party members, diplomats, outstanding inventors, directors of large factories and so on were sentenced to death by firing squad (after Stalin's death, they were all posthumously rehabilitated). In his book on Marshal Zhukov, Colonel Vladimir Karpov, a brave scout who had taken seventy-three Germans prisoner during the war, called Ulrikh 'the most unprincipled and cold-blooded executor of all the tribe of representatives of this damned profes-

Colonel General Vasiliy Ulrikh

sion'. Ulrikh looked like an ordinary man, of medium height, bald with a round face and sweaty hands...

I am digressing, so I will return to my story... When I found room 217 there was only a number on the door but no name. I knocked. I heard someone say: 'Come in.' I went in. There was a lieutenant colonel at the desk. He didn't offer me his hand or say hello, but just told me to sit down. Then he introduced himself: 'I am Lieutenant Colonel Savlin, head of the academy's NKVD special department.'

My heart sank. He started politely asking me where I had fought and where I had served. As I answered I tried to think what I could have said or done to be called to this awful room. And then the lieutenant colonel asked, again politely, if I was taking part in training for the parade and whether I knew that the parade would be viewed by Stalin. I said: 'Yes.' Then looking directly into my eyes, in measured tones he asked: 'So why do you secretly and illegally keep a pistol with cartridges in your suitcase?' At this point I was petrified and began explaining to him in a confused way that I had been keeping the pistol since the war for self-defence.

I was lucky—he was a decent man. The lieutenant colonel didn't see anything criminal in my behaviour, although illegal possession of firearms was a criminal offence and, according to the law, it could be punished by a term of five years in a gulag. This would have meant goodbye to the academy.

You should have seen me flying up the stairs to the third floor of our residence. Everyone I passed was turning and looking back at me. I fetched the pistol. There were no repercussions and nobody else knew about it. Later I took part in the parade. For a long time afterwards I was proud of the fact that I had marched in front of Stalin himself and he had greeted me with his raised hand.

But I couldn't stop wondering who had denounced me to the NKVD. When I had hit the nail with my pistol there had been ten people in our room, three of whom later passed the exams and were accepted into the academy. Which one was the informer? Captain Zinchenko, Hero of the Soviet Union (later my colleague in Zabaykalsky military district)? The senior lieutenant in the telecommunications unit (I don't remember his name)? The lieutenant at the tank regiment's maintenance depot, Myboroda? Which one? Myboroda stood out by the fact that he had heated arguments with everyone whatever the occasion, and by the fact that he was a confirmed bachelor.

After we graduated at the beginning of 1951 we went in different directions in our huge country. Myboroda and I served in different garrisons for a long time, but in the 1970s we both happened to live in Odessa. I was still in military service as a judge for the tribunal in Odessa military district, while Myboroda had retired from the army and was working as a technician at an oil terminal. Twice, perhaps three times a year, we met up and reminisced about the war and our student days in Moscow. Then in 2002 his neighbour called me to come and see him as he was very ill. When I arrived he was lying in bed. He couldn't get up and was obviously dying. He was eighty-two. He told me that he felt that death was approaching and he had only days to live. He wasn't a believer but he had decided to confess to gain peace of mind. His greatest sin was that during the war he had been hired by the NKVD's SMERSH department as a secret informer, or *stukach*, but he insisted that he hadn't informed on anyone while he was studying at the academy. To distract him from his gloomy thoughts I told him a joke:

> In a prison cell one inmate asks another inmate what he has been sentenced for and the other answers: 'I was sitting with my friend and we were telling political jokes. Then we both went home. I thought to myself: "Should I inform on him now, or wait until the morning?" But he didn't wait until the morning. That is why I am here.'

It became clear to me that Myboroda was the person who had informed on me to the head of the academy's NKVD about the pistol. But I didn't say anything due to his poor state of health. He died several days later. I was told about his death but I didn't attend the funeral.

I can tell you another tale which also characterised that hard and troubled time (and could be of interest for those researching our complicated lives in the future). When we were reminiscing about our time at the academy Myboroda told me the following story.

In 1947 the cadets lived in a hall of residence at the academy, with fifteen to twenty to a room. One cadet, Senior Lieutenant Tishenko, opened a letter from his parents in Ukraine in which they wrote about famine in a rural area where people, driven insane by hunger, resorted to cannibalism, killing passers-by, neighbours or even children. The local authorities didn't take any steps to mitigate the famine by giving out food, but heartlessly banished everyone from that area. Tishenko was reading the letter out to Myboroda and three other cadets. While he was reading Myboroda kept making anti-Soviet remarks about the leaders of the state and Communist Party and their inhuman political beliefs. The next day Myboroda was summoned to the academy's political department where an officer demanded a written explanation regarding his anti-Soviet remarks. On the desk were two written denunciations and Myboroda tried to identify the signatures. Which of the four cadets who were present when the letter was read had informed on him?

As he had admitted that he had been an NKVD informer, I realised that Myboroda had been subtly provoking his own comrades into making anti-Soviet remarks so he could inform on them to the NKVD (in return for money, without doubt). The NKVD would then take appropriate measures—in this case, seven years in a gulag, confiscation of property and removal of political rights for five years. But Myboroda's comrades informed on him first. Such was the situation during this troubled time.

Incidentally, Myboroda's story reminds me that during my long military service when talking to my colleagues they would frequently—and in highly confidential tones—come out with vehemently anti-Soviet opinions. At the time I didn't realise that these were deliberate acts of provocation by informers, but my intuition told me that I shouldn't rise to the bait. Perhaps this saved me for otherwise I could be lying in a shallow grave dug into the permafrost at Kolyma or Magadan.

I would like to add that there were 120 cadets in our year at the academy. Of these three were sentenced to the gulag for anti-Soviet propaganda. All three were from my naval department of twenty-three people. After Stalin's death they were all rehabilitated and acquitted of any crime. But their lives had been completely disrupted. I must say that all our state-controlled radio stations, newspapers, journals, magazines, books, cinema, theatre and political information, the political classes at Communist Party offices, not to mention party meetings, party commissions, party conferences, party schools and party congresses were all based on denunciations and round-the-clock propaganda declaring our success. At the same time a second row of barbed-wire fencing was urgently being installed along the western frontier to prevent the Soviet people fleeing from their socialist haven into capitalist slavery.

From Moscow to Zhytomyr, Kiev, Odessa and back to Moscow

'Life may not be beautiful, but it is still full of surprises.' (Anon)

'Judge not lest ye be judged.'

All those who were admitted to the academy had a fortnight's leave to sort out their affairs with their military units. On the train to Zhytomyr I happened to meet another person who had won a place at the academy, Captain Mityuk. Mityuk was the commander of a communications platoon in Kiev. Later he became a major general of law, the chairman of the military tribunal of the Pacific fleet and a military legal counsellor in Cuba and Afghanistan.

The train carriage was overcrowded. We had to stand by the doors at the end of the carriage for the whole night. Mityuk got off at Kiev and I went on to Zhytomyr. On reaching my garrison I heard the startling news—during my month-long absence my regiment and division had been disbanded and the three rifle divisions of the 102nd rifle corps were being merged into one motorised division. So I had to go to a completely unknown military unit which now held all the documents from my regiment. Oh my God! Do you exist at all? It was there that I heard even more startling news. Sudden cuts were being made in the army. Officers who had been heavily wounded, or had received light wounds twice, or had completed intensive six-to-eight-week courses at military schools during the war were being pensioned off into the reserve. By order of the commander-in-chief of the Lvov military district, over a thousand officers from the 102nd rifle corps were to leave the army and join the reserve, including me because I was eligible on all three counts.[6]

I was given a package of my personal documents stamped 'confidential' and sealed with five seals and an order to leave for the Odessa regional military committee to register as an officer of the reserve. Stunned by such unexpected news, I left the building holding the package. Why was destiny so cruel to me? It felt as if I'd been stabbed in the heart. It is especially painful to experience misfortune after happiness. But life wasn't going to finish here. I had to fight! But how? For me it is natural to fight to the end. It's not in my nature to give in. Now I had nothing to lose. Everything was lost. I tore open the package and looked through the papers in my file of personal information. All my references were positive, but the decision of the commanders of the battery, the division and the regiment was that I must be discharged and join the reserve. Only three words are used (*uvolit v zapas*) but they would dramatically change my destiny...

A thought came into my head: you have to find unusual solutions in unusual circumstances. When I was taking my exams I was taken aback by the fact that one in three of those admitted to the academy had never been to the front. For the entire four years of the bloody war they had been taking it easy in the rear—in ministries, various HQs, schools, warehouses and so on. Many of them were the sons of generals or senior party officials or Soviet bureaucrats. Some were chauffeur-driven to the academy in their fathers' cars. One of my fellow students was the son of Lieutenant General Rogov, a member of the Communist Party's central committee and the head of the political department of the USSR fleet. Those types of people would be studying at the academy, but I wouldn't! But I deserved to be a cadet at the academy much more than them.

I remembered the song *Mishka Odessit* (*Mishka the Odessite*), performed by the famous actor and singer, Mark Bernes. But I substituted the name 'Mishka' with my pet name 'Borka'.

> You are an Odessite, Borka.
> It means
> That neither the sea nor the wind can threaten you.
> You are a sailor, Borka, and sailors never cry
> And never lose their nerve.

After all, I was an Odessite and a sailor. I had lived in Odessa for a year during the war and I had been a sailor on a two-mast yacht, the *Decembrist*, for three months while I was in the sports club.

Then a sacrilegious thought entered my mind. What if the phrase to 'discharge and join reserve' (*uvolit v zapas*) was substituted by 'remain in army' (*ostavit v kadrakh*). Only two words would change. But wouldn't this count as deception? Bah! Come what may! I started putting this idea into practice. I don't remember how I managed to get a blank form, or how and where I had these two words typed. But I do remember that I forged the signatures of the commanders of the battery and the division myself, then went to the garrison to find the commander of the regiment who was still in the process of disbanding the unit. He had the regiment's stamp.

I told him that due to an error they hadn't put his signature and stamp on my form. My lie worked. The commander was at home in his pyjamas and was, so to speak, a bit tipsy: he proceeded to sign and stamp my form without looking—God forgive me! But my folder of personal information had been in a packet fastened with five seals. I couldn't turn up at the academy with a torn packet. It would arouse suspicion and there could be undesirable repercussions. And then I remembered Mityuk from the train. As a commander of a separate platoon, he would have a seal. And the fact that his seal would have a different number wouldn't matter because it was unlikely that anyone would check the numbers.

I went to Kiev and found Mityuk. He didn't ask me why the packet was torn and ordered his secretary to seal it properly. While staying in the spa of Shklo, near Lvov, forty years later I came across General Mityuk and reminded him of this episode. He asked: 'Did you present me with a bottle of vodka?'[7] I answered: 'No, but I'll do it now.' So I had to drink a whole bottle of vodka with him. A year later Mityuk died in sad circumstances. He was having a routine operation for the removal of a polyp. He was given a general anaesthetic. But his heart, overstrained by his work in Cuba and Afghanistan, gave out and stopped for ever. May he rest in peace.

I went to Odessa, where my family now lived once more, and walked into their apartment, saluting my father with pride: 'Comrade Colonel, first-year cadet at Military Law Academy Lieutenant Bogachev, present and correct.' Their joy was tremendous!

On my return to the academy, I was admitted to the naval faculty by my own choice. I put on a naval officer's uniform and began my studies. My trickery over the form was discovered ten years later. In 1956 I worked in Moscow as a senior officer in the inspection department of the Military Collegium of the Supreme Court of the USSR.[8] At that time they were checking army officers' personal details. I was summoned to the collegium's personnel department where I was shown a document from the main personnel department of the USSR military department which required me to resign and join the reserve in 1946. Also at that time Khrushchev had launched an initiative to reduce the army by 1,200,000. So a sword of Damocles was hanging over each officer, each with the fear of being pensioned off. This is the end, I thought. Now they've got me. But I must have been born under a lucky star. I wasn't killed at the front but could have been (on a hundred occasions, according to my account),

Boris and Nina on their wedding day, Moscow, 7 November 1949

and I have been lucky in other ways except when playing cards—but I haven't got a gambling habit. Back in 1956 I hadn't served long enough to be eligible for a pension. I didn't have a flat or any civilian occupation. So I would have to start my life from scratch after serving in the army for fifteen years. It's not that easy when you are thirty-two and have a wife and a baby.

On seeing my deep sadness and anxiety, the head of personnel promised to help me. He sent a letter to the Minister of Defence with an explanation of my case and a request to retain me, with brilliant references attached. Sometime later I was called to the personnel department where they read out the order of the Deputy Minister of Defence, Marshal Bagramyam, cancelling the order to pension me off to the reserve. In such a fashion my war and its repercussions were over.

Veterans and comrades-in-arms.

At the end of the war older soldiers and sergeants who had been conscripted to the army and navy were demobilised, then many officers retired, moving to the reserve due to large reductions to the army and fleet. During the first years after the war those who had fought on the front were not exactly eager to keep in touch—they were enjoying the peace. Well, not exactly 'enjoying', as they were immediately put to work at a time when so much had been destroyed and there was so much poverty in our country.

Two decades passed. Much was forgotten about the war. Leonid Brezhnev, who had fought at the front as a political commissar, became head of state. He put great emphasis on imbuing young people with the spirit of patriotism and encouraging friendship among veterans. Veterans' organisations were set up, their membership drawn from military units, regiments, brigades, divisions, corps, armies and fronts. The veterans held their reunions in towns which they had liberated or where their units had been formed. They also helped to set up museums about the war at schools, where they gave talks to pupils and arranged tours of their former battlefields. Hundreds of books about the war, written mainly by colonels, marshals and generals, were published, although these were heavily censored.

Veterans' organisations were formed in the military units that I fought in at the front. In the 1970s our brigade's veteran organisation was established on the initiative of Captain Paul Elshin. Regimental comrades from the brigade met up on a regular basis once every five years in Zagorsk (now Sergiev Posad), where our ordinary sapper brigade became the special assault engineer sapper brigade (which included the new flame thrower battalion) at the beginning of 1944.

Zagorsk was also convenient because quite a few of our regimental comrades—officers, sergeants and rank-and-file—had married or started relationships with the local belles during the three months after our brigade was formed and had settled there after the war and demobilisation. We met at Secondary School No. 6, where everyone greeted us warmly, and the teachers organised our talks to pupils, provided us with free bed and board, gave us presents and so on. After the disintegration of the Soviet Union, and as veterans grew older and unable to travel long distances, these meetings gradually came to an end.

In 1985 I went to Moscow for a reunion of veterans from the 162nd mortar regiment to celebrate the fortieth anniversary of the Victory. On the morning of 9 May I was in a crowd of people crossing Krimsky Bridge over the Moscow river to Gorky Park where regimental comrades from the infantry and mortar units were meeting. Suddenly someone tapped me on shoulder. 'Boris, is it you?' I turned. My God, it was Vladimir Shanin! I had studied with him from 1946 to 1951 at the naval faculty of the Military Law Academy in Moscow and from 1955 to 1958 I had worked with him in the same room in the logistics department of the Military Collegium of the Supreme Court of the USSR.[9] By that time Vladimir had already become an important figure: a colonel of law with a PhD in law, and a chair in legal theory at the law faculty of the Military Institute in Moscow. Vladimir told a man with him that I was from Odessa.

'Oh you're from Odessa are you?' said Vladimir's companion. 'So you're an Odessite.'[10]

'Yes,' I said, 'but I wasn't born in Odessa and I'm not Jewish either.[11] I lived in Odessa before the war and I'm living there now.'

'That still counts as being an Odessite,' he said. 'So tell us something funny.' I told him the first story that sprang to mind.

'Can you tell us another?' I told him another.

'What about a third?'

'Well, this time I can tell you a true story.'

'Go on.'

'In a remote hamlet in Belarus, in the middle of nowhere, some teenagers were gathering mushrooms in the forest when they came across a German container buried in the ground. It had probably been abandoned in a hurry. Inside they found weapons, cartridges and grenades as well as food and alcohol. The lads drank lots of French wine and ate tinned Belgian food, then put on German uniforms, picked up some automatic guns and grenades and went off to the neighbouring village to look for a fight. As it was late, the only person they came across was an old man, who was extremely drunk. He was swaying and holding onto a fence to keep upright. The rest of the village was watching an international football match on TV. The lads threatened to execute the old man by firing squad unless he showed them where the communists lived. The frightened old man pointed to some houses, so the lads divided into two groups and crept up to the buildings. They started firing from their automatic guns and exploded a grenade in a yard, wounding a dog which screamed hysterically, then they went home. But our omnipotent and ubiquitous KGB heard about the incident. The lads were sentenced to fifteen days in prison for hooliganism and the old man was brought before the district people's court for being a traitor and sentenced to one year in a reformatory, taking into account his age and state of health.'

'Bravo! You are a true Odessite!' the man said, and after saying goodbye to each other, we went to our veterans' groups.

Another officer from our regiment who was at our reunion had emigrated from Russia to Israel five years earlier and came to Moscow to see his relatives and former comrades. We asked: 'How much financial support do veterans and war invalids of the Great Patriotic War get in Israel? Twice as much as in Russia, perhaps?' 'Oh no,' he answered. When one of us exclaimed, 'How come? It can't be any worse!', he replied: 'No way, on the contrary, it's ten times better!' then added, 'But don't get upset. There's another category of former officers and war invalids who receive worse levels of support than the Soviets. They are the ones in China.'

After the meeting in the park our group of about thirty went to a nearby café, where, in accordance with our tradition, we continued our celebration. It was interesting—four former commanders of our regiment turned up. They had each taken over the role from the other. They had a lot to talk about and remember. It was at this meeting that I first saw the former colonel of our regiment and Hero of the Soviet Union, Victor Stepanchenko. He had joined our regiment after I had been heavily wounded and sent to the rear. When I went to our regimental comrades' reunions he was absent, and he was present at reunions where I was absent. I took this opportunity to ask Victor how he came to be awarded the title of Hero of the Soviet Union. I had read somewhere he had received this honourable title for his work as a battery commander who had kept killing the enemy and had supported our rifle units' attacks with fire from 120-mm mortars. But such actions were all in a day's work for a battery commander during the war, and were carried out by thousands of mortar batteries at the front. I thought that a Hero of the Soviet Union was supposed to commit an outstanding heroic deed. So what actually happened?

He answered:

Dear boys, you shouldn't believe everything that is written. What happened to me would be impossible to imagine for an author trying to write about war in his study. In mid-October 1943 our troops broke through the German front and we were chasing the German units which were retreating in panic. We aimed to be the first to reach the Dnieper, cross it and take the foothold on the right bank.

It was in this complicated situation that as a lieutenant and commander of a 120-mm mortar battery I was looking for an observation point with two artillery scouts. We ended up in a wood near a road, at some distance from my battery—the range of a 120-mm mortar being six kilometres. Then suddenly we saw a German tank coming along the road towards us with its upper hatch open and a covered, rolled-up flag sticking out. It was obviously a Nazi flag. I was overcome with excitement. What if we got this flag! I was young then—twenty-two years of age. I ordered my scouts to get ready to cover me. When the tank drew level with us I jumped on its armour, snatched the flag out of the hatch and fired some shots inside with my flare gun. I couldn't throw a grenade inside because it would detonate and probably kill me in the explosion. The flare, hissing, smoking and scattering sparks, started zipping around the tank compartment while I quickly jumped off and ran away from the road with the flag. The three-man German tank crew jumped out, their faces distorted with fear, semi-conscious and gasping for breath. My scouts killed them in a burst of automatic gunfire, then stripped the epaulettes from their shoulders and took their documents from their pockets before joining me. We had to hurry because a German tank column accompanied by motorcycles was on the move not far away. After throwing away the flagpole we made our way back to the battery with the flag which we presented to the commander of the regiment and I told him what had happened.

The flag was sent to high command with an explanatory note. It turned out to belong to a tank regiment of the elite 1st SS-Panzer Division Leibstandarte SS Adolf Hitler. So I was awarded the title of Hero of the Soviet Union, the Order of Lenin and a gold star medal. My scouts were awarded the Order of the Red Star. In the 1950s, when I was a cadet at the Military Academy in Moscow, I found out that at the victory parade on 24 June 1945 in Red Square the flag, together with 200 other fascist military flags, was thrown at the foot of Lenin's Mausoleum while Stalin, members of the government and famous admirals and generals watched from the top. Well, the written explanation for my award was appropriate because if they had written that I had destroyed a German tank with my flare gun and captured a regimental flag no one would have believed it and everyone would have just laughed. The general who signed my award certificate was clever and experienced, and he knew what he was doing.

But our reunion ended in tragedy and left us with sad memories for a long time. One of the veterans had been a member of an artillery detachment, then became an engineer at a plant in Siberia after the war. After having a little too much to drink during the reunion he went back to his room on the fifteenth floor of a high-rise hotel, opened the window and threw himself out. Earlier on he had seemed fine; he hadn't said anything to anyone and he hadn't left a note. The reason for his suicide would remain a mystery.

The man who organised our reunions was Senior Lieutenant Korotkov-Kubansky, who lived in Moscow and was the head of the regiment's finance department. When the council of veterans was set up in 1973 there were seventy-five veterans from the regiment on the membership list.

Korotkov-Kubansky's son, Eduard, helped him a great deal and organised events for veterans after his death. In mid-2006

Eduard sent me a letter of farewell, informing me that the council of veterans from our 562nd mortar regiment had come to an end because I was the only member who was still alive. And that was it.

I have already mentioned that the majority of awards were given justifiably and with good reason during the Great Patriotic War. But there were exceptions and here is an example from my fellow cadet at the Military Law Academy, Colonel Vladimir Temerov. In the 1950s he chaired the military tribunal for troops stationed on the island of Novaya Zemlya in the Arctic Ocean where atomic and H bomb tests were being carried out. The deputy political commissar of the military construction battalion on Novaya Zemlya was a major who was a Hero of the Soviet Union. He was an ethnic Lak. The Laks lived in the Caucasus Mountains in northern Dagestan, a remote and inaccessible region, and numbered only several thousand people.[12] Vladimir was very active in the drive to build up patriotism in the ranks and he tried to persuade the major to join in, but with no result. In the end Vladimir asked him point blank: 'You're a Hero of the Soviet Union, aren't you? Why don't you want to tell the soldiers about your heroic deed during the Great Patriotic War?' He was surprised by the major's answer: he turned out to have been a lieutenant and deputy political commissar of a laundry detachment at the front during the war, staffed only by women. He didn't take part in the battles. He committed no heroic deeds. He wasn't outstanding in any way. The title of Hero of the Soviet Union, he was told, had been awarded to him because he was a Lak and his ethnic group had to have someone to be a Hero of the Soviet Union, like all the other groups in the USSR. That was the national policy of the Communist Party. He had no idea what was written in his recommendation for the award. He had nothing to tell the soldiers of Novaya Zemlya and he hated lying. That is why he refused to take to the floor.

FOR THE MOTHERLAND! FOR STALIN!

I would like to finish my story with the words of my favourite poet, Mikhail Lermontov, which he wrote after a bloody battle with mountain tribesmen near the settlement of Valerik in the northern Caucasus.

Heartsick, I pondered the mystery.
I thought: poor people.
What do we want!
The sky is clear,
And under the sky
Is a place for each of us.
But incessantly and needlessly
We fight. Why?

APPENDIX I

TANK CREW VLADIMIR KHLITSOV

On 9 May 2005 I happened to meet Vladimir Khlitsov (born 1926), who participated in the assault on the Reichstag in Berlin. Every time you meet a real-life participant in those formidable events of the Great Patriotic War you learn something new which enables you to understand more fully the truth about the war. Khlitsov is a living legend. I found we had many things in common. We both took part in the battle for Berlin and we were both awarded the medal for taking Berlin. In spite of his age Vladimir was not only in good physical shape, but had kept his clear mind and sharp memory. He remembers events from sixty years ago with as much detail as if they had happened yesterday. I wrote down his story.

After graduating from Saratov tank school, he arrived at the 23rd tank brigade of the 9th tank corps of the 1st Belorussian front as the gun commander of a T-34 tank. The brigade had been fighting battles since the beginning of the war and its members were famous

Sergeant Major Vladimir Khlitsov, T-34 tank gun commander, German
Democratic Republic, 1948

*for their military skill and courage. It was a formidable force. Judge
for yourself: it comprised three tank battalions (fifty-five tanks); a
motorised battalion of assault automatic gunners; machine gun, anti-
aircraft and sapper platoons; and service units. Vladimir particularly
remembers the route taken by his tank company in January 1945
along the enemy's rear during the Vistula-Oder operation, under the
command of Captain Kostyuk.*

We were expecting a German tank counter attack. Our tank
platoon was put into position to carry out an ambush. During
the night we camouflaged ourselves so our tank couldn't be seen
from land or air. At daybreak we heard the sound of engines
from the ravine ahead. We were on alert. Four German tanks
with assault troops holding automatic guns crawled out of the
ravine. I directed the tank gun at a bush on the roadside which
the German tanks would pass shortly. The bush was 150 metres
away. The tank commander ordered me to fire a shell at the last
tank. As it approached the bush we fired. The tank went up in

flames and stopped. The good choice of location for our ambush enabled our platoon to destroy all four German tanks and their troops by sudden firing from a short distance. It was the first German tank that I destroyed.

Our tank company, which comprised seven T-34 tanks, swiftly moved twenty kilometres ahead of the main body of the brigade and corps, avoiding towns and large villages with the aim of damaging communication lines. We were destroying small groups of retreating enemy forces by firing at them while on the move and during short stops. We used our tank caterpillars as well as our guns and machine guns. Our sudden appearance caused panic, fear and horror among the retreating Nazis who ran away in all directions. As we watched our hearts were filled with pride in our army and we believed in our might.

The 23rd front detachment of the tank brigade was advancing on the enemy's rear and in late January 1945 it was sixty kilometres ahead of our infantry units. The corps commander, General Kirichenko, kept shouting over the radio to the tank commanders: 'Advance, my heroes! Go on and on! Don't look back! It's not 1941 now. We won't let you down if you need us.' Then he used four-letter words to describe the Nazis. This ensured that we quickly understood his message, and his 'heroes' didn't involve themselves in long battles but hurried on to destroy the hateful enemy together with their HQs, rear units and storehouses. Those Germans who surrendered weren't held prisoner. Where could we imprison them when we were in the enemy's rear ourselves? Such is the cruel truth of the war, which is not mentioned in books and films.

Ahead we saw the seventy-metre wide River Warta. Our brigade's scouts had learned from local Poles that there was a fort on this river. Knowing only the fort's location with no additional reconnaissance, the front tank's driver mechanic, Polezhaev, used his initiative and resourcefulness to ford the river. Running the risk of driving his tank into holes in the riverbed, he forded the river to make sure that the enemy wouldn't have the opportunity to fortify themselves on the opposite bank before the attack. The other tanks followed Polezhaev, firing as they advanced. It was a great success. If our troops had been crossing such a river under enemy fire it could have resulted in high casualties on our side. For this feat and others, including the courage and skills he displayed in battle, Polezhaev was awarded the title of Hero of the Soviet Union.

Another episode is impossible to recall without a shudder. Our tank battalion of twenty tanks, the head detachment of our brigade, was moving along a country road. We saw a small German town ahead. A railway ran at an angle to the road, covered with anti-snow shields. There was no sign of danger and our driver drove the tank with the front hatch open so he had a better view of the road. Suddenly the anti-snow shields parted, revealing German anti-tank guns which opened fire at our formation. A shell hit the front armour of our tank near the hatch and a large fragment cut the head of the driver, who was sitting underneath. The gun loader was also wounded. The rest of the crew, me included, were seriously shell shocked by the blast. Then two more shells got into the tank, setting it on fire. The assault troopers, eighteen- or nineteen-year-old lads who had been sitting on the armour, were ripped to pieces by the explosion. The German battery was destroyed by our other tanks, and our comrades who hurried over to our burning tank managed to pull us out. I spent two weeks in the brigade hospital, then, once I had recovered, I was sent into action again.

At the end of the war the reward for destroying enemy weapons was paid in cash. So you could get 800 roubles for destroying a German Tiger or Panther tank, or a 'Ferdinand' self-propelled gun; 600 roubles for a Panzer III or IV tank, and so on. At this time the monthly salary of a T-34 tank gun commander was 100 roubles. We had a daily ration of 100 millilitres of vodka. But during an offensive and before battle experienced soldiers, particularly tank crews, didn't drink vodka. This rule was strictly observed. First of all, a sober crew member has a better chance of staying alive: he doesn't have double vision. Secondly, alcohol dilutes the blood, so it's very difficult to stop bleeding, even from a light wound, because the blood doesn't clot. However, after a battle everybody drank (apart from the guards) for themselves and on behalf of their comrades who had been killed. Officers who smoked were given *papirosi* (unfiltered half cigarettes with a paper holder attached), while sergeants and soldiers were given twenty grammes of tobacco a day and they made their own *papirosi* from special cigarette paper (seven booklets a month) which they lit with matches (three boxes a month). It was assumed that there were no hold-ups in supplies, but these occurred quite frequently.

Before an offensive, tank crews were given food parcels designated as 'emergency rations' for three days in case of unforeseen circumstances. The parcels contained tinned meat or fish, salted lard, sugar, dried vegetable soup, dried *kasha*, egg powder, rye rusks, American ship's biscuits made from cornflour and so on. American tins with bright labels were given to us under the Lend Lease scheme; our soldiers called them 'the second front'.

But the tank crews were young men of between eighteen and twenty-five years of age, and they were always on the move in the open air. As soon as we were told about an offensive—and we were usually told about half an hour ahead—we promptly ate the contents of our parcels. Older soldiers among the assault troops who had participated in the Civil War and other wars said it was safer to go into battle with an empty stomach as this gave you a better chance of surviving a stomach wound. But we younger soldiers took no notice.

The T-34 tank was considered the best medium-sized tank of the Second World War. It was a 32-tonne tank armed with an

85-mm gun and two 7.62-mm calibre machine guns. It had wide caterpillars and ran on diesel (German tanks used petrol), with a speed of up to fifty-five kilometres per hour. The T-34 was a moving battery, destroying everything in its path, and surpassed not only medium-sized German tanks but all the medium-sized tanks in the world with regard to manoeuvrability, performance across rough terrain, powerful armour, guns and reliability. The tank gun's shells had a high velocity of 600 metres per second which gave them a great piercing capability. The shape of the tank's body and turret proved to be unique because the thickness of the armour, ranging from forty-five to ninety millimetres, enabled it to deflect enemy shells. For a long time the Germans were afraid to report to Hitler that the T-34 was superior to their tanks. When Hitler learned of this he ordered that the T-34 should be made at his plants. Although the Germans had captured our tanks at the beginning of the war they never managed to replicate them because they couldn't discover how they were made.

I asked Vladimir about trophies. All victors always come back with trophies, I insisted.

What trophies are you talking about? We didn't have any. We didn't have time for trophies. Our aim was just to remain alive. After a battle we were immediately sent to some remote place in a forest, as far away from any settlements as possible, where we would tighten up nuts and so on. Tank crews are a crafty bunch of daredevils, so we have to be kept out of mischief. It's also easier to hide tanks in the forest. German aircraft were specifically searching for tanks because tanks are an army's striking force. And where would we put our trophies anyway? It was cramped enough in the tanks already—you could hardly move. It was really difficult to pull a badly wounded man out of a tank. It wasn't without reason that short people were conscripted into the tank units.

APPENDIX I

The Berlin Offensive

Our part in the Berlin offensive started on 16 April 1945. All the members of our brigade were filled with pride for their part in that operation. In a succession of fiercely fought battles we had to break through several fortified German positions. Our tanks crossed minefields, trawling for mines to create safe passages, while flame thrower tanks with a range of up to 120 metres helped us to advance towards our goal.

Every two hours messages in German on loudspeakers addressed those who were still resisting. 'Achtung! Achtung! Deutsche Soldaten und Officieren! You are surrounded! You don't have artillery, tanks or food! Your days are numbered. Fascist Germany doesn't exist anymore. Stop your senseless resistance, or you will all perish. Hand in your weapons and put up white flags!' But the address had little effect on the German fanatics and only a few surrendered. We had to fight our way past each house down every street.

As we approached Berlin we saw slogans painted on the road: 'Beware Germany! Russia is coming to Berlin.' In Berlin itself, fascist slogans were written on its walls and windows in large white letters: 'Victory or Siberia', 'Berlin will remain German', 'Russians will never come to Berlin'. The last slogan had been amended by someone who had crossed out the word 'never'.

By 21 April the brigade had reached the Berlin suburbs. The Germans couldn't retreat. The city was surrounded by a dense ring of Soviet troops. The Germans announced that Berlin was Germany's Stalingrad and that there would be conscription for all men between fifteen and sixty-five. (After battles we let the teenagers go. Children will be children, and they would have to build a new peaceful Germany after the war.) But this was a very weak version of Stalingrad. Stalingrad held for 200 days and its defence finished with the encirclement of the German troops and Soviet victory, but Berlin surrendered in ten days.

FOR THE MOTHERLAND! FOR STALIN!

The battles in the city grew fiercer. The fascists fired at us from basements, windows, balconies and attics, using all kinds of weapons. Our assault groups were steadily advancing, literally step by step. Buildings were on fire and collapsing in heaps of rubble. Streets and courtyards were covered with dust and smoke. Shell fragments, and lumps of stone and brick rained down on our tank armour, onto the streets and onto the walls and roofs of houses. For ten days and nights the desperate battle for Berlin continued on the ground, in the air, and underground in the U-Bahn, the sewers and cable tunnels.

Imagine what it is like to be in a street with high-rise buildings rammed together on both sides, creating such a strong reverberation that there is an endless rumble of exploding mines, shells and grenades. You can hear shooting from the machine guns and automatic guns of the infantry and the loud fire of anti-tank guns. Our tank guns and our machine guns are deafening. Our 550-horsepower engine is roaring. Amidst the fire and smoke of the burning houses there are shouts of 'Oorah!', curses, groans and cries from the wounded: 'Brother, help me! I'm dying.' Inside the tank it is unbearably hot and stifling—the air is filled with the exhaust gas from recently fired shells, as the tank's air filter doesn't work very well.

Under such conditions we had to be composed so that we could target the enemy and shoot to kill. We were not afraid. To put it more accurately, we had no time to be afraid. We had to be utterly self-disciplined and each of us understood the following: If I don't kill a German, he will kill me. So what if I'm wounded? I'll be alive, I won't die. And if I'm killed—well, that's my destiny.

But I wanted to live. I was eighteen, with all my life ahead of me, and only several hours left before the victory.

At this point we didn't have time for such considerations. The tank commander gave his orders: 'Find electricity pole with slogan ahead. Find machine gun thirty metres to left. Take aim.

APPENDIX I

Fire!' I saw the machine gun through my sight slot, targeted it with the tank gun and pressed the trigger. The tank gun fired, then fired a second time, then a third. The loader could hardly keep up as he loaded the shells into the gun. The shells (fifty-five of them, 85-mm calibre) were on the floor below our feet, behind the driver. We also kept our twenty F1 grenades and our cartridges there. The soldiers called our F1 grenades *limonki* (lemons). Each one weighed 600 grammes, and once activated detonated within three to four seconds. Its fragments dispersed over a 200-metre radius. In other words, it was a powder keg. In fact it was worse than that because not only does it contain powder, but its fragmenting shell is made of robust steel from the Urals. Not without reason were we respected by the infantry, who knew more than anyone else what it was like to fight.

It was almost impossible to understand how we actually fitted into the tank. In the gun turret there was the huge gun mount with two narrow spaces on either side. On one side was a seat resembling a bicycle saddle where the gun commander sat and fired the tank gun. The radio operator sat on an identical seat on the other side and fired the machine gun. The tank commander rested his feet on the shoulders of both men. He was a lieutenant and he was up in the so-called commander's turret where he could observe the battlefield through slots in the tank armour. Under the gun commander's feet, the driver mechanic sat on an armchair, breathing into the steel plate in front of his face. When necessary, I, as gun commander, pressed my right or left foot down on the driver's shoulder to tell him which way to turn. We had a walkie talkie, but it was useless against the roar of battle and deafening gunshots.

In the course of battle, as we in the tank crew ate, drank and slept together (and faced the possibility of dying together), we became so close that we called each other not by military titles or surnames but by familiar first names: Vanya, Pietya, Kolya...

During an offensive we only broke off from battle to carry out light repairs to damaged parts of our tank, to fix caterpillars, brakes and clutches, to get more ammunition, or to refuel.

I remember a tragic incident. In the centre of Berlin, not far from the Swiss Embassy, our front tank came off a bridge across the River Spree which had been half-destroyed by aerial bombing, and sank in the deep water. We couldn't do anything. The iron box became the common grave of our comrades-in-arms, including my friend and fellow cadet, driver mechanic Andrey Ivanov. It was very hard for us. We were filled with sadness as our tank passed the place where that tank had fallen into the river.

The assault and capture of the Reichstag

On 29 April the battle started for the Reichstag (the building of the lower house of the German parliament). The Reichstag was not far from the Chancellery where Hitler, the Supreme Commander of the German army, had been and perhaps still was at that time. In front of us was a massive, gloomy three-storey building with good all-round observation. The Reichstag had been turned into a powerful base of resistance and was one of the most important sites in the defence of the city. Its windows had been bricked up, leaving narrow slots for the muzzles of machine guns and anti-aircraft weapons. Deep moats had been dug around the building and barriers had been erected, equipped with machine guns and other guns. We were in great danger from the anti-aircraft guns and tanks which had been dug into the ground. These fired in direct lines from short distances. The enemy was resisting at all costs, and we were suffering great losses.

We were fighting as part of an assault group. Each tank from our brigade accompanied a rifle platoon fortified by machine gunners, mortar gunners, flame throwers, snipers and anti-tank guns. Each assault group had a banner to hoist over the Reichstag.

My tank was at the front and I was shooting at the enemy firing positions in the square in front of the Reichstag and inside the building itself. Thirty tank brigades, and fifty tank and self-propelled artillery regiments participated in the Berlin operation. But it was our tank brigade which happened to take part in the capture of the Reichstag as part of the 150th Berlin rifle division's attack.

In the counter-offensive near Moscow, 774 tanks took part; at Stalingrad, 1,463; in the Belarus operation, 5,000 tanks and self-propelled artillery guns; and in the battle for Berlin, more than 6,000.

After concentrating our firepower on the square in front of the Reichstag, many of our infantry were ready for the attack. We were given the order to fire only at the windows on the Reichstag's upper floors from which German automatic machine guns and other guns were shooting at our men. We all realised that it was the last battle. That is why we didn't spare shells or cartridges. The battle for the Reichstag was the fiercest in my entire experience during the war. As we learned later, as early as 30 April Hitler had committed suicide with Eva Braun, who became his wife on last day of their lives. Goebbels, together with his wife and five young children, took poison on 1 May, but the Nazi fanatics of the SS (Hitler's elite troops, who were notorious for their extreme cruelty) and cadets from the navy school—a total of 2,000 fighters—kept up their resistance. Drunk, not having slept for several nights and days, on the edge of nervous exhaustion, embittered, brutalised and desperate...

But soon white flags began to appear in different parts of the huge building and calls for a truce. However, our order had come from above—there was to be no truce, only complete capitulation—the turning in of weapons and surrender. The Germans began to surrender from 1–2 May, but only at night. Even after the Germans in the Reichstag announced their surrender and hung white flags or sheets in the windows, shooting could still be heard in the building. Evidently not everyone had agreed to surrender and some were committing suicide.

On the evening of 1 May, two scouts from the 150th rifle division, Georgian Sergeant Kantaria and Russian Sergeant Yegorov, along with the head of their group, the Ukrainian deputy political commissar of the rifle battalion, Berest, climbed up the facade of the building, risking their lives under fierce enemy fire, and unfurled the red banner of victory over Reichstag. For this heroic deed the commander of the 3rd army awarded them with the Order of the Red Banner. Marshal Zhukov considered this award insufficient, however, and recommended Kantaria and Yegorov for the title of Hero of the Soviet Union. And so it happened—two awards for one heroic deed. Yet Zhukov didn't recommend Berest for this title. It was common knowledge that Zhukov didn't like political commissars and the award would signify that this political commissar would be considered a hero. The injustice was corrected sixty years later on 6 May 2005 when Alexei Berest was posthumously awarded the title of Hero of Ukraine.

I was recommended for the Order of the Red Banner, but at HQ it was decided that only officers could receive this award, so I was awarded the Order of the Patriotic War, 1st class. The rest of my tank crew were also given orders.

In Berlin near the River Spree on a high hill in Treptower Park is a monument to the victorious warrior, a monumental sculpture of a Soviet warrior holding a child in one hand and a sword in the other, which he has used to break the fascist swastika. The base of the statue forms a small mausoleum, with a book in a gold box at its centre. The book contains the names of the 7,200 Soviet soldiers who died during the storming of Greater Berlin. I saw with my own eyes people who fought and died defending their motherland, their home, their family, and, having died, these people stepped into immortality.

But life went on. On 2 May all the tanks which were still undamaged, together with their crews, mine included, were put in a separate unit and sent to the city of Posen in eastern Germany (now Poznan in Poland) where battles were still being fought against disparate groups of Germans trying to break through to the west towards American troops. But by the time we arrived the war was over and there was peace at last. We were so happy. We had won. We were alive.

My comrades and I had been brought up in the spirit of internationalism, so during the assault on Berlin we were not acting as avengers of the bloody crimes of the Nazis but as liberators of the German people from the plague of the Brownshirts. After our tank brigade left Berlin for another part of the front our portable soldiers' kitchens were used for feeding the people of Berlin, the old men and children who crawled out of the basements and shelters. Our military medical staff gave medical aid to everyone who turned to them, the wounded and the sick of Berlin. Do the present-day Berliners remember this? Or, to be more exact, do they know about this?

In the Reichstag building, which is now the Bundestag, is a memorial to the Second World War, a wall covered with holes from shell fragments and bullets, and carved with the names of soldiers who reached Berlin in May of that victorious year, with the names of their Soviet towns and numbers of their military units. Some of the German members of parliament were against keeping it, but the majority took the decision to leave this wall as a page from German history which should be remembered by present and future generations in order not to let another war break out.

The author adds:

After the war our historians would consider the assault on Berlin by the Red Army as a golden page in the annals of Soviet military glory, science and the arts. The battle for Berlin was, in fact, the final large

Red Army graffiti in the Bundestag

operation of the Great Patriotic War against the Nazi invaders. Having lost Berlin as its military, economic and political centre, Nazi Germany could not continue its armed resistance and on 8 May 1945 in the Berlin suburb of Karlshorst the representatives of the German high command signed the act of complete and unconditional capitulation.

Writer Ilya Erenburg observed:

War is complicated. It is as dark and dense as an impassable forest. It doesn't look like its description—it is simpler and more complicated. It is felt, but not always understood by its participants. It is understood, but not always felt by later researchers.

APPENDIX II

HURRAY FOR DOGS!

They say that a dog has all man's virtues but none of his failings. It is also said that the more you come to know your fellow man, the more you start loving dogs. The French actor Alain Delon said that a dog has a greater share of man's virtues than a single man can possess. They also say that a dog is man's best friend and not without reason. A wise man said: 'Buy a dog! That is the only way you can buy love.' Only a dog can express such a deep faith in his owner with such limited means of expression. If dogs began to talk, however, man would lose his best friend.

In our brigade there was a separate company of specialist dog handlers who used dogs to search for mines. The company consisted of two platoons, each with thirty handlers, their dogs, a vet with a first aid kit and a field kitchen for the dogs. Each dog was entitled to his own food ration which included bones and meat.

A dog's ability to smell is a thousand times greater than man's; he can smell an explosive buried a metre deep in the ground. The mines were usually covered with two to three centimetres of earth and dogs were taught to detect them in a special school near Moscow. At the front, a handler would lead his dog across a minefield on a ten-metre long leash—a long leash was necessary so that if a mine exploded underneath a dog the handler wouldn't get killed. Once the dog had scented a mine, he would sit down facing it and the handler would put a flag next to the location so that a sapper could disable it later. Sometimes dogs were killed by the anti-personnel mines which could explode even under the slightest contact or pressure. In such cases the brigade's orders contained the following: 'Remove from food ration and withdraw from the lists of the brigade on account of death—bitch Alma, born 1940, dog Bars, born 1939.'

Dogs were not given awards for their dangerous work. Instead their handlers were awarded medals for courage or for merit in combat. But jokers are everywhere so some dogs wore German iron crosses and medals on their collars. The dogs were different breeds, but mainly German Shepherds.

The dogs in our brigade met a tragic end when the war was over. We were stationed in the Austrian town of Tulln on the Danube when we received a command from above to disband the dogs' company.[1] The dog handlers were transferred to another military unit and three or four favourite dogs were left with the battalion kitchens, but we had to get rid of the rest. A way was found. Fifty dogs were taken on boats to the other side of the Danube and left there. But dogs are cleverer than we think. They understood that they were being abandoned. Some started barking and others began to howl, while others rushed into the water and swam for the boats, but fast currents swept them back. That was the end.

I remember another episode with dogs, in contrast to the one described above. In February 1934 the SS *Chelyuskin*, a steamer with an Arctic expedition on board, was crushed by pack ice near the Bering Straits and sank.

The *Chelyuskin's* 111 passengers were stranded on the pack ice, among them seven women and two children. There were also fifty huskies. In the severe conditions of a polar winter with blizzards sweeping over the Arctic, seven Soviet pilots reached the passengers and took them by plane to the mainland. The pilots were all awarded the highest honour of the Soviet Union, the title of Hero of the Soviet Union, which had only recently been created. Among them was Vasiliy Molokov (1895–1982) who had rescued the last group of people.

But the dogs who had faithfully served the people were left on the pack ice. They were doomed. Raising their heads, realising that the people were leaving them to certain death, they howled mournfully, watching the plane leave. Molokov saw everything.

Once he reached the mainland Molokov asked the commander of his regiment for permission to return to fetch the dogs. The commander refused. But Vasiliy Molokov was a dog lover and all dog lovers will know how he must have felt. So, in spite of his commander's order, he went back to rescue the dogs. He couldn't do otherwise.

He was running a great risk. The pack ice could have shifted in a way that would make landing or taking off impossible. Vasiliy risked not only his own life but the plane as well. And he could have been brought in front of the tribunal for disobeying orders.

Once the plane had landed on the pack ice the dogs crowded around Molokov, barking with joy. It is a shame that there was no photographer present—it would have been a unique photograph. The dogs were licking Vasiliy's face and hands, and nuzzling their icy muzzles against his *unti* (fur-covered high boots). Then they jumped through the open hatch into the plane, understanding that rescue had come.

Molokov was given a serious reprimand for acting against his commander's order, but the International Society for the Protection of Animals awarded him a large gold medal for rescuing the dogs. During the war, as Major General of Aviation, Molokov successfully commanded the craft division of night bombers and was awarded nine medals for merit in combat.

For some time a regiment of trained dogs was stationed next to us. While carrying out various errands I used to visit this regiment where, as a dog lover, I saw many interesting things. The regiment comprised three battalions, each consisting of three companies which were made up of two platoons. In each platoon there were thirty trainers with dogs. In the regiment as a whole there were probably 500–600 dogs of many different breeds. Their approach could be heard several kilometres away because of the incessant barking. Not only did they take part in searching for mines in minefields, like our dogs, but they also checked the roads near the front and industrial and agricultural buildings in towns and villages for explosives. With the help of his dog one trainer uncovered sixteen anti-tank and eighty anti-infantry mines, making it possible for our tanks and infantry to advance. He was awarded a medal for courage for this feat.

There were also anti-tank dogs which destroyed tanks. A canvas belt with two pockets containing 4 kilogrammes of explosives and a twenty-centimetre high lever was strapped around the dog. When an enemy tank was 200 to 400 metres away the dog was let off the leash and, as trained, fearlessly rushed towards the underside of the tank where the iron cladding was thinnest. The lever struck the bottom of the tank and the explosives were detonated. The tank exploded, the crew died and, it goes without saying, nothing was left of the dog. An anti-tank dog was trained in a special school using hunger. For two days he was given only water, then was led up to a training tank with a working engine, where bowls of food were placed under the underside.

The trainer let him smell the food before leading him 400 metre away and letting him off the leash along with several other dogs, so that they all ran under the tank. The training lasted for two months. The Germans quickly recognised this tactic, however, and whenever they saw dogs in a combat zone they would shoot them using any kind of weapon. During the war about 300 tanks were destroyed by these kinds of dogs, not just from this regiment but from dozens of other dog regiments.

Dogs from the medical units removed the heavily wounded from the battlefield. Three dogs would pull stretchers which were on runners in winter and wheels in summer. With or without trainers under enemy fire, the dogs made their way to the wounded, who got on to the stretcher which the dogs would then drag to the battalion or regimental medical unit. A first aid kit was attached to one of the dogs, which the wounded man could use if needed. In one regiment a stretcher of this kind took fourteen seriously wounded men off the battlefield, each journey a distance of two kilometres.

Our four-legged friends with their acute sense of smell and hearing were also used for delivering messages, and guard duties. During battles, dogs carried messages from the battalion commander to the regiment commander. One dog delivered 500 messages in a single year. Another dog was wounded while delivering a message. A shell ripped off part of his front paw but he managed to deliver the message using his remaining three paws. These messenger dogs also delivered weapons, food, newspapers, letters and tobacco to frontline troops.

At night or in bad weather, guard dogs protected our minefields from German sappers. A handler and his dog would be sent to a guard post which was 100–200 metres in front of our trenches and consisted of five soldiers headed by a sergeant armed with an automatic weapon and a flare gun. The guards were supposed to be vigilant, looking out for German scouts all through the night. But just you try lying on the ground for a whole night without falling asleep when you are young. A dog handler may have fallen asleep but he rested his hand on his dog's back. On hearing someone approach the dog sat up, strained his lead and started growling quietly. The dog handler woke up, then woke up the others. They set off a flare—unexpectedly for the enemy—and opened fire. The troops in the trench behind them woke up immediately and began shooting.

Soldiers escorting German prisoners to the rear also had dogs with them. It is impossible to escape from dogs. Sometimes a handler and his dog would join a group of scouts going to the enemy's rear. If the scouts discovered any urgent information about the enemy it was encoded then put into a pocket in the dog's collar, and the dog would quickly deliver it to the commanders during the night.

At the victory parade in Red Square on 25 June 1945 there was a formation of handlers and their dogs who, on their four legs, had undergone all the privations of the war. Our dogs, the Almas and Bars,[2] kept in step with their handlers: they had taken 700,000 wounded soldiers and officers from the battlefield; they had found four million mines and explosives; and they had delivered 120,000 combat documents. At the rear of this formation marched a soldier carrying a German Shepherd dog in his arms, resting on a coat. This dog, who was called Julbars, was very famous at the front as he had found a total of 468 mines and he was awarded a medal for merit (this was the only time during the war that a medal had been awarded to a dog rather than a handler).

When the parade was held Julbars was so weakened by illness that he couldn't walk across the square by himself. This was reported to Marshal Rokossovsky and he in his turn reported it to Stalin, who said: 'Let the dog be carried on my coat across Red Square.' So behind the handlers with their dogs marched the leading caninologist, A.P. Malover of the Fédération Cynologique Internationale,[3] carrying the famous Julbars in his arms on Stalin's coat. This was the man famous for the saying: 'People betray but dogs never will.'

In July 1945 dogs in military service were on show in Leningrad (now St Petersburg). The place of honour was occupied by a German Shepherd with clever eyes called Dina. According to the inscription next to her, she had discovered 5,000 mines. In the museum at the military engineering school in St Petersburg, near the Peter and Paul Fortress, is a stuffed dog with anti-tank explosives. In Odessa a stuffed Lurcher with dozens of medals around its neck is on display in the Museum of Miliary History.

The English are well-known dog lovers and experts. In Park Lane in central London stands a monument to the animals who served in the British army in the twentieth century. A bronze horse, two mules and a dog form part of the monument.

Generally speaking, we are indebted to this friendly creature. Throughout the history of mankind, whether at work in times of peace or in battles during war, the dog has walked side by side with man. During times of danger the dog has walked ahead, whether hunting, catching a gangster, racing under a tank, taking part in medical research or space exploration... We remember the dogs Belka and Strelka who were first animals launched into space.

I write so much about dogs because I love them so much and they have always been part of my life. One dog would disappear and her place would be taken by another. When I was fourteen or fifteen years old and we lived in Dnepropetrovsk I had a Doberman Pinscher called Betka, and to everyone's surprise she could follow me up the iron bars of the fire escape to the first floor of the military committee building and come down the same way. I spent much of my time with Betka and didn't do well at school. My father put the blame on the dog and ordered his driver to take her somewhere. I couldn't persuade the driver to tell me where he had taken Betka. I looked for her for over a week and finally found her in a village thirty kilometres away from the city. She was lying near a fork in the road, waiting for me. Our mutual joy was indescribable.

My love for this dog was so great that when we moved from Dnepropetrovsk to Odessa I insisted that Betka should go with us. When we were evacuated from Odessa, we couldn't take Betka with us because we were travelling in a freight train and the carriage was already overcrowded. Some women with children refused point blank to let the dog go with them in the carriage. Betka was left with my father and he kept her in his district military committee office. When a bomb exploded Betka's rear legs were paralysed in the blast: she couldn't walk, she could only crawl.

To stop her suffering my father ordered his driver to shoot Betka before the army was evacuated from Odessa. But the driver couldn't make himself do it and decided to drown her in the lake. He put Betka into a sack with a stone, tied it up and threw her into the lake. But some women who were washing clothes nearby thought that he was drowning a baby, started crying and shouting and made him lift the dog out of the water. So Betka lived with my father until he himself was injured by a collapsing wall and had to be evacuated by ship to Sevastopol. Betka's end is unknown.

An old soldier, no matter what he might be talking about, will always end up talking about the war. As I finish my story about dogs I must point out that other animals also helped us defeat the Nazis, whether they were at the front or in the rear. Millions of horses were used in the army, where there were eighty-five cavalry divisions, and they were even used by the navy.

In the far north there were reindeer brigades which transported soldiers and military equipment on sleighs across the deep snow. In the south near Stalingrad there was a camel brigade: 300 camels were used to transport military equipment. I have already mentioned that oxen were also used to transport military equipment, even weapons and mortars.

APPENDIX II

I cannot resist mentioning another extraordinary episode which happened during the war. In September 1941 when Soviet troops were retreating, all the animals, including hundreds of poisonous snakes from all the world's continents, were released from their enclosures at the Askania-Nova nature reserve, near Crimea. Unaware of this, General Field Marshal Erich von Mannstein's 11th army set up its HQ in the village. During an unexpected air raid by Soviet bombers, German generals and officers hurried to take cover in positions and trenches which had been dug earlier by Soviet soldiers. But there they were met by the snakes which raised their heads, swayed and hissed maliciously, giving the intruders cold, venomous glances. Frightened, the generals and officers decided that they would rather to be blown to bits than face the snakes. So they hurriedly left the trenches!

There was also an amusing incident when the Germans were bombing Moscow and many incendiary bombs fell on Moscow Zoo. The staff at the zoo couldn't extinguish them all so a clever elephant called Shango sucked water from the zoo's reservoir with his trunk and used it to put out the flames.

In Podilsky, a village in the Khmelnitsky region in Ukraine, a daredevil cockerel attacked a German soldier who had come into a yard to steal chickens. Alarmed by this assault, the German started fending off the cockerel with his gun. He was holding the gun by its barrel and it was loaded. The cockerel jumped onto the trigger, firing a bullet straight into the German's heart. As the German died all the onlookers froze with horror because announcements had been made all over the village that for every dead German soldier, 100 local people would be shot. But they got away with it. The other German soldiers, who were eyewitnesses, persuaded their officers that the people were innocent.

So let us be kind to our small brothers.

APPENDIX III

THE HEROES OF THE 16TH ASSAULT RAVA-RUSSKAYA BRIGADE

People must know about their heroes; that is why I give their details. All those mentioned below were awarded the title of Hero of the Soviet Union.

Ivan Katchalko was born on 25 September 1916 in the village of Karlovka (Karlivka), Poltava region, Ukraine, to a worker's family. A member of the Communist Party since 1949, he served in the army from 1937. He took part in battles from December 1942 onwards. On 30 July 1944, in just two hours, Captain Katchalko succeeded in creating a thoroughfare across 800 metres of impassable terrain for military formations. Once they were able to cross the river, the sappers together with the rifle battalion took part in the battles for the foothold. After the war Katchalko continued serving in the army. Now he is a retired colonel living in Moscow. His heroic deeds are described in the books *Podvig vo Imya Rodini* (*Heroic Deeds for the Motherland*), published in Kuibyshev in 1965, and *Sovershennoe imi Bessmertno* (*Their Deeds are Immortal*), published in Moscow in 1976.

Josef Kulik was born on 8 March 1912 into a peasant family in the village of Josipovka (Yosypivka), Kirov region, Ukraine. A member of the Communist Party from 1942, he served in the army from 1934 to 1937 and then from 1941 onwards as a platoon commander. On 30 July 1944 Senior Lieutenant Kulik transported two infantry battalions on dinghies across the Vistula near Annopol (thirty kilometres to the north of Sandomierz) in three hours. By doing this he enabled the foothold on the left bank to be taken. He resigned from the army in 1948 and lives in Yoshkar-Ola. He is written about in the books *Zvyozdi Doblesti Voevoy* (*The Stars of Courage*), published in Lvov in 1968, and *Nashi Geroyi* (*Our Heroes*), published in Yoshkar-Ola in 1985.

Pyotr Zhukovski was born on 18 June 1912 in the village of Nelezh, Smolensk region, Russia. A member of the Communist Party from 1945, he served in the army from July 1941 as a platoon commander. Junior Lieutenant Zhukovski distinguished himself in late January 1945 near Grochowice in Poland. Together with soldiers from his platoon he managed to build a temporary bridge across the River Oder ahead of time after floating the supporting frames to the crossing point, and so enabled the troops to reach the foothold. During the night of 6 February 1945 he and his platoon repelled the enemy's counter attacks near the bridge. He left the army in 1946 and worked as director of a woodworking plant in the town of Kirov. His heroic deeds are written about in the book *Kirovchane—Nashi Geroyi Sovetskogo Soyuza* (*Heroes of the Soviet Union from Kirov*), published in Kirov in 1962.

Vasiliy Dobrorez was born on 31 January 1917 into a working-class family in Russian Manchuria. A member of the Communist Party from 1945, he served in the army from 1941. As a commander of a military unit Senior Sergeant Dobrorez distinguished himself in building a bridge across the River Oder near Grochowice. During the night of 28 January 1945 his unit was ordered to erect two supporting frames for the bridge across the river. The ice on the river had been broken by artillery fire and there were no boats or rafts. In the icy water under enemy fire Dobrorez transported the frames to the site and put them in position, the supports having been previously installed. He resigned from the army in 1946 and worked as a railway engineer in Ufa, Bashkiria (Bashkortostan). He appears in the books *Slavnie Sini Bashkirii* (*Glorious Sons of Bashkiria*), published in Ufa in 1965, and *Sini Otshizni* (*The Sons of the Fatherland*), published in Ufa in 1981.

These heroes' names as well as those of three more Heroes of the Soviet Union from the 16th assault sapper brigade—sapper unit commander Stepanov Dmitry; anti-tank gunner Junior Sergeant Borovkov Pavel; and sapper Immamutdinov Magmud (killed in the battle)—are inscribed on a wall in the Hall of Glory in the National Museum of the Great Patriotic War in Kiev.

APPENDIX IV

SOVIET AND RUSSIAN EXPANSIONISM

The Soviet Union was one of the victors in the Second World War, although with an immense number of casualties (27 million) and a terrible impact on its economy. At the same time the Soviet Union increased its territory and population. During the Second World War the following territories were annexed by the Soviet Union:[1]

1939   Western Ukraine (including Lvov)
       Western Belarus (including Brest)
1940   The Izmail region, including the cities of Izmail,
       Bolhrad, Bilhorod-Dnistrovskyi and others
       Moldova and its capital city of Chisinau
       The city of Chernivtsi in northern Bukovina
       The Vilnius region (populated mainly by Poles)[2]
       The Vyborg region and the city of Vyborg (Viipuri)
       The Pechenga region in Finland

1944   The People's Republic of Tuva in southern Siberia
1945   The mainly German populated Memel region and the
        city of Klaipeda
        The east German region and city of Königsberg
        (renamed Kaliningrad)
        Half of Sakhalin Island near Japan
        The Kuril Islands, Habomai Islands and Shikotan
        Island
1946   The region of Transcarpathia with the city of
        Uzhhorod

This expansion stood in contrast with our allies and fellow victors, Britain and the US, who did not annex a metre of any other nation's territory. It was just the opposite in Britain's case: it transformed its numerous foreign colonies (Australia, Canada, India, Pakistan, South Africa, Singapore and others—more than a billion people) into free, independent states. The only colony that remained British was the Falkland Islands, comprising several small, sparsely populated islands near the Antarctic.[3]

As a matter of fact, statements by Russian, then Soviet, jingoists about the peaceful character of the Russian state or the Soviet Union, and their claim that their nation constantly resisted attacks from its aggressive neighbours, are open to question.

From the fifteenth century onwards, after the removal of the Tatar Mongol yoke and restoration of the Russian state, Russia was constantly annexing new lands and peoples—a policy it continued to implement when it became the Soviet Union. As a result, an initially small Moscow principality, which became Tsarist, then Imperial Russia, developed into the largest state in the world, covering three continents: Europe, Asia and North America (Alaska). Statisticians have calculated that Russia has spent two-thirds of its history engaging in warfare. It has fought wars with sixteen states and regions including Sweden (eight times, for a total of eighty-one years), Lithuania and Livonia (eight times over 110 years), Poland (ten times over sixty-four years), Turkey (twelve times over forty-eight years), Crimean Kazan Astrakhan Khanates (eleven times over forty-two years), Caucasus (twice over sixty-six years), Persia (present-day Iran) (four times over twenty-eight years), the Tatar Mongols (130 years), Central Asia—the Bukhara, Khiva and Kokand Khanates (four times over fifteen years).

The Wars of Russia and the Soviet Union: a Brief Chronology

Below are the wars which Moscow has waged during its history:

1471–96	war against Novgorod
1499	expansionist march across the Urals
1500–03	war against Lithuania
1512	war against Poland
1550	war against Kazan Khanate
1552	second war against Kazan Khanate
1556	war against Astrakhan
1557	war against Crimea
1558–63	war for Livonia
1579	war against Poland
1581	military expedition to conquer Siberia
1590–95	war against Sweden
1598	war against Kuchum Khan of Siberia
1600	military march to River Ob in Siberia
1608–18	war against Poland
1610–17	war against Sweden
1632–34	war against Poland
1637	war against Azov
1634–52	war against China
1654–67	war against Poland

1656–61	war against Sweden
1668–69	war against Persia
1671	march to Astrakhan
1676–81	war against Turkey, Crimea and Moldova
1687	war against Crimea
1689	march to Crimea
1695	march to Azov
1695–97	march to Kamchatka
1696	march to conquer Azov
1700–21	war against Sweden
1711	war against Turkey
1722–24	war against Persia
1733–35	war with Poland
1735–39	war against Turkey, Crimea and Moldova
1741	war against Poland
1741–3	war against Sweden
1741	march to Alaska
1756–62	war against Germany
1768–74	war against Turkey and Moldova
1787–92	war against Turkey and Moldova
1788–90	war against Sweden
1792	war against Poland
1794	war against Poland
1796	war against Persia
1799	war against France
1800	war against England
1804–13	war against Persia
1805–7	war against France
1805–12	war against Turkey and Moldova
1806	march to Sakhalin Island
1808–9	war against Sweden
1812–14	war against France
1813	war against Georgia

1820	march to Kazakhstan
1826–28	war against Persia
1828–9	war against Turkey, Moldova and Wallachia (Romania)
1833	march to Constantinople
1839	march to Khiva (modern Uzbekistan)
1843–59	war with Chechnya, Dagestan and Circassia
1847	march to Kazakhstan
1850	march to Koshkurgan
1853	march to Ak-Mechet
1853–56	war with Turkey, France and Britain in Crimea
1853	march to Kokand (Uzbek)
1865	occupation of Tashkent
1866–68	march to Bukhara
1868	occupation of Samarkand
1873–75	march to Khiva
1877–78	war against Turkey
1880–81	march to Turkmenistan
1884–85	march to Afghanistan
1901	occupation of Manchuria
1904–5	war against Japan
1914–17	war against Germany, Austria-Hungary, Bulgaria and Turkey
1917	war against Finland
1917–18	march to Ukraine
1918	march to Lithuania, Latvia and Estonia
1919	march to Belarus
1919	march to Ukraine
1920–21	marches to Caucasus and Persia
1920–21	occupation of Georgia, Armenia and Azerbaijan
1939	war against Poland
1939–40	war against Finland
1940	occupation of Bessarabia and Bukovina (Romania)
1941–45	war with Germany

1941	incursion of troops in Persia
1944	occupation of Tuva People's Republic (near Mongolia)
1945	march to Japan
1956	march to Hungary
1968	march to Czechoslovakia
1979–90	war in Afghanistan
1992	war in Moldova
1991–94	war on southern Ossetia and Abkhazia (against Georgia)
1992–95	war in Tajikistan
1994–95	war against Chechnya

The Soviet Union followed the same path as Russia. The data from the Soviet Union's participation in military conflicts, particularly concerning casualties, had been classified information, but after the disintegration of the Soviet Union the archives became available.

Below I have listed the participation of Soviet troops in military actions in other states and regions, together with our losses.

1924–29	China
1937–53	China
1938	Soviet-Japanese border conflict: the battle of Lake Khasan (989 killed)
1939	Soviet-Japanese border conflict: the battle of Khalkhin Gol (8,931 killed)
1939	'liberation' march to western Ukraine and western Belarus (1,139 killed)
1939–40	Soviet-Finnish War (126,875 killed)
1941	Iran
1944–53	Ukraine, Belarus, Lithuania, Latvia, Estonia: the liquidation of nationalist groups
1945	Japan
1950–53	North Korea

1956	Hungary (720 killed)
1960–70	Laos
1961–74	Vietnam
1962–63	Cuba
1962–63	Yemen
1962–64	Algeria
1967–75	Egypt
1967–73	Syria
1967–79	Mozambique
1968	Czechoslovakia (96 killed)
1969	Soviet-Chinese border conflict: the Zhenbao Island incident
1970	Cambodia
1972–73	Bangladesh
1975–79	Angola
1977–	Somalia
1977–79	Ethiopia
1978–89	Afghanistan (14,751 killed)
1992	Yugoslavia

The following military units were armed and trained on Soviet territory: two Polish armies; a Czechoslovak force; two volunteer Romanian brigades; Yugoslavian infantry and tank brigades; other military units. The number of these troops acting in the interest of the Soviet Union and the Communist Party totalled 550,000.

NOTES

AUTHOR'S PREFACE

1. In Russian history, the war is actually known as the Second Great Patriotic War, the first one being fought during Napoleon's invasion of Russia in 1812.
2. The term *vzvod* translates as platoon—a group of up to thirty soldiers under the command of a lieutenant—and *vzvodniy* translates as platoon commander. In British army terms, a platoon is an infantry unit, but the equivalent artillery or cavalry unit is called a troop. However, as senior lieutenants in the Red Army cavalry were called troop commanders, *vzvod* is translated as platoon throughout to avoid confusion.

BIOGRAPHICAL DETAILS

1. The Civil War was fought between the Bolshevik Red Army and the White Army of loosely-allied anti-Bolshevik forces.
2. This was where the Bolshevik-organised workers' armed revolt started on 29 January 1918, during the Civil War. The aim of the uprising was to sabotage the elections to the Ukrainian Constituent Assembly and support the advancing Red Army.
3. A military commissar headed a regional office that drafted men for military service, executed plans for military mobilisation and maintained records on military reserves.
4. There were ten school years in the Soviet system. Pupils who completed all ten were entitled to go to university, while those who left at the end

of eighth year could go to technical college. Pupils who failed their end-of-year examinations had to repeat the year.

5. Gumyonka corresponds to the present-day village of Gumenki outside Skopin.

6. During the Terror, Stalin carried out a purge of the Communist Party leadership, government officials, Red Army leaders and other sections of the population, using intense surveillance, show trials, imprisonment and arbitrary executions.

1. EVACUATION TO GUMYONKA

1. A line from a popular Russian song from the 1930s.

2. A reference to the Civil War of 1917–22, and the famines of 1921–22 and 1932–33.

3. The militia or *militsiya* was the official name of the civilian police.

4. Similar to the Scouting movement in the West, the Soviet Pioneer Organisation was a mass youth organisation for ten- to fifteen-year-olds with uniforms, activities and summer camps—although with a Communist Party slant.

5. Odessa was not heavily bombed as the Axis powers intended to use it as a regional base.

6. After a seventy-three-day siege, Odessa fell to Romanian troops on 17 October 1941 and became part of Romanian controlled Transnistria until its liberation on 12 April 1944.

7. During the collectivisation programme of 1928–40, 96.9 per cent of individual landholdings were consolidated into 236,000 collective farms (*kolkhozy* or *sovhozy*). The aim was to farm the collectives using modern equipment and scientific methods, thus increasing the food supply to the urban population, raw materials for processing industries and agricultural exports. There was both passive and violent resistance to collectivization: it is estimated that one million peasant families (the wealthier 'kulaks') were sent to labour camps. (Wikipedia: Collectivisation in the Soviet Union). The upheaval caused by collectivisation was intensified by the dry summer of 1931, leading to the famine of 1932–33 during which an estimated four to five million died

of starvation. (Geoffrey Hosking, *Russia and the Russians: A History from Rus to the Russian Federation* (London: Allen Lane, 2001)

8. Traditional Russian peasant shoes woven out of birch or lime bark. When worn with several *portyanki* or foot cloths, which are worn instead of socks, *lapti* can be warm, durable and practical.

9. An encouraging cry used for oxen: 'Forward! Forward!'

10. After the German invasion, the Red Army desperately needed more soldiers. The navy was one source and two types of unit were created: naval infantry brigades and naval rifle brigades. Although the members of the naval rifle brigades were naval personnel, they were in effect infantry under army command.

11. Author's note: we acted in a similar fashion when we were storming through Germany in 1945. Having broken through to the German rear, we shot German prisoners.

12. Most of these authors are still familiar today, but a few are not so well-known. Thomas Mayne Reid (1818–83) was a Scots-Irish American writer who wrote adventure stories for boys set in the American west. Many of his books were translated into Russian: *The Headless Horseman* was a childhood favourite of the novelist Vladimir Nabokov. James Fenimore Cooper (1789–1851) was the author of *The Last of the Mohicans*. Arkady Gaidar (1904–41) was a Soviet children's author whose most famous work, *Timur and his Gang*, was read in schools until the 1990s. Gaidar was sent to the front as a special correspondent for the newspaper *Komsomolskaya Pravda*, and was killed in battle on 26 October 1941.

2. JOINING THE ARMY

1. Violators of public order were to be arrested and court-martialled, while provocateurs, spies and anyone fomenting unrest could be shot on sight.

2. National heroes who defended Russia from the Polish invasion of 1612.

3. It was extremely cold (in December 1941 the temperature dropped to −28.8°C) and fuel was scarce: people were unable to use their large stoves to heat their homes, so had to rely on small temporary stoves using whatever fuel they could find.

3. TRAINING IN BUKHARA

1. Until recently soldiers did not wear socks (which were time-consuming to manufacture), but were issued with small squares of woollen or cotton cloth, depending on the season. New recruits were taught how to wrap these around their feet; the more inept among them would inevitably suffer from blisters and bleeding feet.
2. The Totskoye range near Orenburg was the site of nuclear tests in 1954. A nuclear bomb was exploded 350 metres above the range, then 600 armoured vehicles, 600 tanks and 320 planes were sent into the epicentre to simulate a battle, with the aim of testing the performance of soldiers and military hardware during a nuclear war. The 45,000 soldiers who took part were not issued with protective gear and were told it was a mock explosion.

4. TO THE KALININ FRONT

1. The Aral Sea was once the fourth largest lake in the world, with an area of 68,000 square kilometres. It has been shrinking since the 1960s, after water was diverted to irrigate the cotton fields of Central Asia, and by 2007 it was 10 per cent of its original size. Aralsk is now forty kilometres away from the shore.
2. SMERSH, whose motto (and extended acronym *SMERt' SHpionam*) was 'death to spies', was the umbrella term for three counter-intelligence agencies set up in the Red Army in 1942 (they were officially founded in April 1943) and dissolved in May 1946. SMERSH recruited a vast network of informers in the Red Army (estimated at between 1.5 and 3.4 million) whose duties included looking out for anti-Soviet elements.
3. In Russia the patronymic, which is derived from the father's name (for example, Nikolayevich (masculine) or Nikolayevna (feminine) from the name Nikolay), follows the given name and is an official part of the name, used both formally and informally.
4. The RGD-33 grenade could be thrown between thirty and forty metres and had a relatively small 'kill' radius of ten to fifteen metres, so could be safely used by advancing troops. In contrast, the F-1 could be thrown thirty to forty-five metres but had a large 'kill' radius of up to 200 metres, so could only be used from a defensive position or during retreat.

5. This depth does not give much protection! Full-size trenches on the western front in the First World War were at least two metres deep.

6. This was the youth division of the Communist Party for those aged between fourteen and twenty-eight.

7. The 50-mm mortar was designed by Shavirin. He also designed other mortars which were used in the army: 82-, 107-, 120-, 160- and 240-mm.

5. THE FRONT NEAR RZHEV

1. The Red Army used the word 'front' to denote an army group, usually containing three to five armies, as well as a geographical military frontline.

2. *Rama* is Russian for frame, as the plane resembles a frame.

3. The Finnish war, or Winter War, began with a Soviet offensive on the east Finnish border on 30 November 1939, and resulted in the expulsion of the USSR from the League of Nations. Finland signed the Moscow Peace Treaty with the USSR on 13 March 1940 ceding 11 per cent of its territory. The battles of Lake Khasan and Khalkhin Gol were fought against Japan, firstly on the Manchurian border in July 1938, secondly on the Mongolian border in August 1939.

6. MY FIRST BATTLE

1. A mass attack of troops without concern for casualties.

2. Author's note: the word 'junior' was not used during battle—there was no time for it.

3. The NKVD, or People's Commissariat for Internal Affairs, ran the regular police service, and, more notoriously, the Main Directorate of State Security (the predecessor of the KGB) and the gulag system of forced labour camps.

7. THE FIRST WOUND

1. Alexander Pushkin (1799–1837) was a famous Russian poet. The epitaph comes from his poem dedicated to Anna Kern.

2. False Dmitri II was the second of three pretenders to the Russian throne who each claimed to be the youngest son of Ivan the Terrible, Tsarevich

Dmitri Ivanovich. The real Dmitri died in 1591 aged nine in uncertain circumstances.

8. MY THOUGHTS ON RZHEV

1. According to the memoirs of the Soviet spymaster Pavel Sudoplatov (1907–96), Soviet military plans for the Rzhev offensive were deliberately 'fed' to the Germans by a double agent, 'Max', to ensure that they sent reinforcements northwards, rather than to Stalingrad. (*Special Tasks: The Memoirs of an Unwanted Witness - A Soviet Spymaster* (New York: Back Bay Books, 1994))
2. Khatyn was a village in Belarus whose inhabitants, mainly women, children and old men, were burnt alive in its church by the Nazis.
3. This is a reference to Stalin's purges of the late 1930s, when Marshal Tukhachevsky and most of the Red Army general staff were executed.

9. THE MORTAR REGIMENT AT VYSHNY VOLOCHYOK

1. Tver is an ancient town north of Moscow. Under Stalin it was renamed Kalinin after the chairman of the Supreme Soviet.
2. A department consists of ten people.
3. This was composed by Vasiliy Agapkin in 1912 in honour of the Slavic women who accompanied their husbands during the 1st Balkan War. It proved popular with the Red Army and was performed during the parade in Moscow to mark the October Revolution on 7 November 1941.
4. The River Lovat formed part of the famous ancient trade route between Scandinavia and Byzantium, via Russia and Little Russia (present-day Ukraine).
5. This offensive was part of the 2nd Rzhev-Sychevka operation of 25 November–20 December 1942. During the campaign, the Kalinin front succeeded in liberating Velikiye Luki, a strategically important town, on 16 January 1943 with the result that the Germans, fearing encirclement from the north, withdrew from Rzhev on 3 March 1943.

10. THE NORTH-WESTERN FRONT NEAR KHOLM

1. These were created by Stalin via Order No. 227 in July 1942. Their troops comprised those convicted of desertion or cowardice (reluctance to fight—those exhibiting cowardice on the battlefield were summarily

executed), liberated Soviet POWs (their sympathies were viewed as suspect) and gulag prisoners. Penal units were deployed in the most hazardous battle situations, including mine clearing—troops were required to run through minefields in attack ahead of the regular troops.

12. IN THE REAR IN TASHKENT

1. Lithuania, Estonia and Latvia were annexed by the USSR in June 1940, in line with the secret protocol of the Molotov-Ribbentrop Non-Aggression Pact of 23 August 1939 which drew up spheres of influence between the two countries. The pact remained in force until the German invasion of the USSR in June 1941.
2. Editor's note: the text specifies 122-mm M1902/30 guns but this model number would apply only to 76-mm guns.

13. HOW I JOINED THE SAPPERS

1. This was a radio-controlled explosion, triggered 400 kilometres away. It was the first time that a long-distance radio-controlled explosion was used in a military operation.

14. ADVANCING INTO POLAND

1. Bogdan Khmelnytsky was a Cossack leader who led an uprising against the Polish-Lithuanian Commonwealth in 1648–54, which resulted in the creation of a Ukrainian Cossack state
2. On 17 September 1939 the Red Army invaded eastern Poland in accordance with the secret protocol of the Molotov-Ribbentrop Non-Aggression Pact. The newly-acquired areas were incorporated into the republics of Belarus and Ukraine.
3. This is spam, which found its way to the USSR via the USA's Lend-Lease policy.
4. This camel was called Kuznechik (Grasshopper) and he was attached to the 120th guards mechanised brigade (formerly the 308th rifle division). It was said that his driver led him to spit on the Reichstag (Vasiliy Grossman, *A Writer at War* (London: Harvill Secker, 2005)). Sadly we cannot find the photograph from *Ogoniok*.

15. THE BATTLE OF GOROKHOV

1. The aims of the Lvov-Sandomierz offensive were to liberate Lvov, clear German troops from Ukraine and capture bridgeheads on the River Vistula (which would eventually enable the Red Army to reach Warsaw and be within striking distance of Berlin). At the same time, the USSR launched Operation Bagration, with the aims of liberating Belarus and forcing German troops out of eastern Poland. The Lvov-Sandomierz offensive would prevent the Germans from transferring their reserves to their Army Group Centre during Operation Bagration.

2. There were actually eighty-five deaths during the storming of Bastille, where 114 soldiers were guarding seven prisoners but the original text has been kept to make the author's point.

3. *Banderovtsi* is a Russian term for the Ukrainian nationalist movement led by Stepan Bandera which fought for Ukrainian independence from Russia and Poland. Bandera had initially supported the German invasion, but the Nazis opposed the establishment of an independent Ukraine and arrested him. He was released in 1944, when the German authorities hoped that he would incite Ukrainian nationalists to fight against the advancing Soviet army.

4. In this conflict the Russian-led alliance contested the supremacy of the Swedish empire in central, northern and eastern Europe.

16. THE VISTULA OPERATION

1. Diplomatic relations between the Soviet Union and the Polish government-in-exile had been established in 1941, following the German attack on the USSR. However, in April 1943 the Germans announced the discovery of mass graves of 12,000 Polish officers at Katyn, near Smolensk, and claimed that the officers had been murdered by Soviet forces. The USSR denied any involvement in the killings and its version was accepted by the Allies, with the exception of the Polish government-in-exile which called for an investigation by the International Red Cross. This prompted Stalin to sever diplomatic relations with the Polish government-in-exile and attempt to persuade the Allies to recognise an alternative pro-Soviet Polish government, with its own resistance army, the Armia Ludowa. From 1943–44, Allied leaders attempted to recon-

cile the USSR and the Polish government-in-exile, but failed, due partly to the Katyn massacre as well as Stalin's insistence that the Polish territories annexed by the USSR in 1939 under the Molotov-Ribbentrop Pact would remain Soviet, and the Polish government-in-exile's opposition to Stalin setting up a communist government in post-war Poland. In 1990 the Soviet Union officially acknowledged responsibility for, and condemned, the killings of approximately 22,000 Poles, including military officers, academics, lawyers, teachers, engineers and writers, at Katyn and other locations by the NKVD.

17. SANDOMIERZ

1. In Polish: *pannur* and *panienek*.
2. Before becoming a full member of the Communist Party, an applicant had a trial period of membership to assess their suitability. The author became a full member in March 1945.
3. From 1932, professional writers in the USSR were expected to be members of the Writers' Union of the USSR. Opportunities for publication without membership were extremely limited. In 1991 the Writers' Union of Ukraine declared its independence from the Soviet organisation.

18. IN THE REAR IN POLAND

1. This was larger and more powerful than the Faustpatrone.

20. A TANK RIDER OF THE 1ST UKRAINIAN FRONT

1. The 4th tank army was originally formed as a part of the Stalingrad front during July 1942 under Major General Kryuchenkin and lost a large number of tanks during its attempt to halt the German 6th army. It fought on the southern approaches to Stalingrad in August before coming under the command of the Don front. The much diminished army was re-designated the 65th army in October, then an abortive attempt was made to re-form it in February 1943 before it finally reappeared as the 4th guards tank army on 15 July 1943.
2. Under this policy, enacted by the Roosevelt administration in March 1941 and operating until 1945, the USA acted as an 'arsenal of democracy', supplying the Allies with weapons and aid. In due course, the

USSR received American jeeps, tanks and other armoured vehicles and aircraft, as well as food and clothing, via Persia. Further Lend-Lease supplies from the UK were brought via the Arctic to the Soviet port of Murmansk.

3. The Kalmyks, descendants of a nomadic Mongol people, lived in the autonomous Kalmyk Republic on the western shore of the Caspian Sea. After the German invasion and the republic's subsequent liberation by the Red Army, the Soviet government accused the Kalmyks of collaboration in December 1943 and deported the entire population to Siberia and to other parts of Central Asia. The Kalmyks were permitted to return to their territory by Khrushchev in 1957.

21. THE ADVANCE INTO GERMANY

1. Author's note: the SS were the elite German troops; like our NKVD they dressed in black uniforms, and they wore a skull and crossbones on their caps.
2. During the war various units were designated 'guards' units after distinguishing themselves in combat and were considered to have elite status.
3. On 8 May 1945 Karlshorst became the HQ of the Soviet military administration. It is now the German-Russian Museum of Berlin-Karlshorst. The Act of Military Surrender was actually signed just before midnight on 8 May, local time, or 9 May, Moscow time.
4. After the Kremlin Wall necropolis, this was the most prestigious burial site during the Soviet era. Many famous people are buried there, including Prokofiev, Shostakovich, Gogol, Bulgakov and Eisenstein.

22. SOLDIER SIDAMETOV

1. In Russian 'who' is *kto* and 'where to' is *kooda*.
2. The Soviet war in Afghanistan lasted from December 1979 to February 1989. The first Chechen war between Russia and Chechnya lasted from 1994 to 1996. The second Chechen war started in August 1999 and ended in May 2000, although Russian troops carried out an anti-insurgency operation in Chechnya which officially ended in 2009.
3. In winter sugar beet, like other root vegetables, was stored in compact mounds covered with earth.

23. THE END IS NEAR

1. They are Russian military heroes. Suvorov (1730–1800) was the gener-alissimo of ground and naval forces who fought against the Ottoman Empire, Poland and French forces in Italy; Kutuzov (1745–1813) was a prominent general under Catherine II who fought in the Napoleonic war; Nevsky (1220–63) defeated German and Swedish invaders and was canonised by the Russian Orthodox Church in 1547; Nakhimov (1802–55) was a famous admiral who took part in the Crimean War; Ushakov (1745–1817) was a famous naval commander and admiral. Stalin also introduced the Order of Bogdan Khmelnitsky.

2. Herriot was leader of the French Radical Party and prime minister in 1924–5, 1926 and 1932. He originally supported the Vichy government before turning against Pétain and supporting de Gaulle. He was subse-quently arrested by the Vichy authorities and interned in Germany.

26. AFTER THE WAR

1. Volhynia is a historic region straddling Poland, Ukraine and Belarus.
2. About one-third of the Jewish population of Berdichev escaped before the German occupation in 1941, but the rest, an estimated 20,000–30,000, were subsequently murdered.
3. Also known as the 1st cavalry army, it was formed by Semyon Budyonny in 1918 during the Russian Civil War as a small force of Cossacks from the Don region. It grew to become a prominent Red Army military for-mation in both the Civil War and Polish-Russian War.

27. MY ILLEGAL TRIP TO AUSTRIA

1. *De Revolutionibus Orbium Coelestium* was put on the Index of Prohibited Books in 1616, during the Galileo affair, and removed in 1835.
2. The official Soviet line on the Holocaust was that all nationalities had suffered equally under Hitler. Of the estimated 1.1 million victims at Auschwitz, at least 960,000 were Jews from Hungary, Poland, France, Holland, Greece and the USSR, 21,000 were Roma and Sinti, and 15,000 were Soviet POWs, in addition to 10,000–15,000 others, including polit-ical prisoners, homosexuals, people with disabilities and Jehovah's Witnesses. (Wikipedia: Auschwitz)

3. The poem is by Victor Lapshin. His actual words are: 'The greatest joy for us [...] is the eternal love of our motherland.'

4. Khrushchev (1894–1971) came from a peasant family living in Kalinovka, a poverty-stricken village near the Russian border with Ukraine, and attended school for four years while working as an animal herder before becoming a metal-fitter's apprentice.

5. This rank was created in 1935. Three of the original five marshals were executed during Stalin's purges and replaced with new men. Budyonny lost his rank during the war.

6. Author's note: the Supreme Court considered the cases of generals, admirals and more senior ranks, as well as those of civilians with corresponding titles and positions. Cases which involved those of lower military ranks and those with corresponding civilian status were considered by regional military tribunals, or fleet tribunals (twenty in total), the supreme courts of the republics (fifteen in total) or by regional courts (175 in total).

28. THE ELECTIONS TO THE SUPREME SOVIET

1. The Supreme Soviet was the legislative body of the USSR. It comprised two chambers: the Soviet of the Union, representing geographical areas of the USSR; and the Soviet of Nationalities, representing the different ethnic groups. Candidates were chiefly drawn from the Communist Party ('independents' were carefully vetted by the party) and served four-year terms. The Supreme Soviet met twice a year and elected members of the Presidium (to act on its behalf when it was not in session), the Supreme Court and Council of Ministers.

2. The Communist Party was known as the Russian Social Democratic Labour Party (Bolsheviks) from 1912 to 1918, the Russian Communist Party (Bolsheviks) from 1918 to 1925, then the All-Union Communist Party (Bolsheviks) from 1925 until 1952, when it became the Communist Party of the Soviet Union.

3. A reference to the collectivisation programme of 1929–40 which its opponents compared to serfdom. With the abolition of private serfdom in 1861 and state serfdom in 1866, the peasants had gained full rights

as free citizens, including the right to own the land which they cultivated.

4. After the end of the war there was a civil war in western Ukraine. 'The Organisation of Ukrainian Nationalists and the Ukrainian Insurrectionary Army were conducting full-blown military operations to prevent the reintegration of Ukraine into the USSR. The scale of the problem was immense: at the end of 1945 the Red Army had deployed over half a million troops against Ukrainian partisans. This armed resistance in Ukraine persisted until well into the 1950s.' (William C. Fuller, *Russia, A History* (Oxford: Oxford University Press, 2002))

5. Most of Lenin's politburo were shot by the NKVD in the early 1930s. Aleksandra Sokolovskaya, Trotsky's first wife, disappeared in 1935, while his sons from his second marriage to Natalia Sedova (who died of old age in Mexico in 1962) were both assassinated: Sergei Sedov in 1937 and Lev Sedov in 1938.

29. THE MILITARY LAW ACADEMY

1. The academy was formed in 1939 from the Military Law Department of the All-Union Law Academy. In 1956 it became the Military Law Department of the Military Political Academy.

2. All organisations had a 'Lenin's room', which was a reading room with a bust of Lenin, tables and books.

3. Largely ignored by the Soviet cultural establishment, Vladimir Vysotsky's fame in the USSR was equivalent to that of Bob Dylan in the US. As well as acting, he wrote and performed his own songs, accompanying himself on a seven-stringed guitar. His lyrics contained social and political comment, and his depiction of the experience of war was viewed by veterans as being far more accurate than that expressed in official patriotic songs.

> Where are your seventeen years?
> On Great Karetny Street.
> Where are your seventeen troubles?
> On Great Karetny Street.
> Where is your black gun?
> On Great Karetny Street.

Where are you not today?

On Great Karetny Street.

Bolshoy (great) Karetny is the street in Moscow where Vysotsky lived as a teenager.

4. The infamous head of the NKVD from 1938–46, then Stalin's deputy from 1946–53.

5. The October Revolution started on 25 October 1917, following the Julian calendar. This date corresponds with 7 November under the Gregorian calendar, which was adopted by the Council of People's Commissars in February 1918.

6. Only officers from active units were eligible to study at the academy. If you were moved to the reserve you would lose your place at the academy.

7. It is a male Russian tradition that if someone does you a favour, you give him a *pol litra* (a half-litre bottle of vodka).

8. After Stalin's death in 1953 all graduates from the Military Law Academy were employed for several years to reassess cases for rehabilitation.

9. This was founded in 1924 as a court for higher military and political personnel of the Red Army and the fleet. It supervised military tribunals and was the supreme authority in military appeals. During the Great Purge of 1937–38 it conducted the major show trials.

10. Odessa was known as 'the capital of humour' in the former USSR and still has this reputation today. A stereotypical Odessite was Jewish, a witty raconteur and joker. Before the disintegration of the USSR, Odessite humour often involved pointing out the flaws and absurdities of Soviet rule. The annual Humorina festival is held in Odessa on April Fools' Day.

11. Odessa had a large Jewish population before the Nazi invasion: in 1939 about 180,000 Jews lived in the city, comprising 30 per cent of the population. Half of them managed to escape before Odessa was captured by German and Romanian forces. Most of those who remained perished in massacres, or in ghettos and Romanian-administered concentration camps set up in occupied Ukraine.

12. By 2010 the Russian Census estimated the Lak population to be 180,000.

APPENDIX II

1. Like Germany, Austria was divided into four occupation zones after the war and was jointly occupied by the US, Britain, France and the USSR. While Germany was divided into East and West in 1949, Austria remained under joint occupation until 1955 when, after promising perpetual neutrality, it was accorded independence.
2. Generic names for female and male dogs.
3. In English, the World Canine Organisation, based in Belgium.

APPENDIX IV

1. The Soviet territorial gains of 1939–40 were part of the secret protocol of the Nazi-Soviet Non-Aggression Pact (the Molotov-Ribbentrop Pact) of August 1939, which divided up Romania, Poland, Lithuania, Latvia, Estonia and Finland into German and Soviet spheres of influence.
2. This has been a contentious issue bound up with the region's history under Russian, Polish, German and Lithuanian control, each with their particular interests. For example, the Polish Census held in 1931 looked at nationality in terms of language, then religion, with the result that Polish-speaking Jews were classed as Poles, while Yiddish or Hebrew-speaking Jews were classed as Jews. Lithuanian nationalists claimed that many so-called Poles were Polonised Lithuanians.
3. Editor's note: to date, Britain has fourteen overseas territories which have never acquired independence.

INDEX

INDEX

INDEX

INDEX

INDEX

INDEX

INDEX

INDEX

INDEX

INDEX

INDEX

INDEX

INDEX

INDEX

INDEX

INDEX

INDEX

INDEX

INDEX

INDEX

INDEX

INDEX

INDEX